Poverty Capital

This is a book about poverty but it does not study the poor and the powerless. Instead it studies those who manage poverty. It sheds light on how powerful institutions control "capital," or circuits of profit and investment, as well as "truth," or authoritative knowledge about poverty. Such dominant practices are challenged by alternative paradigms of development, and the book details these as well. Using the case of microfinance, the book participates in a set of fierce debates about development—from the role of markets to the secrets of successful pro-poor institutions. Based on many years of research in Washington DC, Bangladesh, and the Middle East, *Poverty Capital* also grows out of the author's undergraduate teaching to thousands of students on the subject of global poverty and inequality.

Ananya Roy is Professor of City and Regional Planning at the University of California, Berkeley. She is also the founding chair of a new undergraduate curriculum in Global Poverty and Practice. At Berkeley, Roy is the recipient of the Distinguished Teaching Award and Golden Apple Award for Outstanding Teaching, the highest teaching honors bestowed by the campus and its students. Roy's previous research has provided a close look at poverty and inequality in the cities of the global South.

Poverty Capital
Microfinance and the Making of Development

Ananya Roy

Routledge
Taylor & Francis Group

NEW YORK AND LONDON

First published 2010
by Routledge
270 Madison Avenue, New York, NY 10016

Simultaneously published in the UK
by Routledge
2 Park Square, Milton Park, Abingdon, Oxon OX14 4RN

Routledge is an imprint of the Taylor & Francis Group, an informa business

© 2010 Taylor & Francis

Typeset in Legacy Serif and Bodoni by
Swales & Willis Ltd, Exeter, Devon
Printed and bound in the United States of America on acid-free paper by
Walsworth Publishing Company, Marceline, MO

Library of Congress Cataloging-in-Publication Data
Roy, Ananya.
 Poverty capital : microfinance and the making of development /
 Ananya Roy. — 1st ed.
  p. cm.
  Includes bibliographical references.
  1. Microfinance. 2. Poverty. I. Title.
  HG178.3.R69 2010
  332—dc22   2009048683

ISBN 10: 0–415–87672–9 (hbk)
ISBN 10: 0–415–87673–7 (pbk)
ISBN 13: 0–203–85471–3 (ebk)

ISBN 13: 978–0–415–87672–8 (hbk)
ISBN 13: 978–0–415–87673–5 (pbk)
ISBN 13: 978–0–203–85471–6 (ebk)

FOR MY STUDENTS AT BERKELEY—
WHO TEACH ME THROUGH THEIR PASSION AND SHARP WIT

Contents

Preface

This book has been in the making for several years. Its origins lie in my persistent interest in issues of poverty and inequality. Although my previous research has been concerned with those living under conditions of extreme poverty, this book is different. It studies those who manage poverty, that is, the poverty experts who produce knowledge about poverty and who set the agenda of poverty alleviation. I came to such a project because I wanted to learn more about how international development works. In particular, I wanted to understand how powerful institutions, such as the World Bank, control "capital," or circuits of profit, speculation, and accumulation, and "truth," or the circuits of knowledge production. It was not enough, I felt, to understand poverty at the ground zero of lived experience. It was also essential to make sense of this management of poverty.

The study of poverty is marked by the ethics of distance—of lives that are studied but remain distant from the privileged researcher. The study of power is also fraught with ethical issues, in this case the ethics of intimacy—of complicities and entanglements that are part of the world of development institutions and part of the world of academia. They are intimately about *my* world. Not surprisingly, the production of this book—from 2004 to 2009—is entangled with other projects. During this time, I found myself involved in an effort at the University of California, Berkeley, to establish a new research center and undergraduate curriculum focused on global poverty. As the education director of the fledgling Blum Center for Developing Economies, I came to teach what quickly became one of the campus's largest courses—Global Poverty: Hopes and Challenges in the New

Millennium. In short time, I became an intimate part of the very circuits of truth (and capital) that I sought to investigate and critique. Even so, one thing was clear: the students in my classes, this "millennial" generation, had an intimate relationship with global poverty. It was their issue; it defined their place-in-the-world. In many ways, this project has been an effort to make sense of what I believe will be a key theme in their world: "poverty capital."

I had expected this book to be about Washington DC and the institutions therein that make development. Yet, I quickly realized that the making of development was also taking place in the global South, in sites such as Bangladesh. The Grameen Bank, established in Bangladesh, is now a worldwide phenomenon, hailed as the pioneer of a successful model of poverty alleviation: microfinance. I went to Bangladesh deeply cynical about microfinance, but I came away inspired. Over many summers and winters, I learned an unanticipated set of lessons about this model of development—one that is often packaged and sold as a magical formula of microfinance but that is in fact a quite different logic of human development and social protection.

My initial foray into the world of poverty experts in Washington DC also led me to the Middle East. The post-9/11 world of development was filled with the talk not only of poverty but also of terror. I had to follow the talk, and the money. I chose two sites in the Middle East—Egypt and Lebanon—the former because it is saturated with American money and ideas and the latter because its most prominent development institution is the much feared Shiite militia, Hezbollah. Each of these sites—Bangladesh, Egypt, and Lebanon—led me back to Washington DC, for it remains a central node in the making of development. To indicate this power, I have left the chapter on Washington DC unmarked by location. After all, Washington DC is a global order, one that is not bound by territorial borders and boundaries. All other sites are marked and named.

This book was always about microfinance. Unlike many other development scholars and practitioners, I have no particular professional relationship with the field of microfinance. I had to quickly become fluent in the elaborate and sprawling microfinance debates, even while knowing that I had no intention of becoming a microfinance expert. But the book is also about something more than microfinance. Microfinance is a paradigmatic example of a new moment of development, one characterized by an interest in poverty alleviation and focused on ideas of self-help and empowerment. Microfinance is simply everywhere. It is both the celebrity cause and the ordinary citizen's development tool of choice. Microfinance is also an important frontier of capital investment. The financial crisis of 2008-2009 brought this into sharper view. As Wall Street banks collapsed, so the resilience of microfinance (and thus of the poor) became the topic of much discussion and hope. Thus, microfinance is a window into poverty "truth"—or the accepted knowledge about how poverty and poverty alleviation work—and poverty "capital"—or the types of finance that underpin poverty management and poverty alleviation.

Microfinance is about debt. Academic research also accrues its own debts: both abstract and intimate. This book has been made possible because of the generosity of many different people in many different parts of the world. Amidst busy schedules, development professionals were willing to spare an hour or two to talk to me. Some were willing to do so many times over, patiently answering my repetitive questions. Others shared contacts, made introductions, or let me into a meeting. Organizations made available their archival material, allowed me to attend conferences and workshops, and opened up their libraries. It is impossible for me to list all such opportunities and to adequately register my thanks. But a few debts must be mentioned.

Organizations such as PRODUCT (RED), Whole Planet Foundation, CARE USA and CARE Canada, the Microfinance Investment Support Facility of Afghanistan, and the United Nations Development Programme (UNDP) gave me permission to reprint some of their images and graphs in this book. BRAC, the Research and Evaluation Division, headed by the inimitable Imran Matin, gave me access to its impressive collection of research reports and more generally to the ethos of BRAC. UNDP Egypt facilitated my attendance of the launch of Egypt's National Strategy for Microfinance. I was able to participate in the 2005 Boulder Institute at a discounted rate. At the American University of Beirut, Mona Harb and Mona Fawaz shared their published and unpublished work. At the Grameen Bank, from the very beginning, Muhammad Yunus welcomed me with open arms, greeting me with warmth each time I met him in the global circles of microfinance.

It was the milieu of ideas at the University of California, Berkeley, that nourished the making of this book. This includes the work of many colleagues and friends: Raka Ray, Aihwa Ong, Isha Ray, Mia Fuller, Teresa Caldeira, James Holston, Robert Reich, Richard Walker, Alain de Janvry, Loic Wacquant, Paul Rabinow, Michael Watts, Gillian Hart, Charis Thompson, Ingrid Seyer-Ochi, Peter Evans, Minoo Moallem, Michael Burawoy, Paula Goldman, Saba Mahmood, Annalee Saxenian, and Percy Hintzen.

Also at Berkeley, various departments provided a home for my research and teaching: the Department of City and Regional Planning, International and Area Studies, and the Blum Center for Developing Economics. John Lie insisted that I serve as Associate Dean of International and Area Studies and Shankar Sastry similarly insisted that I take on the role of Education Director of the Blum Center for Developing Economies. The research and writing of this book coincided with these interesting portfolios. It was an insane routine, especially as I juggled teaching, advising, administration, and a book that was always on my mind. But it was also an entanglement that forced me to constantly consider the public and pedagogical relevance of this book. For that I owe John Lie and Shankar Sastry special thanks.

I had the opportunity to rehearse the arguments presented in this book through talks at different venues and I am grateful to have had these opportunities. These include the University of Washington, Seattle (Geography); University of Minnesota (Global Studies); University of Toronto (Geography and Planning/ International Studies); University of California, Irvine (Social Ecology); University of Vermont (Baruch Presidential Lectures); Stanford University (Aurora Forum); Federal University of Rio (IPPUR); and Arizona State University (Architecture and Planning). Some of the ideas presented in this book were previewed in three essays: "In her name" for *Wages of Empire* edited by Amalia Cabezas, Ellen Reese, and Marguerite Waller; "Poverty truths" for *Planning Ideas and Planning Practices* edited by Patsy Healey and Robert Upton; and "Millennial woman" for the *International Handbook of Gender and Poverty* edited by Sylvia Chant.

The scaffolding of this book relies on the work of many scholars. Their research, and friendship, has made possible this analysis of poverty capital. This includes Katharyne Mitchell, Matthew Sparke, Derek Gregory, Oren Yiftachel, Katharine Rankin, Kanishka Goonewardena, Michael Goldman, Pablo Bose, Neil Smith, Manuel Castells, and Janice Perlman.

Various grants provided the funding for this book. UC Berkeley's Committee on Research, the Hellman Faculty Award, and the Prytanean

Faculty Award provided crucial seed funding. A generous National Science Foundation Grant (Geography and Regional Science Program) made it possible to conduct the multi-year and multi-sited research that was necessary to tell the story of poverty management.

My graduate and undergraduate students have played a prominent role in the making of this book. Two outstanding undergraduate students—Lisa Molinaro and Robin Finley—served as research assistants in the early stages of the project. Several graduate students provided research assistance, including Ryan Centner and Gautam Bhan. Pietro Calogero's dissertation helped me understand the terrain of imperialism in Afghanistan. In Beirut, Hiba Bou Akar was an important research guide, sharing with me her ongoing work on Hezbollah. Liz Lee enthusiastically scavenged for the artifacts of millennial development, such as the Benetton microfinance campaign. Sylvia Nam worked on the project for several years, carefully assembling a history of the World Bank and of the circulation of microfinance ideas (complete with her brilliant and caustic analysis).

At Routledge, the conceptualization and production of the book was shepherded first by Dave McBride and then by Steve Rutter and Leah Babb-Rosenfeld. Susan Mannon provided valuable editing advice. I thank Steve for pushing for a book that would be read beyond the halls of academia.

The itinerant nature of this research project was made bearable by family and friends in different parts of the world, especially in Bangladesh, India, Egypt, and Lebanon. My parents, in Kolkata, India, made peace with the long duration of the project as I cut visits short to make yet another research trip to Bangladesh.

At home here in Berkeley, Nezar AlSayyad was also patient—especially when, year after year, I scheduled research trips during every summer, winter, and spring break. As the piles of research material mushroomed all around our house, he heard a familiar refrain: "I'll clean up the mess when the book is over." I guess it is time for me to deliver on that promise. In ordinary and extraordinary ways, Nezar makes possible the work I do.

Two people in particular must be acknowledged. From the very first day that I met him, Syed Hashemi became an important part of this book. His incisive analysis and humor enlivened my "fieldwork." He allowed me to see development through a quite different lens. Stephanie Kim, my graduate student, was there at the very start of this book. She accompanied me on research trips to Washington DC and New York, shared in my interest in the politics of development, and wrote a solid Master's thesis on micro-finance in Vietnam. Stephanie is not here to see this book come to completion and this is a tragedy. She, like many of my students, had a stake in millennial development and its political possibilities. This book is for her and them.

Ananya Roy
Berkeley
June 29, 2009

CHAPTER 1

Small Worlds

The Democratization of Capital and Development

Microfinance is one of the most important economic phenomena since the advent of capitalism and Adam Smith.

(Vinod Khosla, Silicon Valley venture capitalist, 2004[1])

An Encounter in a Grocery Store and in a Classroom

It was the end of a long day at work. I had just finished shopping for groceries at Whole Foods Market in Berkeley, my cart piled high with striped heirloom tomatoes, lush eggplants, and round Asian pears. Then I saw Felicita. She was smiling, a broad grin that was confident, and she bore in her hands a garment with vibrant embroidery. Felicita was the "microentrepreneur" featured that month at Whole Foods Market, her smiling face beaming at us from donation flyers (see Figure 1.1). As I paid for my groceries, I had the option of adding $1 or $5 to my bill for use by the Whole Planet Foundation to "empower the poor through microcredit." But the flyer also told a story: of how Felicita, who lives in Guatemala, "runs an embroidery business and sells her products in the local marketplace." Curious to learn more I came home and browsed the "photo-story" of Felicita on the Whole Planet Foundation website: "Before receiving a microloan, she lacked the capital to buy enough raw materials to make more than a few blouses a week. Now, she has doubled her monthly production, enabling her to buy school supplies for her children" (http://www.wholeplanet foundation.org/partners/microentrepreneurs, accessed July 28, 2008).

Felicita is one of many microentrepreneurs supported by the Whole Planet Foundation and one of millions of women worldwide who today are recipients of microfinance loans given out by a proliferation of organizations. Microfinance, the provision of financial services to the poor, is a highly popular poverty alleviation tool, widely discussed and applied. This broader term, "finance" subsumes within it more specific practices such as the granting of credit in the form of tiny loans, or microcredit.

1

Figure 1.1 Felicita, microcredit client of Banrural Grameen Guatemala and Whole Planet Foundation (photograph courtesy of Alexander Crane).

Felicita is also an example of the "visible" poor, her struggles and successes rendered familiar through the methods of development and philanthropy that are now all around us, even in our grocery stores. This is a "small world"—or as the Whole Planet Foundation puts it, a "global community"—one where the alleviation of poverty is inserted into everyday acts of consumption. Our choices empower, and we are in turn empowered. It is through such forms of intimacy that we make and remake ourselves as world citizens.

Felicita is a microfinance client of Banrural Grameen Guatemala, a Whole Planet Foundation partner. This unusual configuration of institutions itself deserves a closer look. In 2007, the Whole Planet Foundation, Banrural, and the Grameen Trust entered into an agreement to establish a microfinance organization in Guatemala. Whole Planet Foundation is a private, non-profit organization established by Whole Foods Market and it seeks to address the "persistent problem of world hunger and poverty" (http://www.wholeplanetfoundation.org/about, accessed July 20, 2008). Banrural is Guatemala's largest bank. The Grameen Trust is a special arm of the Grameen Bank of Bangladesh, charged with the mission of replicating the Grameen microfinance model around the world. Their partnership yielded

Grameen Guatemala which provides loans to microentrepreneurs such as Felicita. This institutional ecology—a microfinance organization in Guatemala established as an outpost of a microfinance network centered in Bangladesh and financed by a foundation headquartered in Austin, Texas—is also an example of the new "small world" of development.

Most important, Grameen Guatemala, and indeed all Whole Planet Foundation partners, adhere to what may be understood as a Grameen model of micro-finance. Founded by Muhammad Yunus in 1983, the Grameen Bank pioneered a simple model of credit whereby small groups of poor women are able to secure small loans at reasonable rates of interest. The model is meant to serve as an alternative to both formal systems of banking that demand collateral and exclude the poor and informal systems of finance that prey on the poor. Premised on the idea that the poor are inherently entrepreneurial, the Grameen Bank bets on the generation of income and the smooth repayment of such loans. After all, as one treatise on the Grameen Bank puts it in its title, "the poor always pay back" (Dowla and Barua 2006). Women are seen as particularly important conduits of microfinance loans with an altruistic propensity to utilize income for social development, such as the schooling of children, improved household nutrition, or investment in a home. Implemented widely in Bangladesh, the Grameen Bank model is today a global phenomenon. Actively promoted by the Grameen Bank itself, for example through organizations such as the Grameen Trust, Grameen-style microfinance is ubiquitous—connecting the grocery stores of North America to the remote villages of Guatemala. It bears the powerful promise of a model that works, one that can deliver poverty alleviation and the empowerment of women. In recognition of such efforts, Muhammad Yunus and the Grameen Bank were awarded the 2006 Nobel Peace Prize. The Prize committee credited them with the creation of "economic and social development from below." "Lasting peace," the committee noted, "cannot be achieved unless large population groups find ways in which to break out of poverty. Micro-credit is one such means" (Mjøs 2006).

Microfinance, as it reaches poor women such as Felicita, is an example of the democratization of capital. It seeks to transform hitherto exclusionary systems of finance into those that include the poor. In addition, it facilitates flows of philanthropy and investment—from foundations in the prosperous global North to organizations that serve the poor in the global South. But such capital flows also include a vast array of microtransactions: from the consumer at the Whole Foods Market check-out line who makes a $1 donation to the young volunteer who records stories of microentrepreneurs. This is the democratization of development, a widespread ownership of the ideas and practices of development that defies centralized edifices such as the World Bank or even the Grameen Bank. It makes the world small.

I was to be reminded of such small worlds as I completed the writing of this book. When I first encountered Felicita's "photo-story" in that Whole Foods Market in Berkeley, I was already immersed in the study of the globalization of microfinance. Her story was a reminder of a larger story that had become the focus of my research: how a model of poverty alleviation with roots in Bangladesh came to be widely adopted, promoted, and even criticized and challenged. A year later, I returned to the image of Felicita, wanting to reproduce it here, in this book, to narrate a brief account of the reaches of microfinance. I submitted my request to the Whole Planet Foundation, expecting to navigate a tedious maze of permissions and copyrights. It is commonplace for such requests to remain unanswered: organizations have more important issues at hand; often they do not own their images and must iden-tify and seek permission from the photographer. But this time I heard back in a matter of days, from a young man, Alexander Crane, who wrote explaining that he had served as an intern at Grameen Guatemala and that the photograph of Felicita that had caught my eye was taken by him. Alex was no stranger to me. He was enrolled in a class that I was to teach at the University of California, Berkeley, titled "Global Poverty: Challenges and Hopes in the New Millennium." While I had not yet met him, he was one of the hundreds of "millennials" I encounter in this classroom, a generation of world citizens eager to tackle the urgent problem of persistent poverty, brimming with enthusiasm as they spend their summers in Guatemala to Ghana, often convinced by what Alex, in his email to me, called the "transformative power of microfinance." For a riveting moment, Felicita, Alex, and I were bound together in a "small world," a cluster of coincidence and serendipity amidst the millions of women microentrepreneurs who receive loans and the thousands who are photographed by yet thousands of young volunteers and interns.

This book is about such "small worlds." That phrase makes reference to a series of striking compositions produced by early twentieth-century artist, Wassily Kandinsky. *Small Worlds IV* is the cover of this book. I am drawn to the drama of Kandinsky's "small worlds," its complex vectors of movement, its colliding and colluding worlds. For me, the painting evokes the drama that is at work in microfinance and in the making of development. While Felicita's story is of crucial importance, that is not the one I have chosen to tell in this book. Instead, I outline the larger story of the democratization of capital and the democratization of development. Like the drama of Kandinsky's painting, these are intense and furious struggles. Two in particular are central to this book.

First, the globalization of microfinance has generated great interest in microfinance as an "asset class," or as a circuit of investment. While the Grameen Bank promises to alleviate poverty and empower women through a non-profit model of financial services, new models of microfinance institute strict norms of financial sustainability and emphasize profits rather than human development. This, as one famous text puts it, is the "microfinance revolution" (Robinson 2001). It bears a new promise: that the "bottom billion"—the world's poorest—will serve as a "frontier market," opening up new horizons of capital accumulation. Microfinance then is no longer the sole domain of non-profit organizations such as the Grameen Bank; it is the domain equally of commercial banks, investment vehicles, and money markets.

The remaking of microfinance is part of a broader transformation of capitalism itself, what Bill Gates (2008) labels "creative capitalism." This kinder and gentler capitalism seeks to aggressively mine the "fortune at the bottom of the pyramid," but in doing so it also hopes to eradicate "poverty through profits" (Prahalad 2004). It is in this sense that it is possible to think about "poverty capital" and to conceptualize microfinance as a chip or microprocessor in such formations of capital. The complex question at hand, one that animates quite a bit of this book, is whether "poverty capital," and specifically microfinance, will ensure financial inclusion, on fair and just terms, for the world's poor. Can microfinance, as an asset class, sought after by Wall Street investors, maintain this social purpose? Or will it fuel financial speculation, predatory capitalism, and ever-expanding debt?

Second, microfinance is one of those rare development ideas that originated in the global South and was taken up by powerful development institutions in the global North. Pioneered in Bangladesh, by the mid-1990s microfinance had become a development panacea, a globally favored practice of poverty alleviation. This reverse flow of ideas and practices—from the Grameen Bank of Bangladesh to the World Bank—suggests a democratization of development. Yet, as the microfinance revolution has sought to promote "poverty capital" so it has sought to remake paradigms of knowledge. Today, microfinance expertise is produced by the World Bank as much as it is by the Grameen Bank. Indeed, it is the World Bank that controls the portals of knowledge, establishing the norms, metrics, rankings, and best practices of microfinance. World Bank training workshops, texts, and reports disseminate such authoritative knowledge, investing some experts with the authority to be microfinance experts and denying others legitimacy and significance. In short, what is at work is a "Washington consensus on poverty."

In this book, I reveal the workings of the Washington consensus on poverty. But I also demonstrate how such forms of power come to be challenged and contested, how a lively battle of ideas continues in the field of microfinance. While I start at the power nodes of development aid and policy, I eventually journey to the margins of such geographies of power, examining how development institutions in the global South, as varied as the Grameen Bank and BRAC in Bangladesh and Hezbollah in Lebanon, continue to forge a different model of microfinance. Whether or not such ideas have traction, whether or not they represent an original and indigenous version of microfinance, and whether or not they are able to provide robust alternatives to dominant paradigms, are all issues that I tackle in this book.

I believe that such questions—concerned with the democratization of capital and the democratization of development—are important. They speak to the lives of poor women such as Felicita for these lives are now entangled, for better or for worse, with the making of "poverty capital." But they also speak to the hopes and aspirations of "millennials" such as Alex Crane. These lives too are entangled, for better or for worse, with the remaking of development. Will such conjunctures and collisions produce a new set of "small worlds," those that are worth inhabiting and defending? This chapter tells the story of millennial development and its millennials. In doing so, it identifies some of the key issues at stake in the democratization of capital and development: how poverty becomes visible; how markets work or fail; and how development attempts to tackle the uneven geographies of the contemporary world.

MILLENNIAL DEVELOPMENT

The turn of the century has been marked by the emergence of a remarkable global conscience: an awareness of world poverty and the articulation of the will to end poverty. The stark fact that of a world population of 6.7 billion people, 1.4 billion live under the unimaginable conditions of earning less than $1.25 a day, is now common sense (World Bank, PovertyNet, 2008 figures).

Of course, there is nothing new about poverty. The issue is how and why at particular historical moments, poverty becomes sharply visible and serves as a lightning rod for social action and change. This occasional transformation of poverty into a "public" issue has taken place at different times and in different forms. At moments of political conservatism, poverty has been framed as a problem of delinquent behavior requiring moral

6

discipline and the imposition of social order. Such was the case in the 1980s as conservative political regimes on both sides of the Atlantic promoted the stereotype of the dependent and undeserving poor, those dependent on welfare and unwilling to work, victims not of structural forces but rather of their own laziness and lack of responsibility.

At other times in history, poverty has been interpreted as a problem of the national economy and its management. This was the case just after World War II, when a multilateral or multinational system of development—the Bretton Woods order—was established, with the World Bank and the International Monetary Fund (IMF) at its helm. This system sought to "modernize" national economies. It was premised on the idea that development was a ladder with stages of economic growth; some countries were at the top and others had to quickly catch up.

What is unusual about the present historical moment is that poverty has become visible as a global issue. The focus has shifted from the modernization of national economies to the alleviation of the poverty of the "bottom billion," the 1.4 billion people such as Felicita living under the threshold of the international poverty line. There is also a rapid globalization of the responses to poverty—from the global campaigns that are being waged to "make poverty history," to the global dissemination of poverty-alleviation "best practices," to the radical critiques that link poverty to the global economy and thus insist that "another world is possible" and necessary. In short, a new global order, what I call "millennial development," is taking shape.

Millennial development is the confluence of various forces. To begin, there is a remaking of development as a "kinder and gentler" process, one that is as concerned with human development as previous eras were concerned with economic growth. In the 1990s, the World Bank made the alleviation of poverty its top priority. In 2000, the member states of the United Nations (UN) adopted the Millennium Development Goals, an ambitious set of human development goals that were to be achieved through global cooperation by 2015.

As development institutions consider anew the goal of human development, they have developed a new set of development metrics, or development indicators. Instead of focusing on rates of economic growth, there is now the widespread use and tracking of an international poverty line, which binds the world's impoverished in one simple statistic and creates a sense of a common fate. In addition, the Millennium Development Goals have generated an imperative to measure and map progress toward poverty eradication. In the foreword to the 2003 Human Development Report, Mark Malloch Brown, then UNDP administrator, presents the Millennium Development Goals as "a development manifesto for ordinary citizens around the world: timebound, measurable, pocket-book issues they can immediately understand." He continues that "with adequate data, the Goals seek to hold their governments and wider international community accountable for their achievement" (UNDP 2003a: vi). Maternal mortality, primary education, health, and housing are all now crucial ingredients of development, not simply gross national product.

Poverty data is one thing; data on inequality is another. One of the most dramatic diagrams in the 2005 Human Development Report is that illustrating the "champagne glass effect," which shows that the world's richest 500 individuals have a combined income greater than the poorest 416 million (UNDP 2005: 36). In fact, the champagne glass is more like a wide-mouthed funnel, with wealth, income, and consumption disappearing at the bottom (see Figure 1.2).

A focus on inequality is radical because it implies that millennial development cannot simply be about saving the poor; it must also tackle

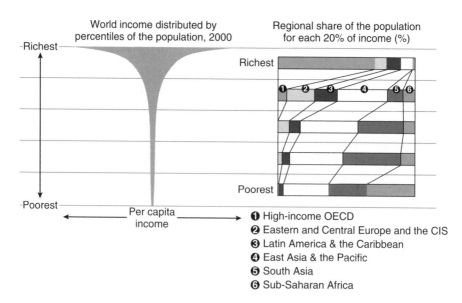

Figure 1.2 Where the money is (UNDP 2005).

the more difficult questions of the distribution of wealth, privilege, and power. There is no simple $1 donation for this, no month-long service learning trip, no church volunteer group. Such a task requires confronting the very ways in which international development functions. Thus, in the frameworks of millennial development, there is a metric of inequality that has gained prominence: the flow of aid from the global North to the global South. Figure 1.3, which appears in the 2005 Human Development Report of the UN, is appropriately subtitled "wealth is growing faster than aid." It shows that while per capita income has been increasing in key donor countries, such as those in North America and Western Europe, overseas development assistance (ODA) per capita has been on the decline.

The United States, while the largest donor of ODA in absolute terms, turns out to be quite stingy, disbursing only 0.22 percent of its gross national income in ODA in 2005, a far cry from the Millennium Development Goal of 0.7 percent (UNDP 2007: 289). When the structure of this assistance is analyzed—to take into account debt relief or contracts to US consultants and companies—the flow of aid from North to South is even more attenuated, more fickle. And such aid is drowned by something else: the substantial agricultural subsidies that Northern countries provide

GDP and ODA per capita, Development Assistance Committee countries, index (1980 = 100)

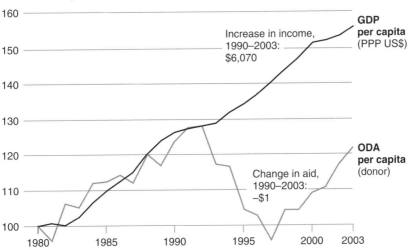

Figure 1.3 Richer but less generous: wealth is growing faster than aid (UNDP 2005).

9

to their own farmers (see Figure 1.4) and that greatly imperil the ability of farmers in the global South to command a fair price for agricultural products in national and global markets.

While the 2001 World Trade Organization (WTO) conference in Doha, Qatar, called for the elimination of such subsidies, they continue to exist, much to the dismay of global South countries. The 2003 Human Development Report of the UN vividly depicts the scale of such subsidies (see Figure 1.4). In this report, Malloch Brown passionately argues that "long term initiatives to halve hunger and poverty will fail without fundamental restructuring of the global trade system—particularly in agriculture." He insists that "policy, not charity is what rich countries can do to meet the Millennium Development Goals" (UNDP 2003a: vi).

Millennial development entails a reform of structures of aid and trade. It also involves the formation of a parallel apparatus of development. Global philanthropic foundations, global justice campaigns, and global non-governmental organizations are leading the fight against poverty, the largest of them commanding resources, power, and influence that far exceed the scope of most nation-states. They are led by iconic figures—Bill and Melinda Gates, Bill Clinton, Bono—global personalities who have become flashpoints for millennial development. These celebrities, and their campaigns, make poverty visible and create a sense of urgency around poverty alleviation. From setting an agenda around poverty (as does the Gates Foundation) to strategically influencing the development agenda of advanced, industrial countries (as does Bono), these figureheads have become decisive actors in the new global order of millennial development.

Many of these organizations and campaigns seek to actively involve ordinary men and women in the struggle against global poverty. The concerts of the rock band U2 have the feel of a Global Studies 101 classroom, with an electronic scroll ticking out the Universal Declaration of Human Rights. Bono is blindfolded and wrapped in an American flag as he laments the human degradation caused by war, poverty, and deprivation. The audience wears white wristbands, for they have pledged to "make poverty history." They are the "everyday Americans" of the One Campaign, a grassroots campaign co-founded by Bono to help eradicate global poverty. They have faith in Bono's (in Sachs 2005: xvii) argument that "[w]e could be the first generation to outlaw the kind of extreme, stupid poverty that sees a child die of hunger in a world of plenty."

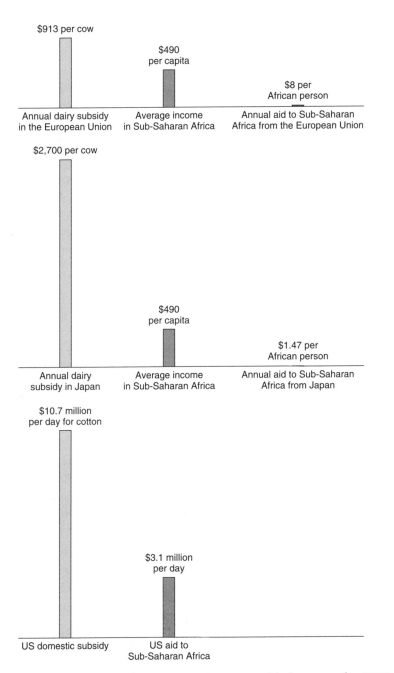

Figure 1.4 Cows and cotton receive more aid than people, 2000 (UNDP 2003a).

Such political mobilization across the ideological spectrum—from evangelical Christians to global liberals—is a hallmark of millennial development. In this way, poverty has become a public issue, with responsibility for its alleviation dispersed among a broad swath of global citizens, especially citizens of the global North. The awareness of poverty defines the West's place in the world. Thus, an account of then World Bank president James Wolfensohn's fight against poverty begins in the following way: "We live in an age when millions of people die because they were born in the wrong place: one section of humanity enjoys $2 lattes and disposable cameras; the other section lives on $2 a day and appears itself to be disposable" (Mallaby 2004: 1). This global conscience is not abstract; rather it has permeated everyday life: the young American school girl who works tirelessly to raise money for anti-malaria bed nets for African families, dollars converted into lives saved, an equation made possible through selfless volunteerism.

Millennial development relies greatly on the modern, Western self who is not only aware of poverty's devastation but is also empowered to act upon it in responsible ways. (PRODUCT) RED is a good example of this virtuous cycle. The message is simple: "Red is not a charity. It is a business model. You buy products. The companies buy pills. Poor people take the pills and live" (http://www.joinred.com, accessed August 15, 2008) (see Figure 1.5). This connection between a consumer buying a Gap t-shirt or a Motorola razor phone at one end and an HIV-AIDS-infected African body receiving medicine at the other end is mediated by the Global Fund, which provides financial support to various development programs. Here too a metrics is essential, this one that establishes "sound performance" and "tangible, measurable results" in "lifesaving work" (http://www.joinred.com/Learn/HowRedWorks/GlobalFund.aspx, accessed August 15, 2008).

But lest we forget, millennial development has another powerful force: global social movements. These movements, through visible and often fierce protest, have served as a catalyst for the new global order. Thus, in 1994, as the institutions established at Bretton Woods—the World Bank and IMF—celebrated their half-century mark, so critics gathered in loud protest, insisting that 50 years was enough and demanding "reparations" for the damages wrought by development (Danaher 1995). The protests and gatherings continued—in Seattle in 1999 against the WTO and the global system of trade, in the annual World Social Forum meetings to insist upon

HOW (RED)™ WORKS

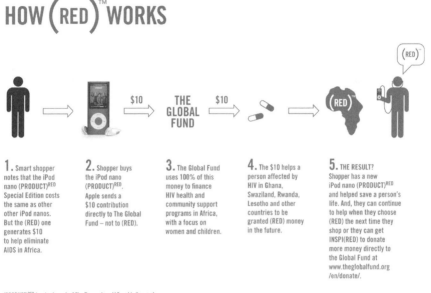

1. Smart shopper notes that the iPod nano (PRODUCT)RED Special Edition costs the same as other other iPod nanos. But the (RED) one generates $10 to help eliminate AIDS in Africa.

2. Shopper buys the iPod nano (PRODUCT)RED. Apple sends a $10 contribution directly to The Global Fund – not to (RED).

3. The Global Fund uses 100% of this money to finance HIV health and community support programs in Africa, with a focus on women and children.

4. The $10 helps a person affected by HIV in Ghana, Swaziland, Rwanda, Lesotho and other countries to be granted (RED) money in the future.

5. THE RESULT? Shopper has a new iPod nano (PRODUCT)RED and helped save a person's life. And, they can continue to help when they choose to (RED) the next time they shop or they can get INSPI(RED) to donate more money directly to the Global Fund at www.theglobalfund.org/en/donate/.

(PRODUCT)RED is a trademark of The Persuaders, LLC and is licensed to (RED) partners. The goods and services of (RED) partners bear the (PRODUCT)RED trademark to support (RED).

Figure 1.5 How (RED) works (courtesy of (RED)).

an alternative to the free-market global economy, outside the G8 meetings to call for a "jubilee" or debt relief for the world's poorest and most indebted countries.

These global social movements are aimed at creating what Global Exchange calls "a people's globalization," predicated on a "democratization of the global economy" (http://www.globalexchange.org, accessed August 15, 2008). The organization Focus on the Global South, headquartered in Bangkok, phrases this in a slightly different way: as a "transformation of the global economy from one centred around the needs of transnational corporations to one that focuses on the needs of people, communities and nations and in which the capacities of local and national economies are strengthened" (http://focusweb.org/who-we-are.html, accessed August 15, 2008). With this in mind, Walden Bello (2007: 210), founder of Focus on the Global South and well-known international activist, argues that the globalist project is in crisis, with the "loss of legitimacy of the key multilateral institutions that serve as the political canopy of corporate-driven globalization." He argues that the "critical factor" has been resistance:

Action is a condition for the emergence of truth. What I mean to say is that for over a decade before Seattle, the United Nations Development Program and other agencies had been publishing data showing the negative impact of structural adjustment programs, neoliberal reforms, and corporate-driven globalization. However, these remained lifeless statistics that were largely ignored by the media, the academy, and policymakers that held on to faith-based assumptions about the beneficial impact of these measures and processes. Seattle, by bringing the message of the protestors so forcefully to world attention, turned abstract statistics into brutal facts . . . It is doubtful if people like the Nobel Prize-winner Joseph Stiglitz or the star economist Jeffrey Sachs or financier George Soros would have detached themselves from the mainstream and begun to criticize corporate-driven globalization so forcefully had Seattle not occurred.

(Bello 2007: 215)

In this book, I take a closer look at the complex ensemble of often contradictory forces and ideas that is millennial development. I examine the key ideas, voices, and policies that have become the hallmark of this moment. Instead of asking: What is poverty? and How is it alleviated? I ask a different set of questions, those that I believe are fundamental. Specifically, I ask: What are the dominant ideas about poverty and poverty alleviation? Are there alternative ideas and if so, how may we learn about and from them? Do the dominant and alternative ideas break with previous models of development? In other words, this is a book about the politics of knowledge at a time of millennial development. It is premised on the argument that certain world views and knowledge paradigms have more purchase than others among poverty experts. This in turn has crucial implications for the allocation of resources and opportunity. As Sub-comandante Marcos (2000), leader of the Zapatista movement, declared from Chiapas, Mexico: "ideas are also weapons."

FROM THE END OF HISTORY TO THE END OF POVERTY

In *The End of History and the Last Man*, an essay originally published in 1989 and then published as a book in 1992, Francis Fukuyama argued that humanity had reached the end of history:

What we may be witnessing is not just the end of the Cold War . . . but the end
of history as such: that is, the end point of mankind's ideological evolution
and the universalization of Western liberal democracy as the final form of
human government.

(Fukuyama 1989: 4)

Fukuyama (1992: xiii) also argued that "liberal principles in economics—the
'free market' have spread," producing "unprecedented levels of material
prosperity" around the world. For Fukuyama, free-market capitalism and
liberal democracy were not simply a reality; they were ideals that could not
be improved upon.

Although Fukuyama himself was to later cast doubt on the "end of
history" thesis, at the time of its initial articulation the paradigm signified
the heady confidence of the gurus of free-market globalization. It was this
audacious revival of "liberal principles in economics," or "neoliberalism,"
that lay at the heart of the "Washington consensus," a term coined by John
Williamson in 1989. Williamson (2004: 7) himself rejects the "perversion
of the term" as a "synonym for neoliberalism or market fundamentalism."
But the Washington consensus came to be seen as a set of rigid strictures
that mandated privatization, deregulation, and liberalization. In a manner
similar to Fukuyama, Williamson (2000: 261) notes that in 1989 there was
"an unusually wide measure of agreement that several rather basic ideas of
good economics were not only desirable but of key importance in the
current policy agenda." In short, both the content and the form of the
Washington consensus were incontrovertible truths. When and how was this
unshakeable certainty about free markets transformed into an awareness of
global suffering? How did the debate shift from the "end of history" to the
"end of poverty"?

In 1994, two years after Fukuyama's book was published, Jacques
Derrida, the legendary French philosopher, published *Specters of Marx*.
Writing against Fukuyama, Derrida (1994: 106) draws attention to an
"obvious macroscopic fact," that "never before, in absolute figures, have so
many men, women and children been subjugated, starved or exterminated
on the earth." In short, the euphoria of the free market was giving way to
the specter of poverty.

In Washington DC, James Wolfensohn as president of the World Bank
declared a post-Washington consensus. In a key speech, titled "The Other

Crisis," delivered to the annual meeting of World Bank Governors in 1998, Wolfensohn argued that while the world was fixated on a financial crisis— at that time the East Asian financial crisis—it had failed to notice that another crisis was looming: poverty (Pender 2001: 402). Soon Joseph Stiglitz, chief economist of the World Bank from 1996 to 2000, emerged as the key interlocutor of such a "post-Washington consensus consensus." Rejecting the "market fundamentalism" of the Washington consensus, Stiglitz made the case for new types of development interventions that relied on the role of the state. Equally significant, he argued that the ideas of this new, emerging consensus could no longer be based in Washington DC and that instead "developing countries must take ownership of them" (Stiglitz 1998: 33). Thus, the "end of history" came to an end. Naomi Klein (2001) writes of a moment of celebration at the first annual World Social Forum in Porto Alegre, Brazil, that great gathering of global social movements: "Many people said that they felt history being made in that room. What I felt was something more intangible: the end of The End of History."

In order to understand the shift from the "end of history" to the "end of poverty" it is necessary to understand two key vectors. The first is the devastation engendered by the market-oriented development policies of the 1980s. Unleashing severe protests against such policies, the crisis also set into motion a new political and academic discourse of "market failure." The second is the emergence of a compelling geographical imagination about sites of poverty, notably Africa. Most often imagined as a "heart of dark-ness," Africa was now seen as a continent wronged by bad development policy, a place that can be fixed through the right interventions. Since 9/11, the Middle East too has been imagined as an "other" geography—a "hot spot" where the rage of the Arab Street has to be somehow tackled and remedied if the home geographies of America and the West were to remain safe and secure.

From Markets to Market Failure

As Fukuyama was writing and defending his "end of history" thesis, a crisis of economy and legitimacy was brewing in many parts of the world. A decade of harsh structural adjustment policies had wrought havoc in many parts of the world such that by the 1990s new policies had to be crafted in order to address growing poverty, unemployment, and indebtedness. Although it was not until the Argentina crisis of 2001–2002 that the IMF was to finally admit the failure of its monetary policies, the World Bank had much earlier distanced itself from the crude structural adjustment paradigm. As global social movements launched protests against the World Bank and IMF, so the World Bank, led by James Wolfensohn, sought to remain one step ahead of protestors (Elyachar 2002). World Bank insiders such as Joseph Stiglitz placed the blame on the IMF, insisting that it had worsened rather than improved the economies of the developing world (Stiglitz 2000a, 2002).

Stiglitz's critique may have proved to be too radical, and in a "showdown" he eventually left the World Bank (Wade 2001). But his twofold criticism of the IMF circulated widely. First, he painted the IMF as a neocolonial institution in which the economic sovereignty of Third World nations was compromised. The IMF, Stiglitz noted, "does not report directly to either the citizens who finance it or those whose lives it affects" (Stiglitz 2002: 12). Second, Stiglitz (2002) argued that the IMF was an instrument of "market fundamentalism," unable to recognize or respond to market failures. Poverty was an instance of market failure, demonstrating the inability of markets to provide collective goods. The Washington consensus, by promoting a free-market ideology was thus unable to successfully promote development. For Stiglitz, the Washington consensus was strongly contradicted by the East Asian case, where strong, developmental states had secured both economic growth and improvements in human development. This contrast between market fundamentalism and developmental states is a key feature of Stiglitz's articulation of a consensus that was to replace the neoliberal Washington consensus. The new order was meant to be a reformed and enlightened globalization with better rules for "global collective action."

If the Washington consensus was associated with the free-market ideologies of Ronald Reagan and Margaret Thatcher, then the post-Washington consensus was consonant with a new political regime, the Third Way philosophy of Bill Clinton and Tony Blair. Clinton (2006), in a speech in London, reflected on the Third Way:

> No one has yet found anything approaching the free market that is as an efficient allocator of goods, services, capital and opportunity. But, the free market left alone ... will not take account of human needs, not equally distribute human opportunity, will not empower people ... unless there is a

role for government to create the conditions, the systems and the tools people need to make the most of their own lives, and to build up their communities.

Clinton's speech seeks to reconcile an ancient tension that lies at the very heart of liberalism: the faith in liberty and free enterprise and the desire for some forms of regulation. In *The Wealth of Nations* (1776), Adam Smith famously espouses a theory of the free market. But Smith is also the author of another key text, *The Theory of Moral Sentiments* (1759), in which he expresses the need for a caring, providing society. Almost a century later, in *On Liberty* (1859), John Stuart Mill also argued for the freedom of the economy. But, like Smith, he also made the case for "public control," for "restraint" such that harm to workers, consumers, and society could be prevented. These ethics of care and restraint, what may be understood as an "ethical economics" (Peet 2003: 10), were lost during the neoliberal policies of the late twentieth century. They are being revived at a time of millennial development.

In his famous thesis of the "double movement" of capitalism, the economic historian Karl Polanyi (1944: 3) argues that the movement to "disembed" the economy from society and create the "stark utopia" of the "self regulating market"—which is essentially what neoliberal policies attempted to do—also generates efforts to recapture and re-embed the economy within social and political control. The "double movement" is thus the tension between "market society" and "society with markets," between a system dominated by market exchange and one where reciprocity and redistribution are possible. It is a struggle that is evident in much of twentieth-century development and within millennial development itself.

In *The End of Poverty*, a text that is iconic of millennial development, Jeffrey Sachs (2005) issues a call for Keynesian interventions in poor countries, thus making the case for an "embedded" liberalism. Persistent poverty, for Sachs, is the visible manifestation of market failure, one that can only be combated through investment in human development infrastructure. Writing against Sachs, William Easterly (2006) in *The White Man's Burden*, argues that the problem with poverty is state failure rather than market failure. Dismissing Sachs as a "Planner" with a "Big Western Plan," Easterly (2006: 60) argues that "free markets work." Such debates also mark the field of microfinance. Vinod Khosla (2004), Silicon Valley venture capitalist, states that microfinance is "the most important economic phenomena after capitalism and Adam Smith" (http://www.gsb.stanford. edu/news/headlines/2004globalconf_khosla_speech.shtml, accessed August 5, 2005). But which version of Adam Smith and liberal philosophy should we reference? Is microfinance a free-market strategy that seeks to harness the microenterprises of the poor? Or is it a response to market failure, an instance of an "embedded liberalism" that is concerned with "social interest" and relationships of reciprocity and redistribution?

Africa Works

If millennial development involves a debate about whether markets work or fail, then it also involves an imagination about places that work or fail. Africa tops the list. In the 1980s, under conditions of structural adjustment, the continent was viewed as the heart of darkness, burdened by corrupt states and failing markets. Today Africa is imagined as a place that was wronged by development and globalization and that must be helped. One of Wolfensohn's first acts as president of the World Bank was to visit Africa (Mallaby 2004: 89). Africa, once understood only in the language of crisis, is now being remade as a "place-in-the-world" (Ferguson 2006: 6).

Take, for example, the July 2007 issue of *Vanity Fair*, which was dedicated to Africa. Guest edited by Bono, the issue sought to present Africa as a "mesmerizing, entrepreneurial, dynamic continent" rather than as a "hopeless deathbed of war, disease, and corruption" (Bono 2007: 32). We are introduced to Africa not so much via Africans as through American celebrities who care about Africa: Oprah, George Clooney, Madonna, Bill Gates, each photographed in stunning fashion by Annie Leibovitz. Particularly striking is the idea, which ran through the issue: that we are all Africans. DNA samples taken from the editors and celebrities chart "individual ancestral paths from their starting point in East Africa." The editor comments: "It is quite moving to see that every person on the planet is linked to this African tribe, and that, as the saying goes, we are all African" (Carter 2007: 28).

The Africa issue of *Vanity Fair* features Jeffrey Sachs and his "millennium villages," which are meant to provide a concentrated dose of development intervention in rural Africa. Sachs's argument about the "end of poverty" is also an argument about places that work or fail. In a recreation of the ideas of development economist Walt Rostow, Sachs envisions development as a ladder with countries at different rungs. Africa, imagined at the bottom of the ladder, has to be given the opportunity to "gain a foothold" (Sachs 2005: 73).

But it is important to note that another geography lurks in the shadows of this remaking of Africa. In the *Vanity Fair* issue, Sachs is presented as "visionary economist, savior of Bolivia, Poland, and other struggling nations, adviser to the U.N. and movie stars" (Munk 2007: 140). That brief and breathless reference to Bolivia and Poland is significant, for Sachs was involved in reconstructing these economies in his capacity as IMF economist. As Naomi Klein (2007: 150) notes, his "shock therapy" for Bolivia "deepened poverty" and "eliminated . . . hundreds of thousands of full-time jobs with pensions," replacing them "with precarious ones with no protections at all." This is the older geography of brutal neoliberalism and market discipline. Millennial development seeks to mitigate the consequences of shock therapy in new zones of experiments such as Africa.

Yet, the geographies shaped by neoliberalism are celebrated as places of progress rather than of devastation. In the world of microfinance, structurally adjusted Latin America, particularly Bolivia, is often presented as a best-practice model, its territories well primed for aggressive privatization and commercialization. Indeed, Latin America, with its history of shock therapy, is seen as the advanced contrast to a more primitive South Asia, especially Bangladesh, home to the Grameen Bank model of microfinance. Thus, the preface to a book on profit-making microfinance declares that Latin America is "a generation ahead of other regions with respect to the development of the microfinance sector" (Jansen 2002: vii).

Microfinance has become a key strategy to lift Africa out of poverty. It makes possible the envisioning of Africa as a frontier of investment and capital accumulation. Thus, a recent CNBC special argues that the current economic crisis may present an unprecedented opportunity to invest "in one of the world's most dangerous places." There is, of course, the interest in Africa's oil, gold, and diamonds. But there is also interest in the micro-enterprises of poor women underwritten by microfinance (http://www.cnbc.com/id/30959351, accessed June 21, 2009). Thus a recent Benetton "global communication campaign" featuring Senegalese singer, Youssou N'Dour, highlights and celebrates a microfinance program in Senegal supported by Benetton. N'Dour proudly states that "Africa doesn't want charity" but rather microfinance (Benetton 2008). His declaration echoes a new set of "African" voices, such as George Ayittey (2004) and Dambisa

Figure 1.6 "Africa Works," United Colors of Benetton (http://www.benetton. com/africaworks-press/en/index.html, accessed January 20, 2009).

Moyo (2009) that seek to set Africa "free"—free from Western aid and state bureaucracies. The Benetton campaign's striking images promise economic freedom, transforming figures of African poverty into microentrepreneurs. They are the new "united colors of Benetton," Africa reconfigured as global chic. They embody the truth that is the Benetton campaign slogan: "Africa Works" (see Figure 1.6).

While Africa draws the celebrities—Brangelina to Namibia, Madonna to Malawi—another geography arouses imperial anxiety: the Middle East. Since 9/11, a wide range of voices across the political spectrum has called for a recognition of the links between poverty and violence; in other words that the "war on terror" must also be a war on poverty. An essay titled "Governance hotspots," written a few days after 9/11 argues: "September 11, 2001 brings to the fore, with perhaps greater urgency than other events, the need for global governance . . . to help reduce poverty and misery, and hence rage, in the global South" (Sassen 2002: 106). The Middle East has been the epicenter of these post-9/11 debates. Globalization enthusiast, Thomas Friedman (2002), has argued that technology-driven globalization, such as the kind in India, can create great prosperity and thus produce "a young generation more interested in joining the world system than blowing it up." Such a theme is prominent also in Sachs's calls for an end to poverty: "To fight terrorism, we will need to fight poverty and deprivation as well. A purely military approach to terrorism is doomed to fail" (Sachs 2005: 215).

Thinking about the Middle East complicates the narrative of millennial development. Although this is a time marked by the call for a reformed and enlightened globalization, it is also a time of imperial war, notably in Iraq and Afghanistan. While there is the body count of universal poverty lines— 1 billion, 2 billion—there is also the body count of military and civilian deaths in these frontiers of imperialism. The simultaneity of war and development presents a challenge. Is the end of poverty the conscientious counterpoint to empire? After all, during nineteenth-century colonialism the colonies were governed not only through military force but also through development. The will to improve, this mission of civilization, a white man's burden, was central to the colonial mandate. Is the end of poverty a revival of this theme of colonial welfare? Francis Fukuyama is not only the author of *The End of History*; until his recent change of heart, he was also one of the key intellectuals of "The Project for the New American Century." Launched in the 1990s, the Project, which included Paul Wolfowitz and Dick Cheney among others, argued that the time had come for an American empire that would spread the values of liberal democracy and free-market capitalism. The wars in Iraq and Afghanistan, waged after 9/11, are often justified in the name of these values. This too is a millennial imagination. It is not surprising then that Afghanistan, which after 9/11 has been incorporated into the geographical imagination of the Middle East, is the site of vigorous development activities such as microfinance as well as war strategies and terrorist hunts.

MICROFINANCE AND THE FRONTIERS OF MILLENNIAL DEVELOPMENT

The world of millennial development has many different agendas and priorities. Of these, microfinance has unusual prominence. In the world of international development, large chunks of budgets do not get allocated to microfinance (infrastructure still rules). It is estimated that even for the largest providers of donor funding for microfinance, the World Bank and the UNDP, the sector accounts for less than 1 percent of annual spending (Rosenberg 2006: 1). Nor is microfinance the largest sector of specialization for international or local non-governmental organizations (NGOs) (many other sectors are common—health, human rights, women). But microfinance is everywhere; it exists in the sub-terrain of almost everything in development. It is the panacea of choice. This ubiquitous idea is lauded and deployed by development institutions and theorists of all stripes and varying ideologies as an important antidote to poverty. Thus, while Sachs and Easterly disagree in substantial ways on how to understand poverty and alleviate it, their disagreement dissipates when it comes to microfinance, for each advocates it as a noble and efficacious policy. The UN celebrated 2005 as the International Year of Microcredit. More recently, in the wake of the global financial crisis, microfinance is being celebrated as the strategy that may yet save capitalism, providing a way to create new markets out of those that business school guru C.K. Prahalad (2004) famously labeled the "bottom of the pyramid."

In this book, I study microfinance in order to study the making of development. As I discussed in my opening story of "small worlds," both the democratization of capital and the democratization of development are implicated in microfinance. Such processes are in turn complicated by the vectors that I outlined earlier: the crisis and opportunity of "market failure," and the geographical imagination of backwardness and marginality about sites such as Africa and the Middle East.

However popular microfinance may be, there is no consensus on how to implement and use microfinance for the purpose of development. Here, I briefly outline three contrasting paradigms of microfinance: Yunus's emphasis on a rights-based, pro-poor approach to microfinance; "creative capitalism" strategies that position the poor as a lucrative market; and sharp critiques of microfinance that reject its impacts on poverty. The three paradigms are about much more than microfinance. They represent struggles within development over issues such as social interest, the regulation of markets, and the nature of capitalism. These are, as I have already argued, key questions in liberalism, shaping the trajectory of economies. They represent the moral dilemmas of the liberal self. The three paradigms reveal what is at stake in millennial development: can poverty be transformed into poverty capital, a frontier of accumulation, speculation, and profit, and if so, will poverty capital serve the interests of the poor?

Credit as a Human Right

Let me start with the foundational idea behind microfinance. Articulated by Muhammad Yunus in the founding of the Grameen Bank, microfinance is premised on the notion that credit is a human right and that it can improve the lives of the poorest. This approach sees microfinance as explicitly distinct from, and even opposed to, commercial banking. Yunus has repeatedly emphasized that microfinance is not banking at the bottom of the socio-economic structure; instead it is about turning banking on its head. In short, it is about remaking capitalism. The idea of "credit as a human right" suggests that microfinance is not simply a development tool but rather an "ethical economics." At a session devoted to microfinance at the 2004 Barcelona Universal Forum of Cultures, Jacques Attali, founder of PlaNet Finance declared that microfinance was key to a "civilized globalization." Similarly, at a microfinance conference held at the Clausen Center for International Business and Policy at my home university—the University of California, Berkeley—John Hatch, founder of Finca International, presented Yunus as the "Gandhi of our times" and microfinance as a force "more powerful than non-violence."

Although Yunus frames his vision of microfinance in the language of human rights, his ideas are in fact concerned with entrepreneurialism rather than redistribution, with opportunity rather than equality. His fierce emphasis on self-reliance creates a model of poverty alleviation that is simultaneously poor-centric and anti-welfare. Thus, Yunus has repeatedly noted that self employment rather than wage employment is the goal of Grameen Bank loans (Bornstein 1996: 331). As he explained at the 2004 microfinance conference at UC Berkeley's Clausen Center: "I say this to the children of Grameen borrowers: Your mother owns a bank. You are different. You must be self-reliant. You must create a job. You must never ask for a job." The theme of self-reliance extends to microfinance institutions as well, with Yunus insisting that the Grameen model is not reliant on either foreign donors or the state. It is not surprising then that when Yunus and the Grameen Bank were awarded the Nobel Peace Prize, Easterly, relieved that the prize did not go to Bono (another "embedded" liberal), celebrated that this was "a victory for the one-step-at-a-time homegrown bottom-up approach" to development (Tierney 2006).

It is a curious combination—of the moral calculus charted by the human rights framework and of the active entrepreneurialism and disciplined self-reliance evoked by the promise of an opportunity society. In an interview (August 2004) that I conducted with him in Bangladesh, Yunus talked about "popular capitalism," which he believed has been overlooked by grand economic theorists. "The market has to be made free for all," he noted. "It is like any other instrument, take for example a knife— one can use it to cut throats or to craft beautiful products. Which will it be?"

The "credit as a human right" framework is often identified with the models of microfinance that are practiced in Bangladesh. But I will later argue in this book that the story of development and poverty alleviation in Bangladesh is more complex. Indeed, "credit as a human right" can be understood to be a "public transcript," obscuring a less visible "hidden transcript" of social protection programs and human development infrastructure. Here, the work of BRAC, which is perhaps the world's largest NGO, is crucial. Like the Grameen Bank, BRAC also uses microfinance as a key instrument of poverty alleviation. However, it embeds microfinance in a vast array of development services. While Yunus, in an interview (August 2004), impatiently noted that "there is no point waiting for the state," Fazle Abed, founder and chairman of BRAC, states that his main goal is to "align government policy to meet the needs and aspirations of the poor" (Covington 2009: 24). Despite their differences, Grameen and BRAC have both manifested what has been recently hailed as "Bangladesh's audacity of hope" (Covington 2009). Chapter 3 of this book tells the story of how development institutions in one of the poorest countries in the world have been able to tackle, to some degree, the challenge of persistent poverty. That story, I argue, contradicts the narrative of a self-reliant opportunity society that has become the "public transcript" of microfinance.

Creative Capitalism

In his Nobel lecture, Yunus (2006a) noted that in order to resolve the problem of crushing poverty, the world has to rethink some of the basic assumptions of free-market ideologies. He called for a new type of entrepreneurship that would be concerned with "social businesses"—those whose bottom line would be about "doing good" (Yunus 2008). At first glance, his speech seems uncannily similar to a host of voices that have called for a market-based approach to poverty. Yet, Yunus has something else in mind. While others place their faith in global capitalism, Yunus recognizes market failures and seeks a development alternative. He finds it in a people's capitalism populated by poor entrepreneurs, facilitated by microfinance.

Standing in contrast to such a view is Bill Gates's (2008: 23) recent espousal of a "creative capitalism":

> It is mainly corporations that have the skills to make technological innovations work for the poor . . . We need a more creative capitalism: an attempt to stretch

25

the reach of market forces so that more companies can benefit from doing work that makes more people better off. We need new ways to bring far more people into the system—capitalism—that has done so much good in the world.

Gates is not talking about corporate philanthropy or corporate social responsibility. Nor is he talking about Yunus's "social businesses." Instead, he is arguing that "there are markets all over the world that businesses have missed" and that the poor constitute a particularly important and lucrative market (Gates 2008: 27). It is a bold vision, which expresses a heady confidence in markets—markets that work rather than fail.

But there are challenges in creative capitalism. On the one hand, the "economies of the bottom billion" are imagined as "short of capital," thereby requiring "private capital" (Collier 2007: 87). On the other hand, the bottom billion are imagined as a "billion bootstraps" (Smith and Thurman 2007). How can the entrepreneurial talents, social capital, and sweat equity of the poor be converted into new forms of capital? This is the "mystery of capital" (de Soto 2000). Microfinance, in particular, seems to contain the magic key to unlock the mystery of capital and enable the transformation of the bottom billion into a new frontier of capital accumulation.

The issue at stake is whether creative capitalism requires a new type of microfinance, one more concerned with financial returns than social returns. It is thus that the Consultative Group to Assist the Poor (CGAP), a donor forum based at the World Bank, has sought to construct a global microfinance industry integrated with financial markets. Such an approach breaks with the Grameen model of microfinance and its emphasis on human development. The case for creative capitalism is pithily expressed in a piece titled "Profit and poverty: why it matters" by Michael Chu (2007), an important microfinance interlocutor and investor. Chu argues that only a profit-making industry with high returns can transform the lives of the "bottom billion": "No longer funds-constrained, the number of poor people reached and the volume of capital disbursed has exploded." It is in this way that the markets, rather than market failure, becomes the key theme of microfinance—a seductive promise of economic freedom and opportunity. Supporters of profit-making microfinance also argue that markets ensure accountability. Thus, Pierre Omidyar, founder of eBay and now micro-finance enthusiast, insists that "there is a difference between undemanding capital—contributed by donors who expect nothing in return—and demanding capital, which requires transparency of financial reporting and an appropriate reward for risk" (Bruck 2006). "Demanding capital," it is implied, will ultimately serve the poor well.

The battle of ideas is fierce. Carlos Labarthe, one of the two CEOs of Compartamos, a Mexican microfinance institution that makes a healthy profit of $80 million a year by serving about 1 million women at 90 percent interest rates, rejects the idea of credit as a human right: "Well, I don't believe that. Opportunity is a human right, education—but credit is for the one that has an opportunity to make something productive with that. This is in a way creating wealth, more than wiping out of poverty. Not bringing up the destitute" (Bruck 2006). Yunus disagrees. Of Compartamos he states: "Microcredit was created to fight the money lender, not to become the money lender" (*Business Week* 2007).

Microsharks

The contrasting approaches to microfinance outlined here share a common theme: an optimism about microfinance and its ability to mitigate poverty. But as microfinance has emerged as an icon of millennial development so there has been a rallying of criticism about the ineffectiveness of microfinance. Surprisingly, microfinance insiders are skeptics. In an interview (October 2004), a senior CGAP advisor argued that there is little empirical evidence to indicate that microfinance is either sustainable or that it reduces poverty. Arguing that the microfinance machine has been driven by "heartwarming images of poor people," he characterized microfinance as more successful in "pulling on heartstrings" than in actually delivering on poverty alleviation. Indeed, a CGAP report makes this point, albeit in less trenchant terms. Evaluating the microfinance portfolio of the World Bank and UNDP, it concludes that "in both agencies, less than a quarter of the projects that funded microlending were judged successful" (Rosenberg 2006: 1). This evaluation is almost identical to that expressed by Thomas Dichter, a development consultant and critic of microfinance. Dichter argues that poverty lending is bad social policy, a bad development strategy, and bad business. While some borrowers never get off the debt treadmill, others squander their credit on consumer goods. The few lenders who can pay their way, he says, rarely serve the poor (Magolis 2007).

Such skepticism runs deep in the Washington microfinance establishment. A high-ranking USAID staffer in the Microenterprise Office noted in an interview (March 2004) that microfinance is now being billed as a panacea—from terrorism to women's empowerment. How could one intervention deliver on all of this? And did the poor really need microfinance? Did they not need a range of financial services, such as savings and insurance, of which credit may be only a small part? Were not the poorest better served by grants rather than loans? In recognition of the popularity of microfinance, she also asked: will the US Congress be willing to hear that microfinance is not magic, that the emperor has no clothes? In various interviews that I conducted between 2004 and 2008, CGAP senior staff echoed these concerns. Were there not limits to what microfinance could achieve? If microfinance was now also meant to address terrorism, was not the problem US foreign policy rather than poverty? Yet others, for example a staffer in the USAID Women in Development office, lamented in an interview (June 2005) that while microfinance has brought attention to the issue of women's poverty, it has bypassed many other issues related to gender equality and empowerment—from women's participation in global labor forces to the legal rights of women. The lament is echoed by critics of Washington-style development who argue that key structural issues remain unaddressed by microfinance:

> As long as microenterprise development is offered as a substitute for meaningful social development . . . for fundamental changes in the economic policies prescribed by institutions such as the World Bank and the IMF, it will only impede progress toward finding real answers to the very real problem of poverty in the South.
>
> (Scully n.d.)

The skepticism about microfinance that seems to unite the anti-development critics and the Washington DC insiders speak to a broader dilemma of millennial development, one that surfaced during Wolfensohn's leadership of the World Bank. From 1995 to 2005, Wolfensohn sought to direct the Bank's work from infrastructure lending to health and education projects. Yet, in the villages of Bangladesh, World Bankers found themselves confronting poor men and women who wanted bridges and roads, who believed that these projects, rather than microfinance, made their lives better. Some World Bankers came to believe that this disjuncture demonstrated that the Wolfensohn World Bank was shaped by a poverty agenda set by NGOs, social movements, and campaigns based in the global North, not by the interests of the poor in the global South: "There could be no better illustration of his institution's identification with its northern stakeholders nor of its deafness to rural clients" (Mallaby 2004: 338–339). This raises questions about the democratization of development. If countries in the global South were to own development, would they choose microfinance? Or is the prevalence of microfinance a sign of mandates imposed by the trustees of development, those with the power to set the agenda?

There is the argument that microfinance does no good, but then there is the argument that microfinance does harm. In India, there is a fierce debate about "microsharks," or microfinance institutions that practice what seems to be predatory lending (Pal 2006). Media reports tell stories of women who have committed suicide because of the inability to pay microfinance loans. In neighboring Bangladesh, home of microfinance, critics portray microfinance institutions as similarly exploitative. They argue that the Grameen Bank deploys patriarchal norms to exact repayment of loans by poor women and that such microfinance lending also increases domestic violence against women (Rahman 1999).

While the proponents of creative capitalism see a global political economy of markets that "eradicate poverty through profits," social theorists such as Heloise Weber, Julia Elyachar, and Katharine Rankin argue that microfinance is a mechanism for deepening financial sector liberalization and simultaneously ensuring social legitimacy. A handmaiden of, rather than alternative to, neoliberal globalization and free-market ideologies, microfinance serves as the social safety net for devastating programs of structural adjustment. Microfinance then is a crucial part of a "new global development architecture," one where the poor are disciplined and appeased through "novel experimentations" such as access to credit (Weber 2002). These theorizations provide a different understanding of creative capitalism: as markets that exploit the poor. They also provide a different understanding of the slogan, "credit is a human right": as a discourse of entrepreneurship and empowerment that obscures the structural exploitations of the poor.

Poverty Capital

In this book, I conceptualize microfinance as "poverty capital." This is a story that transcends millennial development, for it is a story about contemporary capitalism itself. Much of the analysis of *fin-de-millénaire* globalization has been concerned with production capital or finance capital. The recent analysis of sociologist Michael Goldman (2005: 67) has drawn attention to "development capital"—the money that runs through the projects of international development institutions such as the World Bank, USAID, and the UN, and that is often mediated by NGOs and consulting firms. Poverty capital is a subset of development capital. As represented by microfinance, it is a subprime frontier where development capital and finance capital merge and collaborate such that new subjects of development are identified and new territories of investment are opened up and consolidated.

I use the term "frontier" deliberately. The global microfinance industry, led by CGAP, evokes a distinctive imagination of frontiers, billing financial services for the poor as a "financial frontier." A blunt articulation of this approach comes from the title of a 2005 microfinance conference held in Chicago: "Expanding the Frontier: Transforming Microfinance into a Global Financial Markets Instrument" (http://www.chicagomicrofinance.com/ 2005, accessed June 15, 2005). As reported by Elizabeth Littlefield (2007), CEO of CGAP and a director of the World Bank, the microfinance industry is witnessing a "flood of new money from investors and big commercial banks" as well as from the "public commercial-investment agencies, such as the International Finance Corporation." By 2008, there were 104 microfinance funds with total assets under management of $6.5 billion (Reille and Glisovic-Mezieres 2009).

Such flows of investment seek to capture a key frontier: the poorest financial consumers or the "last billion" (Coleman 2008). CGAP reports that while, as of 2006, 500 million people were served by microfinance, nearly 3 billion could benefit from financial services (World Bank 2006b). Thus, a series of reports by the ING Group, a Dutch-based banking, insurance, and asset management firm, is titled *A Billion to Gain?* With covers graced by smiling, entrepreneurial poor women, these reports make the case for why international banks should become involved in microfinance—that microfinance can become "a niche market with competitive profit rates in ten years" (ING 2008: 48). Yet, the reports also express caution—that "international bank involvement in microfinancing may lead to more over-indebtedness" (ING 2008: 35). The cautionary note indicates that micro-finance is a particular sort of global industry, the frontier of what has been billed as a "fourth sector," dominated by socially responsible and development investors (Otero 2008). To harness the energy of this sector, at the 2004 Clausen Center microfinance conference, John Hatch of Finca International proposed a new alliance: between traditional microfinance providers who "control access to the poorest" and commercial banks who "control access to capital." Such alliances lie at the very heart of "poverty capital."

Hatch's vision seeks to establish a direct link between the dispersed millions of impoverished microentrepreneurs in the global South and centralized nodes of financial power in the global North. But the vision also contains a significant tension: that between the financialization of development and the democratization of capital. Can microfinance provide what Stanley Fischer (2003), then Vice-Chairman of Citigroup, asserted a few years ago: "bankers with a profitable business opportunity" and "poor people a stake in the economic future of their countries"? This book tells the story of this strange composition and its inherent struggles.

The globalization of microfinance is also the financialization of development. Under the watchful eye of CGAP, microfinance has been reinscribed as financial services for the poor, a new global industry that can be integrated into financial markets. It is thus that the world's largest banks, from Citigroup to Barclays to JP Morgan, now have a commercial interest in microfinance (Harford 2008). Such financialization requires work. Poverty capital is not only the practice of lending and producing wealth. It is also the practice of producing knowledge. Ways of understanding and explaining the world of microfinance, what I am calling poverty knowledge, go hand in hand with poverty capital. It is here that a metrics of risk assessment and management is forged; it is here that the poor are classified and categorized; and it is here that more generally the business of poverty comes to be "financialized," or transformed into a set of financial benchmarks and indicators. Indeed, by the close of the twentieth century, one benchmark had come to dominate the global microfinance industry: portfolio at risk (PAR), a measure of the outstanding balance of loans that are past due. It is a financial indicator borrowed from the very banking industry that microfinance was supposed to challenge.

Poverty capital is not only financial capital, but also another kind of advantage and distinction. According to the French sociologist Pierre Bourdieu (2005), capital has many different species—organizational, symbolic, cultural, and social. The distribution of such capital exerts a structural effect, conferring power over a system of social relations. Poverty capital is the currency of poverty experts, those who are authorized to produce authoritative knowledge about poverty and its alleviation. This is not simply knowledge; this is the "truth"—the forms of knowledge that come to be understood as certain, legitimate, and undeniably correct. These forms of knowledge, while produced and disseminated by powerful institutions, are also intimate. They are taken up by those who implement development and by those upon whom development is conferred. Indeed, financialization must be understood as "a subjectivity and moral code," "a way to develop the self," "an invitation to live by finance" (Martin 2002: 9, 3).

But the financialization of development involves more than an interest in frontier markets. It also takes place in the language of the democratization of capital. In the centers of development and financial power, such as Washington DC and Wall Street, experts talk with great passion about "breaking down the walls between microfinance and formal finance" (Littlefield and Rosenberg 2004). Yunus talks about humanizing capitalism and how social businesses can create a kinder and gentler globalization. John Hatch imagines a great strategic alliance between (global) finance capital and (local) microfinance NGOs, terming it the "socialization of the world economy." This ethical register may be understood as "neoliberal populism," a phrase that has been previously used by other scholars (Vivian 1995; Gore 2000). Microfinance celebrates the people's economy but it also entails, to borrow a phrase from Marxist geographer David Harvey (2005: 3), an effort to "bring all human action into the domain of the market ... to value market exchange as an ethic in and of itself." By "neoliberal populism" I thus mean the ways in which microfinance seeks to democratize capital and simultaneously convert the microcapital of the poor into new global financial flows. Will the poor benefit from such integration or will their inclusion take place in highly exploitative and predatory ways? This is a question that animates much of this book.

The democratization of capital also raises a more difficult issue: the democratization of development. In this book, I will argue that the agenda of microfinance is established and controlled in monopolistic fashion by the World Bank and its network of experts. This power is challenged and contested, but also in monopolistic fashion, by a handful of influential institutions in the global South. Yet, the promise of microfinance, of its democratization of capital, is that the idea and practice is more widely owned, that we can all participate in it.

That promise is evident in the intimate transactions of millennial development. The Third World poor woman is no longer a figure at a distance. She is now both visible and accessible. The portals of millennial development make it possible to touch her life, give her a microfinance loan, make a difference. On Kiva.org, for example, users can integrate such conscientious practices with the techno-social rhythms of their daily lives. Kiva "lets you browse loans on Facebook, and show off your loans in your Facebook page." There is Kiva for the iPhone, which "lets you get your Kiva fix from anywhere you bring your phone," and Kiva Tweets, which "automatically posts new loans to your Twitter account daily or weekly" (http://www.kiva.org, accessed April 28, 2009). It is the Third World woman, Millennial Woman, who animates this millennial ethics, anchors a global conscience, and transforms the distance of gender and race into a liberal intimacy with the world's poor.

If the democratization of capital and the democratization of development are key themes of the new millennium, then it is worth asking: Who are the users of this new global democracy? Who is thus empowered? An advertising campaign by the humanitarian organization, CARE, is titled "I am powerful." The magazine advertisements and online videos profile Third World poor women. The montage of women's lives is accompanied by an empowering narrative: "I am a woman, poor but proud, invisible but invisible, a natural resource with unlimited potential. Given a chance, a choice, I will improve my community, contribute to society. I am powerful." But the advertisement's key message, "She has the power to change her world" is predicated on an equally important message, this directed to the users of democratized development: "You have the power to help her do it" (http://www.care.org/getinvolved/iampowerful/intro.asp, accessed June 16, 2009) (see Figure 1.7). What is the relationship between democratized development, which is dispersed among thousands of privileged global citizens, and the centralized and powerful institutions of financialized development? The study of microfinance makes possible an exploration of this pressing question.

CENTRALITIES AND MULTIPLICITIES

This is a book about poverty and yet it is not about the lives of the poor. There are many books that deal with the workings of microfinance, that

Figure 1.7 "I am Powerful" (image courtesy of CARE USA and CARE Canada).

evaluate the efficacy of programs, and that debate the value of such an approach. Such scholarship is important but it is not the aim of this book. Rather, this analysis seeks to uncover the dynamics of poverty capital and to chart the historical moment that is millennial development. In order to do so it focuses little on the men and women who struggle under conditions of extreme poverty. Instead, it focuses centrally on those who generate the capital and the expertise around poverty eradication. In describing such processes, I use terms such as "centralities" and "multiplicities" to indicate the monopolistic power as well as political openings that are associated with millennial development. Kandinsky's compositions, including *Small Worlds IV*, are ensembles of centralities and multiplicities. I am inspired by them to study microfinance in these ways.

A particularly useful tool for the mapping of centralities and multiplicities is global commodity chain analysis. Common in globalization studies, this methodology traces the production, circulation, and consumption of commodities (Gereffi and Korzeniewicz 1993). For example, one can study the links in the global chain of an everyday commodity such as coffee—from low-paid small coffee producers in the global South to the trade in coffee futures in New York to the handful of multinational corporations that control the coffee market to the high-profit retail outlets that line our streets. In this way, a global commodity chain links the coffee beans produced by impoverished farmers in Ethiopia to the exorbitantly priced cappuccino that we drink each morning. At each stage, the value of coffee is constructed and managed. In this sense, global commodity chains are also value chains. I borrow the concept of global commodity chains to examine a particular commodity—development, and its circuits of capital and truth.

While the scope of my research and analysis is global, it is also located in specific places, histories, and contexts: Washington DC, Bangladesh, Lebanon, Egypt. At each site, there is the construction and management of development, of its value, of its truths. But together these diverse places also reveal the geography of power and powerlessness, how development is produced on different terms at different places on the map. Here, it is worth paying attention to geographer Matt Sparke (2007: 117): "The Global South is everywhere, but it is also always somewhere, and that somewhere, located at the intersection of entangled political geographies of dispossession and repossession, has to be mapped with persistent geographical responsibility."

To better understand the map of development, I turn to the French philosopher, Michel Foucault (1966: xxiv, xii), who insists on a study of the "space of knowledge," of uncovering the "rules of formation" of such knowledge, and thereby the order of things. The space of knowledge is closely controlled. It is thus that postcolonial theorist, Gayatri Chakravorty Spivak (1999: 191) draws attention to the "problem of the permission to narrate." Who can command and control such permission? In this book, I pay attention to struggles over the permission to narrate and indicate how such contests are inevitably territorialized, making and unmaking a global order. The permission to narrate is also linked to the practice of capital accumulation, to the command and control of surplus value. But such command and control also comes to be challenged and contested by new and alternative frameworks of ethical economics. These are the centralities and multiplicities of millennial development.

Such geographies demand a certain itinerary of research, one that is not limited to a single location but rather spans multiple sites. Over the course of four years, from 2004 to 2008, I conducted over 120 interviews and five life histories with a wide range of actors in the microfinance field, in institutions ranging from the Grameen Bank to CGAP to Deutsche Bank to USAID to Hezbollah, in development agencies, NGOs, foundations, corporations, lobbying groups, universities, social movements, and congressional offices. I selected my interviewees purposively rather than randomly, carefully stratifying my selection to ensure that actors at multiple ranks of each organization—from top personnel to those in the middle ranks to field officers to interns—were interviewed. In some cases, I had the opportunity to conduct interviews several times over the course of a few years and in five cases, such interviews took on the more involved and intense format of a life history.

In Washington DC, Bangladesh, Egypt, and Lebanon, I also collected data and conducted archival research on key microfinance institutions. During this time, I attended major summits and conferences that highlight microfinance, from the 2004 Barcelona Forum to the 2006 Microcredit Summit to the 2005 launch of the Egyptian National Strategy for Microfinance. I participated, as a student, in microfinance training courses, such as the Boulder Institute, the Microenterprise and Development Institute, and the Chalmers Center Christian Microfinance Institute. Keenly aware of the democratization of development, I tracked academic, institutional, as well as popular portals of microfinance, from the Microfinance Gateway to Kiva.org. Indeed, the web was not only a source of important material but also a space of knowledge, one where debates were waged, blogs were maintained, and products were branded. Through such research, I identified three circuits of poverty capital, each of which is constituted through particular centralities and multiplicities.

The first circuit of capital and truth is what I have come to call the "Washington consensus on poverty." I examine how authoritative knowledge about poverty, and especially about microfinance, is produced in the World Bank and other Washington institutions. While it can be argued that the World Bank is increasingly irrelevant to the fate of the global South, with private flows of investment far exceeding ODA, and while its budget allocations in the field of microfinance remain meager, it is nevertheless a "center of calculation" (Falk Moore 2001: 178). In my research, I pay particular attention to how such a centrality is produced and maintained, how from this very particular location a set of "universals"—to borrow Tsing's (2004) term—are generated and disseminated. The World Bank is, in short, the "chief arbiter" of development (Goldman 2005: viii). The Washington consensus on poverty is actively disseminated—through training workshops that circulate best practices and models and data management centers that produce benchmarks and rankings. Yet, in my research, I have sought to reconceptualize this "center of calculation" as fragile, as a terrain of contestation and negotiation, studying how dominant ideas come to be challenged both within and outside powerful institutions. With this in mind, I conducted life histories with a few key interlocutors within the World Bank, those who presented themselves as "double agents." I also extended my research well beyond the World Bank to study how lobbying groups such as the Microcredit Summit were crafting an alternative axis of power centered in Capitol Hill. Indeed, such contestations were a mark of how a quite distant geography—the NGOs of Bangladesh— were making their presence felt and their voices heard at the very heart of power, in Washington DC.

Second, I studied the margins of millennial development: Bangladesh. One of the poorest countries in the world, Bangladesh marks the limits of the "permission to narrate." Despite its pioneering role, the Bangladesh model of microfinance is today discounted and marginalized by the Washington consensus on poverty. These silences too had to be studied. Yet, my research soon became concerned with how Bangladesh has its own distinct centralities and multiplicities. I began to understand how a unique historical conjuncture of development produced, in Bangladesh, a landscape of active civil society organizations that enjoy relative autonomy from both the state and foreign donors. Their experiments with poverty alleviation generate a set of "poverty truths" that are quite different than those of the Washington consensus on poverty. These truths are not confined to Bangladesh, for in rather strategic fashion, the Bangladeshi NGOs work to globalize their models, practices, and ideas. This too is a global order, one where Dhaka becomes the key node in a global policy chain with sites as diverse as Chiapas, Nigeria, Manila, and Queens, New York.

Third, acutely aware that my research was unfolding in a post-9/11 global order, I studied an important imperial frontier: the Middle East. Led to this frontier by Washington DC's "war on terror," I came to examine the ways in which the Washington consensus on poverty establishes itself in and through the reconstruction of Afghanistan and in the economic and political crisis of Egypt. Egypt, saturated with American aid and American ideas, was a key site of investigation. But it turns out that microfinance in the Middle East is not simply managed by Washington DC but also increasingly claimed by other institutions with a quite different history of development. This was most starkly revealed in Lebanon, where the Shiite militia, Hezbollah, is the largest and most authoritative provider of micro-finance and development services. In imagining a global *umma* and garnering resources from a wealthy Shiite diaspora, Hezbollah too crafts a global order, one with its own circuits of capital and truths.

The study of these three circuits of poverty capital—anchored in Washington DC, Bangladesh, and the Middle East—presented its own challenges. In my earlier work, I have been primarily concerned with those who live under conditions of poverty in the cities of the global South. This research, in contrast, was explicitly about those who manage poverty, or those who control what Spivak (1994) terms the dispensation of bounty. To put it crudely, this was a "studying up" rather than a "studying down," one that brought me face to face not with the oppressed poor but rather with an intimately familiar subject, those professionals who research and manage poverty—people like myself.

Thus, rather than seeking to render the strange "familiar"—which middle-class researchers tend to do when they study the poor, I had to make the familiar "strange," paying attention to the forms of power and privilege that I often take for granted in my everyday life. I encountered "zones of awkward engagement" (Tsing 2004: xi). Sometimes the doors would slam shut because I was from the University of California, Berkeley, an academic institution stereotyped as a place of radical politics. At other times, I would be welcomed, because I was seen as a "brown woman," surely possessing the empathy that would allow me to reject Western imperialism. But in most cases I was awkwardly out of place—a theorist and critic amidst the pragmatic technocracy of Washington DC; an American exploring Bangladesh, Egypt, and Lebanon; a Bengali navigating the anti-Bangladeshi microfinance camp; a non-economist in a world of economists; an atheist seeking to understand the discourses of Christian evangelism and orthodox Islam; a researcher of poverty but one unwilling to study poor women, their suffering, and empowerment, rather seeking to study powerful women who manage poverty. I am convinced that these awkward engagements made it possible for me to see the familiar as "strange."

Millennials and the Politics of Knowledge

Large gifts and investments do not garner much attention in the world of microfinance. From securitization deals engineered by microfinance investment funds to allocations made by the Gates Foundation, the talk is usually in the millions of dollars. But one gift bears closer scrutiny. In 2005, Pierre Omidyar, founder of eBay, and director of the Omidyar Network, a philanthropic investment firm, gave $100 million to Tufts University. It was an unusual gift, for it stipulated that the money had to be invested in microfinance and disbursed to micro-entrepreneurs around the world. It meant that Tufts would reap rewards from the gift only if the investments were profitable. Four years later, the gift is "fully invested and paying dividends for students and professors here" (Masterson 2009). In fact, in 2008, the Omidyar–Tufts Microfinance Fund earned a 12 percent return, half of which went to Tufts and the other half was reinvested in the fund. Tufts was able to use this return to "support faculty research, start a loan-repayment program for graduates in public services, and provide student aid." The report thus concludes: "While the economic downturn has battered the university's endow-ment, the microfinance fund's strong performance has put the campus in a position to keep growing." The Tufts president happily states: "It's a wonderful example of what we thought would happen—we would do well by doing good" (Masterson 2009).

It is a compelling win–win story: the university turned philanthropic investment firm; philanthropic investments that yield high financial and social returns; and profitable investments that are immune from the financial crisis. That Tufts has resources to allocate to support faculty and students is compelling for those whose labor takes place in academic institutions and especially for those of us who are in poorly supported public universities. (As I write this, my home university, the University of California, is being drastically defunded.) But this is also a story about how millennial development enters the hallowed world of academia, how it generates new research priorities and curricula, and how, in the unusual case of Tufts, it reconfigures the financial model of the modern university.

Peter Singer (2009) names global poverty as "America's shame." Such a sense is palpable today in American classrooms as a new generation of global citizens flock to service learning opportunities, volunteer abroad experiences, and courses on global poverty. This too constitutes the "space of knowledge" that is millennial development. And it is also a "zone of awkward engagement." As I have conducted the research and analysis for this book, as I have written it, so I have spent time in my Berkeley classroom, watching a new undergraduate course on Global Poverty grow from a handful of students to an auditorium of hundreds. These are the "millennials," the generation that is keen to democratize development. This book is thus inevitably about the intimate act of teaching global poverty in what is also a "center of calculation"—the elite North American university.

In teaching my course at Berkeley I am struck by a contrast. On the one hand, I have students who are brimming with enthusiasm to do good; they want to save the world. They believe they can. On the other hand, I have students who are cynical, those who are able to level sharp critiques of structures of injustice but do not believe that change is possible. I teach in this impossible space between the hubris of benevolence and the paralysis of cynicism. I try to teach the millennials that they must critically reflect upon their eagerness to do good, that the very categories of "donor" or "volunteer" imply privilege, and that in the democratization of development, they will often receive much more than they can ever give. After all, the term voluntarism can be traced to the Latin *voluntas*, which means "will" or "desire." The millennial volunteer seeking to make poverty history is empowered; she is not just a willing subject, but also a willful subject. I seek to remind the millennials of Spivak's (1994) injunction that "responsibility," the driving force of development, cannot suffice. It is necessary to also consider the ethics of "accountability," of being accountable to those who are the recipients of millennial optimism and development largesse. Similarly, I strive to teach the millennials that they can, even in the world's most powerful institutions, even if they have been hitherto denied voice and access, claim the permission to narrate. And I seek to remind them of Jan Pieterse's (2001: 100) brilliant statement that "development is the management of a promise," that development is not only imposed but also desired. That promise, of financial inclusion, of the democratization of capital, of microentrepreneurship, of a better life, of the end of poverty, must be taken seriously. For while these are fictions, like the fictions of finance capital, they have a material reality that is formidable.

This book, like my teaching, is written in the impossible space between the hubris of benevolence and the paralysis of cynicism. It is a space marked by doubleness: by both complicities and subversions, by the familiar and the strange. I write it in the figure that most often strikes a chord with my millennial students, as a double agent, shaped by centralities and multiplicities.

NOTE

1   Vinod Khosla, remarks at the Global Business and Global Poverty Conference, Stanford Graduate School of Business, May 19, 2004 (http://www.gsb.stanford.edu/news/headlines/2004globalconf_khosla_speech.shtml, accessed August 5, 2005).

CHAPTER 2

Global Order

Circuits of Capital and Truth

We live in an ocean of money . . ..

(Muhammad Yunus, founder of the Grameen Bank, 2009[1])

At Lookout Mountain, Microfinance Evangelicals

A few years ago, an event listed on the popular web portal, the Microfinance Gateway, caught my eye. The Chalmers Center for Economic and Community Development at Covenant College, Georgia, USA, was going to hold a training conference on Christian microfinance and microenterprise development. The flagship college of the Presbyterian Churches of America, Covenant College, offers both on-site and online courses for missionaries, churches, and ministries working in the "Two-Thirds World," their term for the global South. Microfinance and microenterprise development, as it turns out, are central elements of such training. Indeed, as noted by Brian Fikkert (2003: 5), the director of the Chalmers Center, many of the important and large "Christian relief and development agencies are operating large-scale microcredit programs (e.g., Food for the Hungry International, Opportunity International, World Concern, World Relief, World Vision International)." Fikkert notes that hundreds of Christians in the industry have gathered regularly for global conferences on Christian microenterprise development.

The Covenant College training conference, with about 100 attendees each year, is meant to provide rigorous training to Christian missionaries in this field. Run by a professional staff, many of them with doctorates in economics from the Ivy Leagues, it is an intriguing combination of the latest academic debates about microfinance and poverty alleviation on the one hand and the mandates of evangelism on the other hand. Eager to learn more I registered and began the journey to the scenic isolation of Lookout Mountain, arriving amidst a flock of the faithful and a flurry of prayers. My secular Indian upbringing had done little to prepare me for coursework on the tenets of Presbyterianism. But I wanted to

41

understand how the idea of microfinance had traveled from the villages of Bangladesh to this missionary gathering at Lookout Mountain. Embraced lovingly by anxious evangelicals who thought of me as a lost soul, here is what I learned at Lookout Mountain.

At first glance, Christian microfinance seemed familiar. Instructors presented the key principles as the following: relief, rehabilitation, and development, participatory development, and assets and need-based development. But Christian microfinance is also meant to be an instrument of proselytizing, a means of consolidating new frontiers of evangelism. Missionaries at the training conference were working in frontier territories, from Afghanistan to Malaysia. They were drawn to microfinance, and particularly to the solidarity group model, because it seemed a particularly effective way of mitigating poverty and promoting Christianity. Thus Fikkert (2003: 42) writes: "There is enormous power in getting people into groups, and Christians in particular should see groups as opportunities for evangelism and discipleship." Yet, at this conference, missionaries expressed concern about microfinance, especially the emphasis on lending to women. Although the instructors presented the familiar, gendered arguments of microfinance—that "the quickest way to alleviate poverty is financial services for women," the participants asked: "How can we lock out men by defining them as non-performing assets?" They insisted that Christian microfinance has an obligation to be patient with men, to discipline and disciple them.

There were other dilemmas as well. Christian microfinance, as presented at Covenant College, starts with a conceptualization of poverty. It is a deeply contradictory framework, one that seeks to reconcile biblical ideas with structural analysis. Poverty is a result of the Fall, of a separation from God, and of the pollution of all relationships. Poverty is thus marked by dependency and disempowerment, for the poor have lost their sense of being created in God's image. Poverty is not only economic, it is also spiritual and therefore cannot be alleviated solely through material interventions. To work with the poor is to work to restore the relationship of the poor with God. But poverty is also the lack of assets and the lack of income. It reflects Robert Chambers's (1983) concept of the deprivation trap, and it is the analysis presented in the World Bank's *Voices of the Poor* (Narayan and Petesch 2002), both frameworks used in Chalmers classes. Can these contradictions, between the narrative of sin and the narrative of structural vulnerability, be reconciled? Here is Fikkert's (2003: 9) attempt to do so: "Both the Scriptures and empirical evidence indicate that oppression of the poor is often a factor in their poverty. It takes the power of Jesus Christ over sin . . . to remove the oppressor. His power is the answer, and the poor need to cling to this hope." Such ambivalences are not unique to Christian microfinance. They exist at the very heart of microfinance, in the struggle to reconcile an intervention aimed at the structural causes of poverty with the insistence that the poor must help themselves through entrepreneurship.

But what is perhaps unique to Christian microfinance is a deep anxiety about debt. And it is here that Christian microfinance, in surprising and perhaps unintended fashion, calls into question the premises of millennial development. Central to the Covenant College training is the argument that development can do harm, that burdensome debt and high interest rates can place poor people in systems of bondage, that well-meaning missionaries can indeed hurt entire communities. With this in mind, the Covenant instructors rejected various forms of development. They provided a scathing critique of short-term Christian missions to the Two-Thirds World, dismissing them as "disaster tourism" that "dumped relief supplies" on poor communities. And most important, they rejected the dominant framework of microfinance, arguing that the emphasis on commercialization and financial sustainability was incompatible with their mandate to avoid doing harm. It is thus that a training conference on microfinance ended with the surprising recommendation that Christian evangelicals should eschew microfinance and instead promote church-centered credit and savings associations built around indigenous solidarity groups. In the face of a brave new frontier of poverty capital, the missionaries asserted a Christian truth, rejecting sleek Wall Street models of finance for the seemingly primitive form of rotating savings and credit associations that are present in so many poor communities.

Like these fierce proselytizers, the global microfinance industry has pursued microfinance with evangelical zeal (Rogaly 1996; Woller, Dunford, and Woodworth 1999). Interestingly, and as I will show, this industry has been less inclined than its religious counterpart to express existential doubt about the idea of microfinance. In the global order of microfinance, a handful of authoritative ideas and best practices rule. This is a fundamentalism of sorts, not unlike the "market fundamentalism" critiqued by Stiglitz (1998) in his call for a reform of globalization. Indeed, the global order of microfinance is increasingly committed to market models and strategies, seeking to position microfinance as an asset class, or a circuit of investment, speculation, and profit embedded within the broader workings of finance capital. The moral struggles of Christian microfinance provide a glimpse of the ethical quandaries that lurk in the shadows of this global order. They suggest the need for a thorough interrogation of such market fundamentalisms.

GLOBAL ORDER

The Globalization of Microfinance

In 1995 an unusual development institution arrived on the scene in Washington DC: The Consultative Group to Assist the Poor or CGAP. Initially titled The Consultative Group to Assist the Poor*est*, it was housed in the World Bank. The establishment of CGAP is a testament to the energies of the Wolfensohn World Bank and its formal commitment to a poverty agenda. Wolfensohn's remaking of the World Bank as a kinder and gentler institution harks back to a previous era, the years when Robert McNamara as president of the World Bank sought to implement an agenda of poverty alleviation. Ismail Serageldin, one of the key founders of CGAP, acknowledges that his inspiration for forging a poverty agenda came from his own personal experiences as a young World Banker serving under McNamara (personal communication, December 2005).

From the beginning, CGAP's poverty agenda has been synonymous with the microfinance agenda. This is possibly the case because Serageldin and other founders were influenced by the work of Muhammad Yunus, founder of the Grameen Bank, who served initially on the CGAP Advisory Board. This is also possibly the case because microfinance represents the confluence of various Wolfensohn agendas, notably small enterprise development and gender empowerment. As Wolfensohn (2000: 5) explained:

> Poor people themselves view small business as a critical means of inclusion in economic activity, enabling them to use their savings and labour to earn enough to survive on a daily basis, as well as to grow out of poverty. Microfinance helps the poor to maintain and grow those small businesses and to cope with the fluctuations and crises that dominate their lives.

The Wolfensohn World Bank set out to focus on women and development, conceptualizing women as a final frontier of inclusion (Bergeron 2003a, 2003b). Microfinance, with its emphasis on lending to poor women, was thus crucial. It became, as Scully (2001) notes, Wolfensohn's most common response to the question: "What has the World Bank done for women lately?"

Yet, the CGAP agenda was ultimately to have little to do with either small enterprise development or gender empowerment. Instead, it was to focus on financial services and the integration of the poor into financial markets—what CGAP calls "inclusive financial systems." CGAP's mission statement reads: "At the core of microfinance is a fundamental belief that access to financial services empowers the poor by reducing their vulnerability and giving them choices" (http://www.cgap.org, accessed June 9, 2008). CGAP also marks a break with the Bangladesh model of micro-finance and its emphasis on human development. It calls for a "minimalist" microfinance, one that is concerned solely with access to finance. The prominence of CGAP thus indicates a shift in the center of the microfinance world from Bangladesh—and its famous institutions such as the Grameen Bank and BRAC—to Washington DC, specifically the World Bank.

Also unusual about the establishment of CGAP is its relationship to other donors. CGAP presents itself as "a consortium of 33 public and private funding organizations—bilateral and multilateral development agencies, private foundations, and international financial institutions" (http://www. cgap.org, accessed June 9, 2008). Yet, in many ways CGAP is a World Bank entity, with half of its annual $12 million budget coming from the World Bank (CGAP 2003) and its director serving on the World Bank Board of Directors. In short, CGAP has no legal status independent of the World Bank (CGAP 2003). What CGAP embodies then is not only the poverty agenda of the 1990s, but also the power of what can be understood as the "Washington consensus on poverty." I coin and use this term deliberately, as a counter-point to Stiglitz's (2008) argument about "a post-Washington consensus consensus," a new consensus that declares the end of "market fundamentalism." There may indeed be such a new consensus, focused on poverty. But I argue that it is centered in Washington DC and that it promotes a market-based approach to poverty.

What is at stake here is much more than the control and allocation of budgets; it is the control of knowledge by the World Bank. So it is the case in microfinance. After all, the World Bank reputedly allocates only 1 percent of its budget to microfinance—although this figure is disputed by Elizabeth Littlefield, CEO of CGAP. She argues that taking into account the Bank's policy work in the financial sector and investments by the International Finance Corporation (IFC), the figure is closer to 6 percent, making the World Bank the "world's largest microfinance donor" (Littlefield 2006). But what is crucial is that CGAP presents itself as a "potent convening platform for a wide range of stakeholders to reach consensus on standards and norms" (http://www.cgap.org, accessed June 9, 2008). Although various Northern donors, ranging from USAID to the British Department for International Development (DFID), establish and implement their own poverty policies, it is CGAP that establishes the "performance-based benchmarks" in microfinance (Wolfensohn 2000: 7). It is CGAP's best practices that are taken up by practitioners around the world, its "pink book" the holy grail of microfinance. Thus, it is CGAP that controls how microfinance is understood, or what we know about microfinance. In this sense, CGAP controls the truths about microfinance.

Mohini Malhotra, one of the founders of CGAP, now working elsewhere in the World Bank, notes in an interview (June 2004) that "knowledge management was a CGAP goal from the very beginning." The idea was never to increase aid budgets but instead to shape the ways in which aid is allocated—through performance-based grants that allow CGAP to develop benchmarks and guidelines, through the training of microfinance practitioners, and through the dissemination of key ideas that establish the terms of debate and educated donors. After a while, one could travel to almost any part of the microfinance world, Malhotra notes, and find that practitioners in the field were familiar with CGAP, its principles, and the issues presented in its focus notes. No other microfinance donor can wield such intellectual influence, building "near-universal consensus," its "best practice microfinance becoming standard practice" (Helms 2006). Thus, during an interview (October 2004), one senior CGAP staff noted: "What is measured, is what is managed. We script. We manage. We control."

In a June 2005 interview, Elizabeth Littlefield presented such production of knowledge as a "unique public good." It is a statement that echoes Wolfensohn's insistence that the World Bank has to be a "knowledge bank," producing the public good of development knowledge (Stiglitz 1999). On the one hand, the argument about a "unique public good" suggests a democratization of development knowledge. But on the other hand, such development knowledge is legitimate and authoritative only when endorsed by CGAP and its poverty experts. It must be asked: can there be a consensus on development if it is not generated by Washington DC?

Such issues were sharply evident at a microfinance training workshop (June 2004), in which a Nepalese practitioner confronted the instructor of the course, a CGAP staff member: "What price do we have to pay to use your tools and ideas? Do we have to hire CGAP and World Bank consultants?"

The instructor responded that all CGAP knowledge products were public goods. But the audience, each paying a hefty fee for attending this workshop, was not convinced. After all, they are now consumers of a Washington consensus on poverty.

The Democratization of Capital

At the heart of this "unique public good," or these knowledge products, is the financialization of development. At CGAP, the very concept and practice of microcredit is being transformed. If the Bangladesh model of microfinance, epitomized by the Grameen Bank, seeks to invent and implement systems of service delivery and human development managed by NGOs, then CGAP seeks to construct a global financial industry. What is at stake here is a crucial shift from the idea of development as social services and the improvement of human capital to development as integration into global financial markets. CGAP's (2004a) widely disseminated document, *Key Principles of Microfinance*, endorsed at the 2004 G-8 summit, skillfully crafts a set of market norms for "best-practice" microfinance: from the repudiation of interest rate ceilings and donor subsidies to the emphasis on financial transparency. A new set of indicators and benchmarks now dominate microfinance, measuring financial performance and producing what can be understood as a "new politics of calculation" (Mitchell 2002: 8). In this way, financial norms come to supersede social norms in the making of development.

Led by CGAP, the Washington consensus on poverty emphasizes a more limited role for government – as an "enabler, not direct provider" (CGAP 2004a). CGAP presents the "early pioneer organizations" of microfinance—"the nonprofit socially motivated nongovernmental organizations"—as outmoded and outflanked by "financially sound, professional organizations" that are a "fully integrated part" of "mainstream financial systems" (Littlefield and Rosenberg 2004: 38). In the field of financial services, CGAP thus hopes to promote "institutional diversity" with an important role ascribed to savings and credit cooperatives, commercial banks, community finance institutions, consumer credit companies, and insurance companies. CGAP thereby presents a new institutional model for microfinance: financial institutions. But such an ideology is at odds with the reality that leading microfinance institutions are "nearly twice as profitable as the world's leading commercial banks" (Hashemi 2006) and much more able to withstand financial crisis than commercial banks (Rawe 2003).

These strategies are not unique to CGAP. The USAID's showcase project, the Global Development Alliance (GDA), established by the Bush administration, envisioned a new set of institutional partnerships: between the private for-profit sector and the non-governmental sector, with USAID as a facilitator and mediator. Praising the success of the GDA at the 2006 National Summit of the Initiative for Global Development, then President George W. Bush noted that "some of the best work in fighting poverty is accomplished in partnership with private institutions" (http:// georgewbush-whitehouse.archives.gov/news/releases/2006/06/2006 0615.html, accessed April 24, 2007). The GDA is part of a larger remaking of development, one where overseas development assistance is dwarfed by flows of foreign direct investment. In an interview (June 2005), USAID's GDA director, Dan Runde, noted that "USAID had suddenly become a minority stakeholder in the development business."

Although CGAP hopes to construct "sound and deep market infrastructure," its enterprise is not necessarily the standard neoliberal ideology of free markets and profit-driven capitalism. As CGAP puts forward a set of economic claims about financial markets and their role in development, so it puts forward a set of ethical claims about the "democratization of capital." In its most basic iteration, the democratization of capital means "inclusive financial systems." CGAP prides itself on "breaking down the walls between microfinance and formal finance" (Littlefield and Rosenberg 2004) and thereby including the poor who have been hitherto unserved by financial markets. Thus, Marguerite Robinson, whose "red book," *The Microfinance Revolution* (2001: 25), published by the World Bank Institute, is one of the key texts of the Washington consensus of poverty, presents microfinance as the "reclaiming of finance for society at large—the true democratization of capital." She, like others, argues that state-led development is captured by local elites while development via financial markets is more egalitarian. Particularly compelling is the argument that models of NGO or state-led development impose a myriad of rituals and conditions on the poor whereas financial markets liberate the poor from such forms of supervision and surveillance. The democratization of capital is thus about the economic freedom of the poor, about reconceptualizing the poor as financial consumers. With this in mind, Robinson (2001: 92–93) rejects the

Grameen Bank model of microfinance noting that it "assumes that the poor must be taught to save and that they need to learn financial discipline."

Such ideas are prominent in the "Ohio School" of economics (Hulme and Mosley 1996: 2). Rejecting both the role of the state and of institutions such as the Grameen Bank, the Ohio School economists have maintained faith in informal financial markets. According to them, institutions such as the Grameen Bank impose a heavy burden of opportunity costs (forced savings) and transaction costs (weekly meetings, membership of an organization), which are inequitable and inefficient. Such economists argue that poor women have to expend valuable time at meetings, pledge allegiance to organizations, and manage the finances of village groups. "Do you and I, as women borrowing from a bank, have to do this when we take out a loan from the Bank of America?" asked a USAID consultant of me during one of our interviews (March 2004). "Why do poor women?" she continued. "And how can this pass as women's empowerment? True empowerment is to have choice; to be able to purchase a service without all these conditions and rituals."

In the writings of microfinance experts such as Elisabeth Rhyne, managing director of the Center for Financial Inclusion at Accion International and former director of USAID's microenterprise division, such freedom takes on even deeper normative dimensions. Invoking Nobel Prize-winning economist Amartya Sen's framework of development as freedom, Rhyne (2001: 183) argues that access to finance is the ultimate means of engendering freedom, economic capacity, and social choice. Such ideas are ubiquitous in the world of microfinance. It is thus that in Egypt the director of a microfinance organization stated with great passion during an interview (December 2005) that

> women did not need empowering; they were already empowered. This is about financial services and we must provide the best possible services. You Americans want to talk democracy. Well, this is financial democracy. Don't come here and ask our clients why they are not sending their children to school or how they are spending their money. Let them make their own choices.

But as the idea of development knowledge as a public good is not without contradictions and paradoxes, so the democratization of capital is fraught with ambiguity. The NGO model of microfinance, pioneered by the

Grameen Bank, is centrally concerned with risk. Shaped by the assumption of "good women" and "risky men," this model ensures loan repayment through peer groups, patriarchal discipline, and the presence of a massive NGO in village life. Here risk is managed through gendered and intimate techniques of rule. But the new financial markets envisioned by the Washington consensus on poverty cannot remain embedded in such institutional forms, village groups, and gendered intimacy. In order to achieve global scale, they require new technologies of risk management, those that will create transparent financial markets. This too is the important work of CGAP. Risk scoring models now seek to ascribe risk to different categories of the poor, mimicking the character-based lending that undergirds consumer credit systems. These models rate variables such as age, sex, marital status, and occupation, thereby creating scores that facilitate or limit access to credit. Such systems have, of course, historically redlined the poor, inscribing them as high-risk borrowers. Yet, they are now being deployed to promote the democratization of capital.

The Creation of an Asset Class

As the Washington consensus on poverty rejects the rituals of older forms of microfinance, so it inaugurates its own rituals. One such ritual is the annual announcement of the "Global 100"—a ranked list of the "top performing microfinance institutions throughout the developing world" (http://www.themix.org/publications/2007-mix-global-100-rankings-microfinance-institutions, accessed June 12, 2008). The list is created by the Microfinance Information eXchange (MIX), a virtual microfinance market-place established by CGAP and supported by Citigroup Foundation, Deutsche Bank, the Omidyar Network, Open Society Institute, and the Rockdale Foundation. MIX seeks to link microfinance institutions with investors and donors in "a transparent information market" (http://www.mixmarket.org, accessed October 13, 2008). To do so it creates "heat maps" that provide real-time credit ratings of microfinance institutions. The visualization tool for creating such heat maps is ironically titled "Panopticon" (http://www.panopticon.com, accessed October 13, 2008). A panopticon is the ultimate icon of modern discipline and punishment—the prison designed by nineteenth-century liberal philosopher, Jeremy Bentham, to maximize the power of the prison guard's surveilling gaze and to ensure that prisoners internalize this gaze and take up practices of self-discipline.

The heat maps are the new millennium's panopticon, means to enact financial discipline upon NGOs.

The "Global 100" list ranks microfinance institutions on the basis of outreach, scale, profitability, efficiency, productivity, and portfolio quality. Strikingly absent, of course, are criteria that are explicitly concerned with impacts on poverty. Often released through Wall Street outlets—for example at a Deutsche Bank luncheon in New York city—the Global 100 reinforces the consensus of the CGAP guidelines. It validates and invalidates particular models of microfinance, celebrating financial efficiency and scarcely considering pro-poor innovations. The pioneers of microfinance, Grameen Bank and BRAC, are deemed successful in terms of their scale of outreach— millions of borrowers and depositors—but unsuccessful in terms of efficiency. The Global 100 is a condensed version of the heat map; it directs the heat of global investment funds to what have been designated as the best institutions and the best practices. Other lists have now emerged, such as one started by Forbes in 2007. The Forbes list of 50 "winners" explicitly states that its rankings "attempt to measure financial performance, not the social benefits of any microfinance institutions" (Swibel 2007). Such lists inaugurate what has been called an "asset class," or a circuit of investment, in the world of microfinance.

The lists indicate that the management and mitigation of risk is no longer confined to poor subjects. Equally important is the mapping of risk in relation to a distinctive subject: microfinance NGOs. Conceptualized now as MFIs, microfinance institutions that are financial intermediaries, these organizations must compete for investment funds and must prove their financial worthiness. They too are entrepreneurial subjects, as are the poor to whom they lend. They must in turn be rated, compared, and constantly assessed according to the norms of global financial markets. This in turn requires constant experimentation with different technologies of trans- parency and visibility. In this sense, visibility is both an ideology and practice of millennial development—the rendering visible of the bottom of the pyramid and its structures of risk and returns. The heat maps and ratings, the new panopticon if you will, are important elements of this system. Standard & Poor, for example, is now launching a global rating of microfinance institutions, a project sponsored by the Inter-American Development Bank. A director at Standard & Poor explains the endeavor thus: "To unlock these sources of capital in both international and domestic markets, investors require transparent and globally accepted credit analysis" (*PR Newswire*, February 6, 2008).

Information technology plays an important role in the global order of microfinance. Replacing the face-to-face relationship between the microfinance client and the loan officer is now a web of transactions mediated by credit scores, smart cards, biometric identification, and information flows. Take for example, one of the showcase projects of USAID's GDA, a partnership between credit card giant Visa and village banking pioneer, Finca International. It is an alliance being billed as the future of development:

> Visa will provide product platforms, technological processing capabilities, and technological expertise and will train Finca's credit officers. Finca will provide access to clients through its network of village banks and train its clients on the use of electronic payment solutions and share its expert knowledge.
>
> (http://www.usaid.gov/press/releases/2004/
> pr040124.html, accessed May 10, 2005)

Here then is the dream geography of the Washington consensus on poverty:

> Once a week, Ana Silva Velasquez travels from Bolivia's capital city of La Paz to the Chilean city of Iquique to buy toys for her wholesale business and small toy shop. Before leaving, she stops by one of the branch offices of Prodem, a private financial fund. At an optical scanning device—similar to an automatic teller machine—she swipes her smart card and verifies her identity by placing her thumb in an electronic fingerprint authenticator attached to the card scanner. She removes paper currency from the automatic teller and, with the money tucked safely in her purse, starts off on her shopping trip. "I don't have time to stand in line at a bank," explains the microentrepreneur.
>
> (Silva 2002: 33)

For the global microfinance industry, such technological infrastructures bear the promise of a mapped and connected lending industry, one where credit scores, credit histories, and credit transactions are made transparent, where the remote frontiers of Bolivia are rendered instantaneously visible for institutions such as the MIX. The biometrically scanned body of the Third World woman anchors these circuits of capital and truth. "'We have succeeded in bankizing people in rural areas,' Prudencio, general manger of Innova, Prodem's technology development affiliate, explains" (Silva 2002: 33–34).

It is no longer enough then to talk about microfinance as a sector of development. Rather it is essential to talk about it as an industry where the commodity that is being produced, traded, and valued is debt. Syed Hashemi (2006), a senior microfinance specialist at CGAP, notes: "Microfinance has actually matured into one of the most successful and fastest-growing industries in the world. In Africa alone, its growth is probably second only to that of cell phone use." This is the new frontier of capital accumulation.

With the construction of microfinance as an asset class, the microfinance business is booming. This is evident in the emergence and growth of microfinance investment funds, of which there were 104 by the end of 2008 (Reille and Glisovic-Mezieres 2009). The returns range from an average of 8 percent for structured finance vehicles at the highest, to as low as 0 percent for some young funds (CGAP 2008b). These microfinance funds have been growing rapidly, reaching a total of $3.5 billion in 2007 and $6.5 billion in 2008 (Swibel 2007; Reille and Glisovic-Mezieres 2009). They are concentrated mainly in Europe, with the largest being Procredit, a German holding company that invests in new, "greenfield" microfinance banks. Another important "frontier" organization is Blue Orchard Finance, a Geneva-based asset manager that specializes in microfinance. In 2006, Blue Orchard's Loans for Development funded five-year loans to 21 microfinance institutions in 13 countries. The transaction was billed by Morgan Stanley, at the 2006 Microcredit Summit, as the first "fully open market investment" in microfinance organizations, one that was not underwritten by government guarantees.

For all of the talk of free, open, and global markets, markets are in fact idiosyncratic, uneven, and closed. Such too is the case with microfinance, where issues of risk remain pressing. As microfinance institutions must manage the risk of lending to the poor, so global investors must price and mitigate the risk of lending to microfinance institutions. Donors have stepped in to underwrite this debt industry and absorb the losses that may be generated by MFIs unable to yield high rates of financial returns. In 2008, the Norwegian government launched the Norwegian Microfinance Initiative, a $117 million microcredit fund, with 50 percent of the fund provided by the Norwegian government and the rest provided by private financial groups, banking groups, and insurance companies (Stoltz 2008). Yet another instrument is the Deutsche Bank Microcredit Development Fund. A project led by Asad Mahmood, the director of Deutsche Bank's Community Development Group, this $50 million debt fund is set up as such that donors can provide the first-loss cushion. It turns out that the construction of new markets requires the absorption of risk by governments. It is in this sense that the economic historian, Karl Polanyi (1944: 146) observed in brilliant fashion that "markets are planned."

At the 2004 microfinance conference at the University of California, Berkeley, Jonathan Lewis, a microfinance consultant, noted the prevalence of risk aversion: "Americans don't care to invest in places where they are scared to drink the water." It is not surprising then that the flow of microfinance capital has been clustered and concentrated rather than widespread and fluid. Much of the microfinance investment, so-called "microfinance fever" (Swibel 2007), is geographically concentrated in Eastern Europe and Latin America (CGAP 2004b; Littlefield 2007), where "one can drink the water." And much of it is institutionally concentrated in a handful of microfinance institutions, those that have been deemed winners by global mappings of risks and returns.

As microfinance is transformed into a global financial industry, there is also a growing risk aversion to lending to the poor. Here too flows of capital seek out market winners—the segment of the poor that are deemed to be creditworthy and entrepreneurial. In a dramatic interview (October 2005), a staffer at the United Nations Capital Development Fund (UNCDF) argued that the extremely poor are "unbankable." "If you take the poorest of the poor, that's some feeble minded, half-minded cripple. Do you think this person needs a loan? No." He drew a diagram depicting a sharp and certain line demarcating the "bankable" and "economically active" poor from those who are "unbankable." Here then is the inescapable contradiction of microfinance as an asset class: the redline. Such redlining is the very thing that microfinance set out to mitigate.

In addition to the risks associated with lending are the risks associated with collection. As commercial banks and equity funds enter the field of microfinance, so they must confront the perils of enacting financial discipline on the poor. Thus, in an interview (March 2005), a top-ranking Wall Street banker noted that global investment banks face an intractable challenge in collecting on loans:

"Can you imagine the field day that the press and you academics will have if a Wall Street bank goes after poor, rural Bolivian women and tries to press loan repayment? We cannot do what the microfinance NGOs have done so successfully, which is to use a variety of social sanctions in order to ensure that the poor repay.

In order to hedge such moral risk, the Washington consensus on poverty promotes linkages between commercial banks and microfinance institutions. Such relationships outsource the practices of discipline and punishment to NGOs, thereby allowing banks to enter frontier markets. Although the Washington consensus on poverty emphasizes themes of self-sufficiency and chides microfinance NGOs for their primitive dependence on donors, the sleek giants of Wall Street remain dependent on incubated government funds and the disciplinary hand of those primitive NGOs.

The paradoxes, ambiguities, and contradictions that mark the making of microfinance as an asset class echo those that are inherent in the very structure of World Bank-style development. From its inception the World Bank has been indelibly shaped by capital markets—for it is in these markets that the Bank, enjoying "quasi-sovereign" status, floats its bonds and is judged by conservative financial investors (Miller-Adams 1999: 25). The Bank has in fact earned the coveted AAA ratings of Moody's and Standard & Poor's on its bonds since 1959—the same agencies that now are interested in rating microfinance institutions. As the World Bank (2000) itself notes, its work has been overwhelmingly profitable, recording healthy profits every year since 1947 with profits exceeding $1 billion per year for the past 15 years, hitting close to $2 billion in recent years. Bondholders in the global North benefit from the interest payout on such revenues (World Bank 2000: 3).

But the World Bank must also manage risk, seeking to reconcile its bond ratings with the enterprise of making loans to countries "where one cannot drink the water." As development scholars note:

[T]he Bank's substantial skill in maintaining strict financial policies and performing well in purely financial terms has allowed it to act as an intermediary through which the resources of the world's most conservative investors can be channeled to developing countries for what, under other circumstances, would be considered distinctly risky ventures.

(Miller-Adams 1999: 25)

In this sense, the World Bank is not unlike a microfinance institution or a microfinance investment fund. It seeks to cross the redline into new frontiers of lending. Yet it must also move money through circuits of capital, securing financial returns and earning high ratings on global heat maps. The financialization that seems to be a new feature of millennial development turns out to be an old logic, deeply embedded in the financial model of CGAP's home, the World Bank. It is a story to which I will return later in this chapter.

The "Accomplishments of Truth"

The financialization of development is a project, one that is actively constructed through the deployment of technology and the management of risk outlined here. But such a project also requires the production of knowledge such that the principles and norms of financial markets become central to the practice of development. Here, it is important to draw a distinction between information and knowledge; knowledge is a sorting and categorizing of information such that normative frameworks and arguments take center stage. In outlining a Washington consensus on poverty, I am interested in what may be understood as "authoritative knowledge" (Falk Moore 2001)—those ideas that become the commonsense expertise, the dominant paradigm, the taken for granted worldview. Authoritative knowledge not only produces truth but also consent to this truth. But such circuits of truth are also sites of political contestation. As noted by the French sociologist, Pierre Bourdieu (1985: 729, 731), there is a struggle "for the power to conserve or transform the social world by conserving or transforming the categories through which it is perceived," to preserve the "monopoly of legitimate naming." This is the power of CGAP, and more generally of the World Bank. But it is power that must be constantly updated and maintained.

French philosopher Michel Foucault (1969: 106) notes that to analyze a "space of knowledge," it is necessary to study the "enunciating subject." He asks: "Who is speaking? . . . What is the status of the individuals who—alone—have the right, sanctioned by law or tradition . . . to proffer such a discourse?" (Foucault, 1969: 55). It is this capacity to speak that Yunus laments Bangladesh lacks. In an interview that I conducted in 2004, he talked with great passion about how "those with the pen shape development ideas," and of how institutions such as CGAP articulate and disseminate the "Wall Street perspective" of capitalism. With this in mind, I now provide a brief glimpse of the "enunciating subjects" of the Washington consensus on poverty and the institutional sites from which they put forward their ways of knowing.

The phrase "accomplishments of truth" comes from Michael Chu's endorsement of Marguerite Robinson's (2001) book, *The Microfinance Revolution*. Chu writes:

> In the past five years the enormous promise of access to capital as an effective tool for the world's poor has erupted into the world's consciousness. But the facts have often come intertwined with myth and legend, until oft-repeated misinformation threatens today to debase the accomplishments of truth. In this fog Marguerite Robinson's book, *The Microfinance Revolution*, arrives as a beacon.

Robinson's book is indeed a marker, if not a beacon. Published in 2001 by the World Bank, and widely disseminated and received, it represents the core ideas of the Washington consensus on poverty. Thus, the book is a key artifact in the making of microfinance knowledge. Robinson, herself a social anthropologist by training, is a fixture at sites of knowledge production, often wearing a name badge that simply reads "Consultant."

In the knowledge order of microfinance, perhaps no site is as important as what is commonly known as "Boulder." Originally sited at Naropa University in Boulder, Colorado, this is a microfinance training program now held each summer in Turin, Italy. Fees are steep—nearly $10,000 for three weeks of tuition, board, and lodging. The shift in geographical location took place after 9/11 and is meant to facilitate the attendance of participants from the global South who may have difficulty procuring a US visa. A CGAP project, the Boulder Institute is led by Robert Peck Christen, formerly a senior advisor at CGAP and now director of Financial Services for the Poor at the Gates Foundation.

During a conversation in Turin (July 2005), Christen noted that the Boulder program is not so much about training as it is about "conceptual frameworks and ways of thinking." Every morning, for the three weeks of the Boulder program, Christen presents the key ideas and principles of "best-practice" microfinance. In the afternoons, students attend courses taught by other experts. Since 1995, there have been hundreds of participants who have been trained by the Boulder program. They are sponsored by the donors who anchor the Washington consensus on poverty—the World Bank, UNCDF, USAID, and CGAP—and it is generally understood that microfinance organizations receiving grants from such donors are expected to send their top practitioners to Boulder to be trained. It is thus that every summer, CGAP produces a new cohort of authorized experts, trained in "best-practice" microfinance and in the "accomplishments of truth."

Like CGAP, the Boulder Institute is focused on the theme of building financial systems for the poor. At the 2005 program, Christen articulated the intent of the institute thus: "to impress on the growing microfinance community the need for financial sustainability as a precondition for attaining massive outreach." Not surprisingly, the Boulder plenary sessions and courses are saturated in ideas that seek to reposition microfinance as "microbanking"—as suggested by the title of the MIX's *Microbanking Bulletin*. Thus at Boulder one hears a great deal about indicators such as PAR and other standards of commercial banking. And one hears very little about poverty. Indeed, Robinson, in her course, clearly noted that "we teach not with a poverty focus but about going to scale." The scale question positions microfinance as a global industry: "If Coca Cola and FedEx can get their products to the end of the world why not microfinance?" asked one microfinance consultant.

Such a paradigm prevails not only at Boulder but also at other microfinance training programs. Launched in 1999, the Microenterprise and Development Institute (MDI) at New Hampshire initially presented itself as a poverty-focused, anti-Boulder venue. Yet the curriculum at MDI, while seemingly less prone to a recitation of CGAP "best practices," is also largely devoted to the theme of financial sustainability. In a class that I took at the 2004 MDI, we were trained to analyze the microfinance sector as a competitive global industry and to develop strategic financial positions for microfinance institutions. The language—of financial benchmarking, of financial performance indicators, of capital and cost structures, of portfolio at risk—was the language of the financial industry, and it was now the defining framework for microfinance as well. While some faculty expressed disappointment with such a curriculum, arguing that MDI was meant to be an alternative to a rigid and ideological Boulder Institute, others felt that microfinance practitioners were demanding a Boulder-style curriculum and this need had to be met. Here too microfinance was being strategically positioned as microbanking.

The Boulder Institute is more than a performance of "best-practice" microfinance. It is a site of knowledge production where a complex and sophisticated narrative of microfinance, and indeed of development, is produced. Robinson (2001: xxxiii), for example, presents the microfinance revolution as the shift from donor-funded "poverty lending" institutions in South Asia to "sustainable, financial intermediaries" or "microbanking" in Indonesia and Bolivia. This is a powerful narrative—of how institutions work and fail, but also of how places work and fail. In his daily morning session at the Boulder Institute, Christen traces the arc of microfinance from ancient lending practices to modern banking. He locates the roots of microfinance in tenth-century Buddhist temples in China, in the Maimonides principles of the twelfth century that encouraged financial assistance to the poor, and in fifteenth- and sixteenth-century merchant funds in England that were meant to lend to entrepreneurial borrowers. His argument is simple: that all societies and cultures have a history of microfinance and that today's microfinance practitioners are a part of this "long and illustrious" history. Christen analyzes modern microfinance as similarly differentiated, with three key genres: the South Asia model that seeks to provide credit to the poor through non-profit organizations; the Latin American model where the emphasis is on microenterprise and the generation of employment; and Indonesia where a more generalized, rather than targeted, model of banking and savings is well established. This is a historical geography that is also an argument about which microfinance models are most amenable to financial sustainability.

While Robinson (2001: xxxi) dismisses the Grameen model as dependent on donor funds, drawing a sharp line between institutions that depend on subsidies and those that do not, Christen provides a more nuanced debate about subsidies. In one of the Boulder sessions, Christen "defended" Yunus and the Grameen Bank. Noting that Grameen covers its operating costs, thus achieving operational self-sufficiency (OSS), he credited Yunus, "despite all the smoke and mirrors," for having produced "the pioneering institution that provides financial services to the poor." But he also noted that Grameen fails to achieve financial self-sufficiency (FSS) and insists on providing subsidized interest rates that do not reflect the real cost of money. Christen argued that Grameen would have to raise its interest rates in order to achieve FSS, a choice that Grameen has been unwilling to make. Grameen's choice was compared to that of the Bolivian market leader, BancoSol, whose effective interest rate of 46 percent is considerably higher than Grameen's 12 percent.

Such benchmarking is a powerful knowledge practice for it establishes global norms and fixes the parameters for evaluating institutional choices. After his animated "defense" of Grameen, Christen posed the questions that seal the deal:

> Should not those most worried about a poverty alleviation agenda be those most committed to full financial sustainability, to an industry that reflects the real costs of money? If they really care to reach the greatest number of poor families, would they not also care to ensure the most efficient use of subsidies?

It is in this way that, at Boulder, high interest rates come to be presented as a key "best practice" of microfinance and that in turn the practice of high interest rates is seen to be an essential component of "democratized capital."

At first glance, the Boulder Institute's "accomplishments of truth" are taken up enthusiastically and even with awe by microfinance practitioners around the world. The attendance of the Boulder Institute is a stamp of validation, a mark of authority. At MDI, disgruntled participants complained that the course was not as "cutting-edge" or "rigorous" as Boulder. And yet, the reception of Boulder ideas is more complicated than the establishment of a consensus would suggest. At the Boulder Institute, as at MDI, many of the participants, especially those from sub-Saharan Africa were central bankers seeking to learn how to regulate microfinance. For them the microfinance portfolio lacked prestige; it was an assignment that they hoped to quickly leave behind as they moved on to more valuable posts in central banking. There were other groups of disinterested microfinance practitioners, for example, those who were operating new microfinance institutions in Iraq and Afghanistan. In these frontiers of imperialism, where war and aid operate simultaneously, the development business is an important livelihood for a decimated middle class. Microfinance just happened to be the flavor of the times. For these practitioners, as for the central bankers, the swipes at the Grameen Bank, the debates about subsidies and sustainability, were all a yawn—many had never even heard of the Grameen Bank.

But for others the battle of ideas mattered. At Boulder, I met an Italian banker who rejected what he termed the "ideology of the Washington consensus" and noted that in Italy Yunus was widely loved—that he was "as popular as parsley." I also met a development consultant from Germany who lamented the deafening silence on the Millennium Development Goals at the program and expressed her shock at the scarce attention given to issues of poverty. And at MDI, I met several students, many of them from India, who had chosen MDI over Boulder because they were concerned about the latter's exclusive emphasis on financial systems. In the MDI classes, they made considerable trouble, calling into question the principles of "best-practice" microfinance and the norms of the Washington consensus.

The more significant crack in the Washington consensus has to do with the "accomplishments of truth" trumpeted at Boulder. Our Boulder packages included a piece by Chris Dunford, Director of Freedom from Hunger. Titled "Microfinance: a means to what end?" this 1998 essay reads, in part:

> We have lost our nerve; we have abdicated moral and intellectual leadership of the microfinance movement to financial engineers . . . Microfinance donors are driving practitioners to scramble for profitable mass production of methodologies pioneered over a decade ago without knowing enough about who we are reaching and with what effect. Today our fascination with "best practices" is more about institutional performance than the best possible outcomes for poor families. Best practices increasingly means adopting the performance standards of the commercial banking industry. Now there is a wonderful irony. We, the NGOs, are starting to emulate the standards of the very industry that has largely failed to meet the enormous demand among the poor for financial services . . . Market failure for the poor is the history of banking worldwide.

Dunford's essay casts doubt on the Boulder truths. Boulder's dominant message, that microfinance will and should be fully absorbed into commercial banking, misses the very real threat that the poor will once again be redlined and marginalized. Robinson's retort has been that it is not for the banking industry to reach the starving; rather microfinance institutions, such as BRAC, can improve the lot of starving people enough to make them bankable. It is this priming for bankability that has intrigued the Ohio School, which, while criticizing the high opportunity and transaction costs of microfinance, has also recognized that a revolution is afoot in this type of lending to the poor. At his Boulder course, Claudio Gonzalez-Vega, an Ohio School economist, thus framed microfinance as a "revolution," one that "stopped using property as collateral and instead started looking at people, at intangible futures." It is a frontier of capitalism that is opened up because, in the words of J.D. Von Pischke, yet another Boulder instructor and Ohio School economist, "Dr. Yunus was able to monetize the promise of a poor woman who had never touched a coin."

Gonzalez-Vega's argument is intriguing: that rather than microfinance being absorbed into commercial banking, in the future, banking itself will look more and more like microfinance. In a global economy driven less by physical assets and more by human capital, in a global economy of uncertainty where the standard methods of managing risk will be undermined by great volatility in occupations and livelihood, the banking industry itself will have to turn to the tricks and techniques of microfinance—to what Von Pischke designates as the "mystical and transcendental practice" of "monetizing the promise of a poor woman." This practice is "poverty capital." It is not the primitive past of modern finance capital; rather it is the face of the future.

THE END OF POLITICAL ECONOMY

The debates at Boulder, as well as the silences at Boulder, provide a glimpse of a much broader terrain: the intellectual agenda of millennial development. Three questions dominate this agenda: First, do markets work? Second, what are the ways in which development converts one form of capital into another, thereby producing what I have called poverty capital? Third, what is the role of poor women in development? All three questions are at stake in the conceptualization and implementation of microfinance such that the microfinance debates can be seen as a microcosm of millennial development.

Markets for the New Millennium

The shift from late twentieth-century free-market ideologies and austerity policies to a twenty-first-century ensemble of ideas and practices concerned with poverty and human development is marked by the rise of a discourse around market failure. For the key interlocutors of millennial development, such as Jeffrey Sachs (2005), the "poverty trap" is an example of such market failure. Breaking with his earlier role as an IMF operative implementing the neoliberal Washington consensus, Sachs now insists that markets are not sufficient to create the "Big Push" needed to end poverty. Such ideas also animate the work of another Washington insider, Joseph Stiglitz. Rejecting the neoliberal Washington consensus as "market fundamentalism," Stiglitz (2002) argues that the role of the state is essential—in both economic development and in ensuring the democratic and equitable distribution of the benefits of development.

Yet microfinance sits uneasily with the call for a "developmental state." Although it can be argued that microfinance emerged as a response to the failure of credit markets to reach the poor, the microfinance framework remains ambivalent about the role of the state. In general, microfinance does not involve state investments in physical or human capital. Indeed, as a development narrative, microfinance writes out the role of the state and instead focuses on the creativity of poor entrepreneurs and the success of local institutions in enabling such entrepreneurship. At sites such as the Boulder Institute, the analysis of market failure is prominently missing, drowned in a loud call for financial markets that serve the poor.

This faith in "pro-poor markets" is not unique to microfinance. It lies at the heart of one of millennial development's most famous debates: Easterly's scathing critique of Sachs's call for a "Big Push." As Sachs presents his solutions to market failure, so his New York neighbor, William Easterly (2006) rejects this approach as a "Big Western Plan," utopian social engineering for the twenty-first century. Easterly argues that the tragedy of poverty is not market failure but rather that the West has spent billions of dollars on trying to address this market failure and has not made a dent in poverty. Instead of Planners, Easterly calls for Searchers, those who, in incremental and piecemeal fashion, search for solutions. Easterly (2006: 27) argues that "the poor are their own best Searchers" but he is particularly interested in how the market is a mechanism of Searching. Thus, according to Easterly (2006: 60), development does not work, but "free markets work." Easterly's diagnosis of poverty is quite different from that of Sachs and Stiglitz: he believes that the rich have markets, the poor have bureaucrats. For Easterly (2006: 59), microfinance is a solution to this problem—it rids the poor of bureaucrats and solves the problem of credit by creating markets for the poor.

Easterly's analysis points to key conceptualizations of poverty that animate millennial development: that the poor *have* assets and that the poor *are* assets. In *The Mystery of Capital*, Hernando de Soto (2000) writes that the poor are heroic entrepreneurs who are part of the solution, not the problem. He argues that the poor own trillions of dollars in assets, the value of which far exceeds any amount of foreign aid that has been or can be transferred to the developing world. Why then are these asset-holders poor? De Soto argues that the reason is that the poor hold their assets in defective form, dead capital, and that the capture of such value is made more difficult by the red-tapeism of bureaucratic states. In short, he presents a diagnosis of state failure. Not surprisingly, at sites such as the Boulder Institute, de Soto's analysis is a common fixture. Instructors often refer to it to make note of the "immense value of savings among the poor." This is a powerful imagination, that of a new financial frontier that has hitherto gone unnoticed and untapped and that can serve the interests of the poor.

The compelling narrative of pro-poor markets is perhaps most famously outlined in the work of C.K. Prahalad. Noting that there is a "fortune at the bottom of the pyramid," Prahalad (2004: 1) argues that it is time "to stop thinking of the poor as victims or as a burden and start recognizing them as resilient and creative entrepreneurs and value-conscious consumers." Although this may be seen as creating opportunities for the poor, Prahalad (2004: 1, 5) argues that such an approach also opens up a "new world of opportunity" because "the poor represent a 'latent market' for goods and services." His analysis of microfinance thus focuses on the emerging alliances in India between profit-making banks such as ICICI and self-help groups. Prahalad (2004: 129) celebrates these arrangements because banking for the poor "is no longer viewed as a mere social obligation. It is financially viable as well."

The "bottom of the pyramid" framework has important implications for microfinance. It leads, in obvious fashion, to "mass-minimalist" microcredit, provided by "innovative, cost-conscious" lenders that use "scale economies" to provide a "simple, mass-produced financial product" and that are concerned with "business success and financial discipline, not empowerment" (Reinke 1998: 553). Yet, such models also have to be pro-poor, concerned with social value as well as financial value. Thus, one of the most popular concepts in the millennial reimagining of microfinance is the idea of the "double bottom line" (Tulchin 2003). The sentiment is pervasive. Michael Chu (2005: 14) writes:

> At this intersection of business and society, microfinance is an illustration of the power of harnessing the markets to deliver dual returns. On the one hand, the market made possible the creation of economic value: the superior returns—Return on Assets and Return on Equity—that accrue to the first movers that know how to do it right in a new and huge industry. On the other hand, the market also allowed the creation of social value—the maximizing of the disposable income of the poor.

It is possible to read millennial development as a fierce battle of ideas, an irreconcilable divide between those who are concerned with how markets fail the poor and those who advocate pro-poor markets. CGAP's reliance on market strategies of finance falls at the latter end of the spectrum. Yet, a closer look reveals that the divide may be less stark and that a more broadly rooted "consensus on poverty," indeed one that stretches beyond Washington, may be at work. For the language of pro-poor markets is not only the talk of Easterly, Prahalad, de Soto, and Boulder experts. It is also the talk of those associated with an older microfinance paradigm. In his speeches on microfinance and in interviews, John Hatch, founder of Finca International, simultaneously rejects and affirms the CGAP framework—expressing solidarity with the Grameen model and its emphasis on social performance and yet also stating that he is "suspicious of government." His reliance on "poor entrepreneurs" is an echo not only of de Soto's (2000: 4) image of a world "teeming with entrepreneurs" but also of Yunus's (2009) provocative line, that "we live in an ocean of money" (http://knowledge.wharton.upenn.edu/article.cfm?articleid=2243, accessed May 30, 2009). Likewise, although Muhammad Yunus expresses skepticism about a capitalism centered on the free market, he calls not for state solutions to market failure but rather for new, inventive forms of capitalism that combine the maximization of profit with the maximization of social value. His hybrid "social business" sounds quite a bit like the "double bottom line" or pro-poor markets that inform millennial development. Indeed, the idea of the "double bottom line" itself comes out of the work of the Grameen Foundation USA and is widely promoted by this organization and other allies seemingly opposed to the CGAP model. Yunus's approach puts forward the argument that the cause of poverty is the lack of capital and that by addressing this deficit, microfinance can allow the poor to fully participate in a more humanized capitalism (Fernando 2006).

This uncanny convergence of ideas does not indicate the imposition of a Washington consensus on poverty on organizations such as Finca and Grameen. Rather, it signals a common optimism about the democratization of capital and a common suspicion of the role of the state. As it turns out Stiglitz's ambitious insistence on a post-Washington consensus, with its call for a developmental state, marks the margins, not the center, of millennial development. Stiglitz's use of the prefix "post" is either premature or overly hopeful, since millennial development maintains the strain of market fundamentalism that he sets out to reject. Free markets are now being repackaged as pro-poor markets. The Washington consensus on poverty may in fact be a global consensus.

The Convertibility of Capital

The transformation of free markets into pro-poor markets requires work. Here, the ideas and practices of millennial development rely heavily on the concept of social capital. If the early years of international development emphasized physical capital (investment in infrastructure), and if the McNamara years were focused on human capital (investment in education and other basic needs), then millennial development foregrounds social capital. The World Bank defines social capital as "the internal social and cultural coherence of society, the norms and values that govern interactions among people and the institutions in which they are embedded." It argues that "social capital is the glue that holds societies together and without which there can be no economic growth or human well-being" (http://web. worldbank.org/WBSITE/EXTERNAL/TOPICS/EXTSOCIALDEVELOPMENT/ EXTTSOCIALCAPITAL/0,,contentMDK:20185164~menuPK:418217~ pagePK:148956~piPK:216618~theSitePK:401015,00.html, accessed July 14, 2008).

The broad interest in social capital partly stems from a concern with a particular type of market failure: information problems. "Incomplete information," along with "incomplete contracts" and "incomplete markets," takes center stage in the Nobel Prize-winning work of Joseph Stiglitz (Fine 2001: 8). In a lengthy Nobel lecture, Stiglitz (2001: 473) reminisces about his first visits to the developing world and a stay in Kenya that made an "indelible impression" on him. He was struck, he recalls, by "the imperfection of information, the absence of markets, and the pervasiveness and persistence of seemingly dysfunctional institutions." In the "information paradigm" promoted by Stiglitz, institutions matter. Social capital, which Stiglitz (2000b: 59) defines as "including tacit knowledge, a collection of networks, an aggregation of reputations, and organizational capital," is such an institutional solution, "a social means of coping with moral hazard and incentive problems." For him "peer monitoring," for example in the Grameen Bank's microfinance model, is an example of institutions that provide efficient ways around information asymmetries. In other words, social capital is not an alternative to markets but rather a non-economic means to alleviate market failure and improve market efficiencies. But Stiglitz (2000b: 68) also expresses ambivalence about social capital, noting that while there is an "important public role in the enhancement of social capital" it remains unclear how such a role is best pursued.

A more decisive statement on social capital is made by the World Bank in a poverty assessment report, titled *Cents and Sociability* (Narayan and Pritchett 1997: 1). It emphasizes the role that social capital plays in improving income and that such a role far exceeds the role of investments in human capital such as education. In development circles, group-based microcredit and indigenous rotating savings and credit associations (RoSCAs) are seen as examples of the "fruitfulness of social capital" (Woolcock 1998: 183). It is as if "the traditions of Third World cultures" are no longer an obstacle to "monetization and modernization" but rather have a new value—as a "potential source of social capital for those economies" (Bergeron 2003a: 165). But not all traditions and norms are seen to be valuable. The authoritative analysis of Robert Putnam (2000) draws a distinction between "good" and "bad" social capital. Such ideas are echoed in Woolcock's statement that not all types of social capital enable development. Group-based, women-focused microfinance is seen to activate and mobilize "good" social capital.

Social capital can be conceptualized as a remedy for market failure, as a non-economic "glue" that holds societies together. It is thus that a 2003 UNDP report on *Subjective Poverty and Social Capital* in Egypt focuses on the "informal institutional arrangements . . . including customs, norms, values, religious beliefs, and social and solidarity networks" that "structure the poor's access to employment, commodity markets, and housing, services, personal safety and security, as well as wider social support." But social capital, specifically "good" social capital, can also be converted into economic capital (Fine 2000: 62). The interlocutors of millennial development, such as Francis Fukuyama, thus turn to "culture" and "premodern" traditions and norms (Fine 2000). Bundled together as social capital, such traditions and norms are unmatched in their capacity to perform "double duty"—"as a counterweight to the unfettered individualism of the market and, simultaneously as a means to gain advantages in it" (Portes and Landolt 2000). Thus BRAC, one of Bangladesh's largest development NGOs, emphasizes "process capital": "the greatest power of microfinance lies in the process through which it is provided" (Abed and Matin 2007: 4). Such views present a challenge to CGAP's market minimalism, for they indicate that institutional innovations are as significant as financial innovations; that "development finance must also be defined as building social capital" (Capital Plus 2004: 5).

Conversions across economic, social, and cultural capital are shaped by and reinforce processes of class power and advantage. In other words, the "capital" in social capital is not innocent (Rankin 2002: 99). The World Bank's interest in social capital can be seen as a "depoliticization of development," one that seeks to "represent problems rooted in differences of power and in class relations as purely technical matters that can be resolved outside the political arena" (Harriss 2001: 2). The traditions, norms, and associations bundled together as social capital by millennial development turn out to be a hierarchical, stratified, and power-laden world. Easterly (2006: 79) defines social capital as "trust"—"that is, how much people follow rules without any coercion." But trust itself is "enforceable trust"—"trust exists in these situations precisely because it is enforceable through the power of the community" (Portes and Landolt 2000: 534). Such forms of domination and enforcement are of course easily evident in microfinance—from the explicit and subtle patriarchies that make possible the financial discipline of poor women in South Asia to the penal collection apparatus of microfinance in the Middle East. The conversion of social capital into economic capital and ultimately into global finance capital is thus underpinned by practices of discipline and punishment. This is the key to poverty capital in the age of millennial development.

In Her Name

The global order of millennial development, with its imagination of pro-poor markets and the convertibility of capital, is also a gender order. To a considerable extent, the new poverty agenda hinges on the "Third World woman." From health and population programs to environmental management initiatives, she has emerged as the key agent or "instrument" of development (Jackson 1996: 489). If, as feminist scholar Chandra Talpade Mohanty (1991) once argued, the Western eyes of development constructed the Third World woman primarily as the victim, now she has become an icon of indefatigable efficiency and altruism. This interest in poor women is partly related to a commonsense recognition of the "feminization of poverty," that the world's poor are disproportionately women. While sex-disaggregated statistics are hard to come by, an oft-quoted figure is that 70 percent of the world's extreme poor are women (Chant 2008: 166). It is thus that scholars have declared women in poverty to be a "global underclass"—not only income poor but also burdened by a range of vulnerabilities that are especially exacerbated in female-headed households (Buvinic 1997). Millennial development has made gender a key theme in discussions of poverty. Two of the eight Millennium Development Goals are explicitly concerned with gender inequalities. Goal 3 seeks to "promote gender equality and empower women," operationalizing the mandate in targets such as gender disparities in primary school education and women's political participation. Goal 5 features maternal health as a key indicator of human development. Such mandates are reinforced in a series of UN documents. In ambitious fashion, various UN reports have insisted that "gender inequality is a major factor in holding back achievement of the MDGs [Millennium Development Goals]" (UNIFEM 2008: 14).

The struggle to make women's poverty a visible and urgent part of the new poverty agenda is an important part of "global feminism" (Molyneux 2006: 432). The poverty agenda itself is preceded by a long-standing effort known as Women in Development (WID). In the 1990s, various UN summits, such as the Cairo Conference on Population and the Beijing Conference on Women, became arenas for the activism of thousands of NGOs, advocacy groups, and activists affiliated with the field. But the nexus of gender and poverty is tricky. On the one hand, millennial development draws attention to systematic and structural patterns of gender inequalities. But on the other hand, millennial development yokes gender to poverty, seeking to integrate poor women into development programs. These instrumental practices of integration can reinforce rather than dismantle gender inequalities. It is thus that various poverty programs, such as Oportunidades, Mexico's highly praised cash transfer program, position motherhood as the key to success (Molyneux 2006: 432). Oportunidades pivots on the idea of "co-responsibility," making mothers "primarily responsible for securing the program's outcomes." Is this "female altruism at the service of the state" (Molyneux 2006: 434, 437)?

I term this instrumentality a "feminization of policy," thereby indicating the ways in which development operates through women-oriented policies that in turn serve to maintain traditional gender roles of social reproduction and create a third shift of voluntary, unpaid labor for women. In other words, such policies can deepen what has been identified as a "feminization of responsibility and obligation" (Chant 2006: 206). Recent research indicates that "women's disproportionate share of the 'altruistic burden' within low-income households appears to be increasing rather than declining." This is the case despite rising female labor force participation rates in the global South, involving poor women in an "ever-expanding portfolio of maternal obligations" (Chant and Brickell 2010: 2). Such "altruistic burdens" take place not only within households but also in communities. They are the responsibility of Millennial Woman, the iconic figure of millennial development.

The nexus of gender and poverty is a complex one, of course. As some feminist theorists have critiqued the instrumental approach, so others have argued that such an approach may indeed have significant human development impacts. They make an "instrumental case for investing in gender equality," noting that such investments may improve the "social pathways through which women's access to resources might operate to improve their own and their children's welfare" (Kabeer 2005: 2). As discussed in the next chapter, such instrumental programs are also a terrain of contestation and negotiation. For example, a study of microfinance programs in Nepal reveals how poor women engaged in "loan swapping," "sustaining long-term debt financing by taking loans from multiple lenders." Such practices can be critiqued as "repaying credit with debt." But they can also be understood as the "skillful manipulation of a development technology" by poor women in order to support "subsistence and social investment activities" (Rankin 2008: 1971).

Despite such contestations, it is important to note that there is a very specific way in which millennial development has come to be centered on poor women. Their inclusion is made possible by what is perceived to be their inherent talents and abilities as entrepreneurs (Rankin 2001). It is an entrepreneurship that manifests itself primarily in the small-scale and informal sectors of the economy or "microinformality" (Elyachar 2002). In his autobiographical account of the Grameen Bank, *Banker to the Poor*, Yunus (1999) locates the origins of alternative development in the disjuncture between the elegant economic theories of his classroom and the reality of poverty just outside the university. The solution for him was not top-down development but, rather, giving credit to the poor, whom he saw as entrepreneurs. Rural, poor women figure prominently in this account. In every written text, interview, and speech, Yunus tells the origins story as a story of the women in the village of Jobra just outside the university at which he taught economics in the late 1970s. He describes watching these women weave stubborn strands of bamboo to make stools and baskets, icons of hope in these dilapidated villages of poverty, small brown hands making beautiful, luminescent objects. These objects, and these women, were bound in a system of exploitative moneylending, a system that Yunus set out to end. The liberation of rural, poor women came through the transformative power of money:

> The day finally comes when she asks for a first loan, usually about 25 dollars. How does she feel? Terrified. She cannot sleep at night. . . . When she finally receives the 25 dollars she is trembling. The money burns her fingers. Tears roll down her face. She has never seen so much money in her life. . . . All her life she has been told that she is no good, that she brings only misery to her family . . . that she should have been killed at birth. . . . But today, for the first time in her life, an institution has trusted her with a great sum of money. She promises that she will never let down the institution or herself. She will struggle to make sure that every penny is paid back.
>
> (Yunus 1999: 64–65)

Jeffrey Sachs (2005: 14) lauds Bangladesh's human development achievements, noting in particular "a new spirit of women's rights and independence and empowerment." Here, the entrepreneurialism of poor women that is celebrated by Yunus is converted into empowerment and ultimately into human development, even economic capital.

71

It can be argued that the CGAP model moves away from this focus on women and that in particular it seeks to incorporate poor men, formerly the "non-performing assets" of microfinance, into credit markets through the use of new technologies of transparency and visibility. Indeed, the financialization of development can be partly interpreted as the demise of the feminization of policy. With the growing emphasis on the financial sustainability of NGOs and on the minimalism of service provision, concerns about household patterns of spending and consumption, the role of mothers, and the realm of social reproduction are possibly fading. And yet, the Third World woman persists—in image and in text—as a haunting. Thus, *Capital Plus*—the 2004 report of the Development Finance Forum— has her on its cover, and the CGAP annual reports place an image of her in every section. On the first page of the 2003 report, she is the indigenous peasant woman, photographed with both "primitive" abacus and "modern" calculator, a figure that transcends primitivism to adopt modern, calculative technologies. She is a fetish, a magical object. The financialization of development takes place "in her name."

Money, Not Work

In his definitive text on the modern world, *The Order of Things*, French philosopher Michel Foucault charts a shift from classical conceptions of wealth to a modern analysis of political economy. Foucault (1966: 190) notes that in the classical age of mercantilism money was "the instrument of the representation and analysis of wealth" and that conversely wealth became the "content represented by money." In this system of circulation and exchange, value was established through equivalence—the equivalence of the pure fiction that is money as well as through the equivalence that is necessity. Foucault (1966: 241) notes that "a man's labor was in fact equal to the value of the quantity of nourishment necessary to maintain him and his family for as long as a given task lasted. So that in the last resort, need— for food, clothing, housing—defined the absolute measure of market price." In the nineteenth century, a new understanding of the economy was to emerge, one "whose object would no longer be the exchange of wealth (and the interplay of representations which is its basis) but its real production: forms of labor and capital" (Foucault 1966: 245). In this framework of political economy, value "ceased to become a sign"—it became a "product," produced by the "worker's energy, toil, and time" (Foucault 1966: 276).

The great texts and voices of millennial development are deafeningly silent on the matter of production, converting the figure of the worker into that of heroic entrepreneur. It can be argued of course that in the millennial age, production itself is pure fiction, materializing only in the volatile circuits of finance capital rather than in the fields and factories of the nineteenth and twentieth centuries. Indeed, de Soto (2000: 6–7) presents capital not as a relationship of production but rather as a "representational process." For him the poor are not workers but rather latent entrepreneurs who own assets, albeit those rendered impotent by faulty representation. De Soto (2000: 216) writes: "Marx would probably be shocked to find how in developing countries much of the teeming mass does not consist of oppressed legal proletarians but of oppressed extralegal small entrepreneurs with a sizeable amount of assets." The conversion of such "dead capital" into economic capital is de Soto's mission. His work marks the silence of millennial development on the "worker's energy, toil, and time." It indicates the end of political economy.

Yet, from time to time, millennial development finds itself confronting the laboring body. A recent article on microfinance co-authored by Stiglitz pays attention to the gendered nature of labor and subsistence. It shows how poor, rural women in developing countries face social and economic impediments to participating in formal labor markets. Microfinance, the authors argue, allows female labor to become "productive," i.e. to earn financial returns (Shahe, Morshed, Mahbub, and Stiglitz 2007). What the article couches in the language of microeconomic decision-making—within households and in labor markets—is the brutal political economy that has been obscured by millennial development: the toil of workers, the dispossession of the landless.

The persistent poverty of the bottom billion can only be tackled if the truths of political economy are also confronted. Three in particular are implicated in the microfinance debates: how markets fail the poor; how social capital operates through processes of power and domination; and how poverty interventions create an altruistic burden for the world's poorest women. While such truths are sometimes glimpsed in the debates and struggles of millennial development, for the most part they remain obscured by the great optimism regarding financial inclusion and the democratization of capital.

A KINDER AND GENTLER WORLD BANK

While millennial development is a distinctive historical conjuncture, a rather unique ensemble of ideas and practices, its lineage can be traced in the archives of twentieth-century development. Millennial development more generally and the Wolfensohn World Bank, in particular, repeats and reiterates many of the key principles of an earlier era of development, that of basic needs and "redistribution with growth," and thus of an earlier World Bank, that led by Robert McNamara from 1968 to 1981. It is useful to briefly reflect on this historical precedent, its engagement with poverty, its crafting of circuits of truth—all of which play out once again in millennial development. Such a history also reveals a set of striking challenges and contradictions that hound the World Bank's efforts to play a lead role in the efforts to end poverty. While millennial development is a terrain of action much broader than the single institution of the World Bank, I remain focused here on this singular actor because of its dominance, through CGAP, in setting the microfinance agenda and thereby establishing the Washington consensus on poverty.

Global Liberals at the Bank

CGAP was founded in 1995 by Ismail Serageldin, who also served as the first vice-president of the World Bank's Environmental and Social Sustainability Division. In an interview (December 2005), Serageldin talked at length about how he had been drawn to the work of Yunus and had come to believe that it was time to "mainstream" microfinance in the world of development. CGAP was to be this vehicle, with Yunus as the first chair of its Policy Advisory Board and Serageldin as its first chairman. Serageldin's recounting of the early days of CGAP reveals the tensions that continue to mark the field of microfinance: the CGAP agenda was meant to counteract the "bad habits of European donors who were pumping money into subsidized government programs," and instead it was to focus on sustainable development. This was possible since the World Bank staff had a "natural inclination to act as custodians of the financial sector." But it also had a primary goal of poverty reduction, one that drew inspiration from the Grameen Bank. In other words, in its early years, CGAP was to some extent a counter-establishment institution.

But perhaps the most striking aspect of Serageldin's account is that it links his leadership in establishing CGAP with his experience as a young professional in the McNamara World Bank:

> The only reason I stayed at the Bank was McNamara. I had come to the Bank with misgivings and I was keen to work at the ILO [International Labour Organization] on human education. The Bank seemed a terrible place for someone interested in education since the Bank's education programs did not fund literacy or girls' education, all the issues I cared about. But then McNamara appeared. I remember the Nairobi speech, with its focus on the poor. McNamara started a 530 club—100 of us, all young, met at 5:30 pm in Room 530. And McNamara told us that we would have to transform this place. We did—through rural development projects, slum upgrading, health, education, women and development.

Serageldin's narrative reveals not only the unique moment of the McNamara World Bank but also a sense of the Bank itself as being dramatically reshaped at various historical conjunctures, the sense of closures and openings, of centralities and multiplicities. For Serageldin, an important opening came with the protests around the Narmada Dam and the withdrawal of the World Bank from the project:

> We were severely attacked at the 50 Years is Enough gatherings. And it was time to review our resettlement policies. Until this point, the Bank had counted money, not people. The protests—Narmada, 50 Years—made it possible for people like myself to fight battles within the Bank. This was the high point of my career.

Robert McNamara was himself the product of a larger historical moment. His engagement with poverty can be seen as a globalization of the American war on poverty (Finnemore 1997: 206). Inspired by John F. Kennedy, McNamara was a "global liberal" (Milobsky and Galamabos 1995). An architect of the Vietnam War, he was convinced that "by alleviating the poverty of others, rich nations could create a more stable and secure world for themselves" (Finnemore 1997: 211). The theme of security is important, for in his speeches and approach, McNamara repeatedly stressed the relationship between security and development (Kraske et al. 1996).

What has been described as McNamara's "missionary zeal" (Caulfield 1996), can also be found in Wolfensohn and his efforts to reshape the World Bank of the 1990s to focus on poverty alleviation. On his first day on the job, Wolfensohn held a press conference where he declared that "poverty alleviation is the single most important problem" and that the Bank must be a force for "social justice" (Mallaby 2004: 88). Like Serageldin, Wolfensohn was quite directly influenced by the McNamara era. But as emphasized by Serageldin, the moment was also ripe for a new focus on poverty. An emergent global civil society, made up both of NGOs and social movements, was clamoring at the doors of the World Bank, calling for a prioritization of poverty alleviation. Internally, the Bank's culture itself needed reform, with high levels of dissatisfaction among Bank staff. Thus, by the 1990s, the World Bank faced a "crisis of relevance" (Rich 2002: 28).

The changes undertaken by Wolfensohn bear uncanny similarity to those initiated by McNamara almost two decades earlier. Under McNamara, new departments, such as Agricultural and Rural Development, Urban Projects, and Population, Health, and Nutrition carved out new spaces of action (Ayres 1983). Such too was the case with Wolfensohn's initiatives: Human Development, Poverty Reduction and Economic Management, Environment, Rural, and Social Development (Rich 2002: 37). Equally important to both the McNamara and Wolfensohn World Banks was the transformation of development knowledge. The signature report of the McNamara years was the 1974 World Bank report, *Redistribution with Growth*. It represented a culmination of the ideas put forward by poverty-focused critics. So has it been with the Wolfensohn World Bank, where Joseph Stiglitz was to reject the "market fundamentalism" of the 1980s and call for a new approach to development.

The McNamara era also previews some of the contradictions that mark the current moment of millennial development. Now, as was the case then, there is more ease in discussing "absolute poverty" rather than "relative poverty." The former is seen as a degradation of the human condition, therefore demanding of all of us an urgent response. But relative poverty is a structural logic of inequality and its mitigation demands more radical means (Ayres 1983: 77). It is that wide-mouthed funnel, with much at the top and little at the bottom. It is a funnel through which little trickles to the bottom. The *Redistribution with Growth* report, produced in the McNamara years, sets relative poverty beyond its ken: "Relative poverty 'means simply . . . that some citizens of a given country have less personal abundance than their neighbors. That has always been the case, and granted the realities of differences between . . . individuals, will continue to be for decades to come'" (Ayres 1983: 77). In his 1977 annual address to the Board of Governors, McNamara presented the argument thus: "Closing the gap was never a realistic objective in the first place . . . Nor is it one today" (Ayres 1983: 81).

Yet another contradiction lies in the question of how absolute poverty is to be alleviated. Although the McNamara and Wolfensohn World Banks set out to reject simple solutions of economic growth, they remain firmly tied to a market paradigm that seeks to reduce poverty by increasing income, productivity, and output. In the McNamara years, the World Bank put its "primary emphasis not on the redistribution of income and wealth . . . but rather on increasing the productivity of the poor" (Caulfield 1996: 100).

It is not surprising then that this global liberalism with its focus on absolute poverty was to be quickly erased during the Clausen presidency that followed. With its talk of the "productivity of the poor," it perhaps even set the stage for it. Previously the head of the Bank of America, the world's largest commercial bank, Clausen moved the World Bank away from "redistribution with growth" to an ideology of neoliberal supply-side economics. Years later, at the 2004 microfinance conference held at the Clausen Center for International Business and Policy at the University of California, Berkeley, Tom Clausen introduced Muhammad Yunus, lauding the role of microfinance in a world of poverty. In doing so, Clausen traced an interesting genealogy, arguing that in its early years the Bank of America itself was not unlike a microfinance institution, embedded in a community and making small loans. His narrative presented finance capital as a people's economy, thereby sounding the themes of entrepreneurship and pro-poor markets that are central to millennial development. This is now the new global liberalism of the World Bank.

A Knowledge Bank

Under Wolfensohn, and earlier under McNamara, the World Bank was organized as much as a "knowledge bank" as a "poverty bank." During the McNamara years, a series of policy papers outlined poverty concerns in various sectors—rural development, basic education, basic health, low-cost housing (Ayres 1983). And as in the case of millennial development, then too there was a focus on poverty maps, body counts, and the sheer facts of poverty. McNamara himself acknowledged this obsession:

> Because our product is advance of people. Social and economic advance of people, and not just one person but large numbers of people . . .We are in the business of dealing with numbers—numbers of people, numbers of dollars, numbers of tons of food produced. How on earth can you run this place without thinking in those terms?
>
> (Kraske et al. 1996: 173)

Under McNamara, the research capacity of the Bank expanded significantly and in 1975 the establishment of the Operations Evaluation Department signaled "an effort at self-criticism and evaluation" (Ayres 1983: 6). The McNamara Bank also created its own transnational "knowledge-generating machinery," such as the Consultative Group on International Agricultural Research (CGIAR), which partnered research and policy centers in the global South with American universities and most important with the lending agenda of the Bank (Goldman 2005: 85–87). Similar efforts were once again underway in the Wolfensohn years. Eager to shake up what he called the Bank's "marshmallow middle," Wolfensohn created new training courses that would expose staff to poverty, make them spend more time in the field, and also organized them into knowledge-sharing networks and technical groups (Mallaby 2004: 165). It is important to interpret the role of CGAP in this institutional context.

The argument for a "knowledge bank" has been made most passionately by Joseph Stiglitz. In keeping with his general account of market failures, Stiglitz (1999: 588) argues that "what separates more developed from less developed countries is not only a scarcity of capital, but a disparity in knowledge." Institutions such as the World Bank, he notes, are "public institutions, designed to facilitate collective action at the global level." Bridging the knowledge gap is one such important form of collective action; "knowledge is one of the central international public goods" (Stiglitz 1999: 578, 590). Stiglitz (1999: 590) thus concludes that "working more broadly to close the knowledge gap, is the special responsibility of the World Bank."

But important contradictions also mark this production of knowledge. What does it mean for the World Bank to bear "special responsibility" for knowledge, including poverty knowledge, at a time when it is also seeking to ensure that developing countries take "ownership" of development? Wolfensohn's hallmark initiative, the Comprehensive Development Framework, launched in 1999, is guided by the idea that development goals and strategies are based on "local stakeholder participation" and that "governments take the lead in preparing and implementing development strategies to shape the future of their countries" (http://web.worldbank. org/WBSITE/EXTERNAL/PROJECTS/STRATEGIES/CDF/0,,pagePK:6044 7~theSitePK:140576,00.html, accessed June 20, 2008). For low-income countries, such ownership takes material shape in the Poverty Reduction Strategy Papers. For the World Bank, it takes the form of the less tangible idea of "listening to the poor," a favorite theme of the Wolfensohn World Bank. In order to facilitate, or even require, such listening, Wolfensohn sought to change the internal culture of the Bank. By moving more of the staff, including country directors, into the field, Wolfensohn hoped that he could create a "new atmosphere of hope," where, as he stated in a 1996 speech, "we can tell our kids we make a difference . . . that we can cry about poverty . . . that we can embrace our clients, that we feel them" (Mallaby 2004: 167).

But such ideas of country ownership and listening to the poor raise urgent questions. How then can this democratized knowledge production be reconciled with the idea of a knowledge bank? In fact, it can be argued that the Comprehensive Development Framework only deepens the Bank's monopoly over development knowledge. Such issues also seem to have plagued the McNamara Bank. One account presents McNamara as "a conscientious pastor . . . visiting his flock, the poor of the world" but that "like most missionaries, McNamara believed that he was there to teach, not to learn" (Caulfield 1996: 97). If the World Bank is intent on teaching rather than learning, then it must be asked if it can accept and incorporate diverse ideas, including those that may run counter to its own ideologies. If it cannot—if it "conducts its own research without benefit of peer review, evaluates its own projects, and sets up think tanks around the world" (Pincus and Winters 2002: 22), then what is the knowledge produced by such an institution? Surely, this is not the unique public good that Stiglitz has in mind or that Elizabeth Littlefield, CEO of CGAP, so forcefully affirmed as one of the contributions of the World Bank. Indeed, critics of the World Bank have argued that the idea of a "knowledge bank" manifests unequal power relations in international development. "When you go into your bank, the clerks do not tell you that you have a knowledge gap and they are going to fill it. You would regard this as an impertinence" (Standing 2000).

Moving Money

There is a striking symmetry between the imperatives of the World Bank and the field of microfinance. The Bank must move money. So too must microfinance. While McNamara sought to remake the World Bank as a "development bank" and Wolfensohn in turn sought to remake the World Bank as a "knowledge bank," both eras reveal the particular dictates that accompany the sheer fact that the Bank is a bank.

In its early years, the World Bank, as it was established at Bretton Woods, functioned primarily as a conservative financial institution, raising money on Wall Street and making market-rate loans to creditworthy developing countries for projects whose risk could be clearly assessed. The World Bank received, and successfully maintained, AAA ratings for its bonds. In his speeches, McNamara repeatedly noted that World Bank loans bypassed the "poorest 40%" and that it was time to rethink the "investment banking model of development" (Goldman 2005: 68). With the establishment of the International Development Association (IDA), the World Bank was able to fulfil the new poverty mandate by taking in donations from donor governments and directing such soft money on soft terms to poor countries using soft—or in other words social—criteria. Such transactions increased the amount of money moved by the World Bank, with lending increasing from $2 billion in 1969 to over $12 billion in 1981 (Miller-Adams 1999). The expansion of development capital also required new forms of knowledge production. The new truth that McNamara had to establish was that "investing in the poor" was the most efficient route to growth with equity in the global South (Goldman 2005: 77).

The remaking of the World Bank as a development and knowledge bank came with its own problems. The poverty agenda itself lacked clarity. How much of the World Bank's expanded portfolio actually made it into the hands of the poorest 40 percent? What were the real effects on poverty? In a scathing critique of the McNamara era, Michael Goldman (2005: 87) argues that the

> rapid growth of the Bank's loan portfolio . . . eventually led to crippling effects
> in the South: high external debt, loss of diverse food production, the

dollarization and Americanization of food production, and plummeting food prices due to a worldwide glut in agricultural commodities.

He concludes that McNamara's "end poverty" decade "ended with a highly indebted South and a highly stratified farming system . . . Poverty grew as a result of the Bank's development industry." Similarly, during the Wolfensohn years, the World Bank's own Operations Evaluation Department concluded, in 2001, that "despite the Bank's poverty reduction mission, poverty has been a relatively minor explicit consideration in budget allocation" (Rich 2002: 36).

The moving of money by the World Bank draws attention to some of the dilemmas of millennial development, in particular the tensions between an investment banking model and a development banking model. Today's Washington consensus on poverty, with its mandate of the financialization of development, harks back to the conservatism of a World Bank driven by Wall Street ratings. Financial performance, in this case, trumps all other measures of performance. The high risks of lending to the poor cannot be accommodated in such a framework. These contradictions lie at the heart of World Bank lending, including in the two eras that came to be focused on poverty reduction. In an address to the Bond Club in New York, McNamara noted:

> The World Bank is not only a financial institution—it is a development agency . . . But having said that, I must make equally clear that the World Bank is a development investment institution, not a philanthropic organization and not a social welfare agency. Our lending policy is founded on two basic principles: the project must be sound, and the borrower must be creditworthy.
>
> (Kraske et al. 1996: 182)

In trying to change the "culture" of the World Bank, Wolfensohn put forward the idea that the effectiveness of the Bank's work had to be judged by the smile on a poor child's face and not just by the World Bank's bond ratings. This was the nature of development banking, which he, in a manner similar to McNamara, distinguished from investment banking. And yet, as he was often reminded by his staff, the World Bank does not lend directly to the poor or even to the NGOs that work with the poor. A senior manager thus confronted Wolfensohn at a 1995 meeting and asked that as a merchant bank with governments as clients, the World Bank must "stop talking about the environment, about women in development, about poverty alleviation, and so on as priorities" (Rich 2002: 52).

Such contradictions plague microfinance. CGAP seeks to strip away the human development aspects of microfinance and insists on a minimalist model of banking. Its argument, as I have already noted, is made on grounds of efficiency but equally on grounds of freedom, agency, and sovereignty—that the poverty conditionalities not only impede the freedom of microfinance institutions but also impose the will of poverty experts on the poor. How should such models of development banking be judged? Is microfinance effective when it moves money or when it alleviates poverty?

On a broader scale, what is at stake is not so much the democratization of capital as the democratization of development. Millennial development is a moment of unusual organizational density and diversity. Global poverty campaigns such as the One Campaign involve "everyday" people in the struggle against poverty and the reform of development. More radical organizations and movements such as Global Exchange, the World Social Forum, or Focus on the Global South make a similar argument about a people's globalization, one that exists in contrast with corporate-led globalization and neo-imperial development. This dispersed ownership of development promises to put an end to the monopolistic control of development.

Yet, Third World governments have argued that the new poverty agenda represents a new hegemony and impedes their right to economic development. This is a new "overload" of conditionalities—everything from the rule of law and participation to women in development and environmental considerations (Kapur 2002: 69). Poverty reduction is the "foremost conditionality" in the new "global development architecture" (Weber 2002: 538). Mark Malloch Brown, one of Wolfensohn's chief advisors and later UNDP administrator thus characterizes this agenda as a neo-colonialism of sorts. He compares the influence of poverty NGOs on the World Bank to the time when the British East India Company allowed Christian missionaries into its territory. These nineteenth-century missionary societies then proceeded to stamp out native practices that they perceived to be barbaric and uncivilized. "Nearly two centuries later, the modern missionaries of the NGO movement aimed to turn the World Bank into a crusader" (Mallaby 2004: 264). The conditionalities, some believe, threaten the viability of the World Bank. Malloch Brown's cautionary note signals what has been dubbed the "Chinese rebellion," the desertion of the World Bank by borrowers who can access private capital, money that is not burdened by poverty conditionalities. With private financial flows far exceeding ODA, the World Bank faces a new challenge of moving money and reinventing the role of development capital.

Ethical Capitalism

This chapter started at Lookout Mountain with the story of a covenant. There proselytizing missionaries took up the mission of saving the world's poor but also cast existential doubt on popular poverty alleviation ideas such as microfinance. In doing so, they broached the crucial issue of ethical development: in their case, can Christian values be reconciled with the role of the church as a loan collector?

The ethics of development is also an important theme in a kinder and gentler World Bank. Wolfensohn cast his speeches to World Bank staff as a call not only for change but a call for changing the "inside"—the "bureaucratic, cynical, distrustful" inside of institutions such as the World Bank (Mallaby 2004: 146). This call is steeped in a hopeful moralism—of better and more committed development professionals who can create a better type of development. And yet, as indicated in this chapter such a mandate can be in tension with other goals of development, such as moving money. Is there such a thing as ethical capitalism?

In the world of microfinance, these are fierce debates. As CGAP seeks to promote pro-poor markets, so questions have arisen about the functioning of such markets. Take for example, the controversy about Compartamos, a microfinance institution in Mexico. Compartamos, once a Catholic NGO is now a profit-making financial institution. In its initial public offering on the Mexican stock market, Compartamos raised $458 million. Private Mexican investors, including the bank's top executives, pocketed $150 million from the sale. More than half of the public offering proceeds went back to development institutions that had invested in Compartamos when it moved from being a non-profit to a commercial venture in 2000. One of them was Acción International, a Boston-based non-profit organization that provides technical assistance and capital to microfinance institutions. Acción invested $1 million in Compartamos in 2000 and sold half its 18 percent stake at the time of the public offering for $135 million. Reaching almost one million borrowers per year, mainly poor women, Compartamos has a portfolio of about $400 million and reaps an annual profit of $80 million. Most important perhaps, Compartamos defines a new frontier of capital accumulation. "This has got Wall Street's eye, London's eye, Geneva's eye," said the manager of a microfinance fund, "to say that if all the dots got connected this can be quite profitable" (Malkin 2008). In the midst of the financial crisis, in 2009, the *Wall Street Journal* (April 21, 2009) reported that Compartamos was posting a growth in net profits of nearly 25 percent. Yunus's statement—that we live in an ocean of money—seems indeed to be true.

The founders of Compartamos claim that the integration of microfinance with finance capital and stock markets will help the poor. Alex Counts, president of the Grameen Foundation, disagrees, arguing that Compartamos's poor clients "were generating the profits but they were excluded from them" (Malkin 2008). Surprisingly, a CGAP study, while defending the initial public offering (IPO), agrees with Counts, noting that to the extent that "higher charges to borrowers correlate directly with higher profits captured by investors, including private investors . . . there is a direct and obvious conflict between the welfare of clients and the welfare of investors" (Rosenberg 2007: 10). Central to the debate is the fact that Compartamos charges an annual interest rate of nearly 100 percent, not necessarily that much higher than interest rates in Latin America but significantly higher than the pro-poor institutions in South Asia that were initially the public face of microfinance. Yunus has thus lashed out at Compartamos as a "moneylending" operation. But microfinance economists such as Jonathan Morduch have argued that as long as such profit-making institutions are serving poor clients they are doing good (Harford 2008).

The Compartamos controversy echoes a long-standing debate in microfinance about "mission drift." Women's World Banking, a global network of microfinance institutions and banks, which had enthusiastically embraced the commercialization of microfinance, recently published a report expressing concern that "the influx of private capital into the microfinance industry may be . . . diluting the poverty-alleviation focus of transformed microfinance institutions in the face of increased pressure to generate profits." The study found a significant decline in the percentage of women clients served by commercialized microfinance institutions and called upon the microfinance industry to find ways to avert such trends (Frank 2008). A *Time* article on this report thus ran with the headline: "Microfinance: women being cheated?" (Kiviat 2008).

Faced with such critiques, CGAP is now discussing the establishment of a Code of Ethics. Along with Deutsche Bank and the Boulder Institute, CGAP convened a meeting in May 2008 in New York to "develop a common ground and set of principles that would help microfinance navigate between commercialization and its social mission." Elizabeth Littlefield, CEO of CGAP, made the argument thus:

"Without firm commercial foundations, microfinance cannot become the profitable business that it needs to be in order to survive. But without firm ethical principles and a commitment to benefit poor people's lives first and foremost, it will no longer be microfinance" (http://www.cgap.org/p/site/c/template.rc/1.26.1881/, accessed August 28, 2008). Littlefield had already expressed concern about seeming success stories such as Compartamos, arguing that microfinance could not simply be about transferring money from North to South or about creating a new asset class; it also had to be about "developing local financial markets that serve their own citizens" (Alexander 2007). Dubbed the Pocantico Declaration, the code is meant to "distinguish microfinance from other providers of financial services who lack the social motivation that drives the microfinance industry." Asad Mahmood, General Manager of Social Investment Funds at Deutsche Bank, notes that such action is necessary because of the "potential reputational risk" to the microfinance industry (http://www.cgap.org/p/site/c/template.rc/1.26.1881/, accessed August 28, 2008).

How should we make sense of such forms of "ethical capitalism," a term that has been used to signal the foregrounding of ethical concerns by business (Barry 2004: 195)? CGAP sounds the slogan of the democratization of capital, promising financial inclusion for the world's poor. But the workings of organizations such as Compartamos reveal that these pro-poor markets are new subprime frontiers of capital accumulation. CGAP's "Code of Ethics" seeks to regulate such forms of poverty capital. It also acknowledges the difficulties of extracting profits from the bottom billion in a world that also seeks—as the last line on the cover of Prahalad's (2004) book reads—to "enabl[e] dignity and choice" for the poor. The "ocean of money" may not be so easy to navigate after all.

CGAP's Code of Ethics can be interpreted as a sign of the ongoing debate that exists within the World Bank. It is perhaps an instance of the democratization of development. Indeed, the Wolfensohn World Bank may "have created grounds for redefining development in the struggle over the meaning of inclusion and social justice" (Finnemore 1997: 165). After all, Washington insiders such as Joseph Stiglitz repeatedly voice dissent, calling into question the discourses and practices of development. These auto-critiques often express sympathy with the protest movements that stand aligned against the World Bank and IMF; they often seek to put forward a more humane and inclusive agenda of development; and they usually work to foreground issues of poverty and inequality. Millennial development, in other words, may at once be facilitated by and facilitate the work of "double agents." The very strength of such auto-critiques derives from the "insider" status of these double agents: that they speak from within the project of development.

Yet, it is precisely this politics of position that also reaffirms the legitimacy and authority of the Washington consensus on poverty. It is thus that Stiglitz's auto-critique challenges development ideologies of "market fundamentalism" but simultaneously consolidates the role of the World Bank as the "knowledge bank" of millennial development. Committed to the idea of the public provision of collective goods, Stiglitz positions the World Bank as a global institution that can claim such a public purpose. The rebellion of World Bank staffers against Paul Wolfowitz, George Bush's appointee, has similar features. The dissent ultimately forced this World Bank president to resign, thereby also disrupting the power exerted by the US President over such appointments. However, the uprising once again marked the limits of the "political." World Bank staffers did not reject the legitimacy of Wolfowitz because he was the architect of an illegitimate war in Iraq. Instead, Wolfowitz was pushed out on grounds of corruption, on the charge of having inappropriately supervised and compensated his girlfriend. The disjuncture between such nepotism and his campaign as World Bank president to fight corruption was stark, and enough of an excuse for World Bank directors and staffers to demand his resignation (see Wolfowitz 2007). The incident demonstrated that World Bank staffers were much more than passive and obedient technocrats. However, its terms of debate consolidated the image of the World Bank as an institution independent of ideology and politics, one that would not comment on war and occupation. It also consolidated the image of the World Bank as the honest broker, an institution committed to fighting corruption, and one that could act as the keeper of global norms and rules. This is the "doubleness" of these types of dissent—that they simultaneously challenge and renew the role of the World Bank as the arbiter of development.

In a similar vein, CGAP's Code of Ethics may be a sign of dissent and debate, but it may also indicate a new, revised Washington consensus on poverty. Thus, a survey of CGAP members conducted as part of an evaluation showed the widespread concern that CGAP would "take over" new ideas (Forster, Maurer, and Mithika, 2007: iv). Indeed, a closer look at the few pro-poor innovations introduced by CGAP reveals that they all have roots in other institutions, such as BRAC in Bangladesh. Will CGAP be able to give due credit to the authors of such ideas or will it, in the name of ethical capitalism, appropriate such innovations? Will CGAP, for the sake of its Code of Ethics, impose a new consensus, a new regime of mandates and benchmarks on its "stakeholders"?

Such issues are about much more than microfinance. They lie at the very heart of millennial development as a new order of global liberalism. They hark back to the long history of the World Bank and its moments of transformation. They reveal the making of development—through the moving of money and through the production of knowledge.

NOTE

1 Muhammad Yunus in an interview at the Wharton School of Business, University of Pennsylvania, May 27, 2009 (http://knowledge.wharton.upenn.edu/article.cfm?articleid= 2243, accessed May 30, 2009).

CHAPTER 3

Dissent at the Margins
Development and the Bangladesh Paradox

<hr>

Poverty is like pornography—you know it when you see it.

(John Hatch, founder of Finca International, 2006[1])

Fall from Grace?

In 2006, Muhammad Yunus and the Grameen Bank were awarded the Nobel Peace Prize. The prize brought new attention to the role of the Grameen Bank as a pioneer of microfinance. Those opposed to the Grameen model of microfinance had to acknowledge its contributions to development. "Yunus was one of the early visionaries who believed in the idea of poor people as viable, worthy, attractive clients for loans," said Elizabeth Littlefield, CEO of CGAP, a donor forum based in the World Bank that advocates a market-based approach to development. And "that simple notion has put in motion a huge range of imitators and innovators who have taken that idea and run with it, improved on it, expanded it" (Dugger 2006). For a moment, the Washington consensus on poverty, anchored by institutions such as CGAP, seemed shaky.

The most elaborate celebrations unfolded at the Microcredit Summit held in Halifax, Canada, in November 2006. From the speeches to the imagery, the summit sought to promote the Grameen Bank's model of microfinance, showcasing an unyielding focus on human development and the role of microfinance in achieving such goals. Each session was inaugurated by a videomontage, the "Faces of Microcredit," usually of a poor woman and how her life has been transformed by microfinance. "We are here because of the women," announced Sam Daley-Harris, director of the Microcredit Summit Campaign, at the opening ceremony. Behind him played a song, "Hear Me Now," by the international band, The Green Children, the video featuring Yunus with a Grameen borrower. Milla Sunde, the lead singer, celebrated the changes in the life of this poor woman: "A smiling face that tells the story of a changing place . . . a tone in her voice wields the power of choice." Queen Sofia of Spain was on stage in her signature Grameen *gamcha*, the "royal shoulder," as Yunus noted, carrying this 20 cent humble cloth made by poor women as a "symbol of dignity and enterprise." Peter Mackay, now a Cabinet minister in Canada, hailed "microcredit as the vaccine for the pandemic of poverty," one that could address the important issues of "human rights, freedom, democracy, and private sector development." Even in Afghanistan, Mackay noted, microfinance could put "financial power in the hands of poor women."

When Yunus, the Nobel laureate, took the stage, the nearly 2,000 delegates from 100 countries erupted in standing ovations. In a sharply worded speech, Yunus declared victory:

> We are no longer a footnote in the financial system of the world. So those who doubted us, I hope that they will now be with us . . .The era of showing profits is over. The focus on the poorest is back . . .We will measure our success not on the rate of return on investment but by the number of people coming out of poverty.

It is thus that John Hatch, founder of Finca International, could insist that microfinance was a "movement, not an industry," and that this summit was the "biggest self-help event in history." "We have created globalization from the bottom up and it is bigger than globalization from top down."

The representatives of the Washington consensus on poverty were also present at the Halifax Summit. They spoke the words of caution, outlining the limits of microfinance, and seeking to temper the eager enthusiasm of the delegates. Kate McKee, formerly head of USAID's microenterprise division and now a senior advisor at CGAP, asked the summit to reflect on the "audacious" nature of the Microcredit Summit's goals and argued that we need to know much more about how microfinance impacts poverty. But the summit was to have little of this. In a bold announcement, Iftikhar Chowdhury, Bangladesh's ambassador to the UN, cited a World Bank report indicating massive improvements in human development in Bangladesh and attributing such achievements to microfinance organizations. Chowdhury went further, arguing that such forms of development also engendered peace and that microcredit thus "drained the marshes of terrorism." The Nobel Prize seems to have reinforced "microfinance evangelism," the "hard-selling" of an "anti-poverty formula" with "destitute women" featured prominently (Rogaly 1996). It is this rhetoric and imagery that dominated the Halifax Summit.

But the Nobel Prize was not a surprise. At the 2005 Boulder Institute, various key figures in the CGAP circuit talked about how if microfinance were to receive the Nobel Prize, then the prize should go to BRAC. "If I were in charge of Nobel Prizes," declared Marguerite Robinson, World Bank consultant, "then I would give it to Fazle Abed and his extraordinary institution, BRAC." These declarations anticipated the inevitable: that Yunus and the Grameen Bank were the public face of global microfinance, and that a Nobel Prize would undoubtedly be conferred upon them. BRAC, while much more favored by the Washington consensus, did not enjoy the same global recognition. BRAC was not—as one of the Italian attendees at Boulder had put it so elegantly—as beloved and well-known as is parsley in Italy. Even Robert Christen, a key CGAP figure, in one of his plenary sessions at the Boulder Institute, had to admit that it was only after his mother had watched a PBS documentary on Yunus and the Grameen Bank that she came to understand the concept of microfinance and the work he did.

And yet, what followed on the heels of the Nobel Peace Prize was not simply celebration and adulation but equally a sharp critique of microfinance. For example, an essay in *The New Yorker* argued that while "microloans make poor borrowers better off . . . they often don't do much to make poor countries richer." Rejecting Yunus's argument that the poor are entrepreneurs, the author notes that microloans are more often used to smooth consumption and that they rarely generate new jobs for others. A "missing middle"—small- to medium-sized enterprises—was seen to be the "real engine of macromagic" (Surowiecki 2008). In a bold articulation of this position, one published the week after the Nobel Prize was granted to Yunus and the Grameen Bank, *New York Times* columnist John Tierney (2006) argued that "the Grameen Bank is both an inspiration and a lesson in limits." Wal-Mart, according to Tierney, has done more than any other organization to "alleviate third world poverty," for it provides factory jobs to poor villagers, jobs that may seem to be "sweatshop" jobs but that allow workers to work their way out of poverty. In a similar vein, an essay in the *Wall Street Journal* presented Yunus's ideas as an "ameliorative" rather than "transformative" entrepreneurship. "Can turning more beggars into basket weavers make Bangladesh less of a, well, basket case?" "The poverty of countries like Bangladesh derives from their comprehensive backwardness," the authors concluded (Bhide and Schramm 2007). Such critiques frame the Grameen Bank as an outdated native economy, a primitive life form to be soon superseded by forms of economic organization more conducive to global capitalism.

Microfinance's fall from grace had been underway for a while, well prior to the granting of the Nobel Peace Prize to Yunus and the Grameen Bank. As the

Washington consensus on poverty sought to remake microfinance into a new financial industry, so the old-type microfinance, focused on poverty, came under attack. In a series of editorials and articles that were published in May 2004, the *New York Times* warned that "no one should be lulled by this microfinance boom into believing that it is a cure-all for global poverty" (*New York Times*, May 5, 2004). Yet, about ten years ago, it was the very same editorial page that had lauded microcredit as a virtual "cure-all," "a much-needed revolution in anti-poverty programs" (*New York Times*, February 16, 1997). And in 2003, the editorial page reiterated its confidence, stating that "microcredit is a proven development strategy."

Such shifts in opinion mark a transfer of allegiance from a Bangladesh model of microfinance, epitomized by the work of the Grameen Bank, to the Washington consensus on poverty. The 1997 editorial explicitly sided with the Microcredit Summit and its efforts to reach 100 million people by 2005 and to increase the share of microfinance in the world's development and aid budgets. Recognizing Yunus as the founder of the "microcredit movement," this editorial listed the Microcredit Summit's goal as a "worthy" one that "the United States should support." In 2003, the editorial expressed support for the Microcredit Summit goal of expanding outreach but also echoed the language of CGAP—that a "real microfinance revolution," i.e. of financial services and a financial industry led by "large global banks" could even further "empower the world's poor" (*New York Times*, November 19, 2003). The 2004 editorial was unequivocal. It broke sharply with the Microcredit Summit and its efforts to push poverty-focused microfinance legislation in the US Congress, a controversy that I discuss in greater detail later in this chapter. It was preceded by an article filed from Bangladesh that argued that "there is little rigorous evidence judging whether the very poor benefit from microcredit" (Dugger 2004). The article solicited numerous letters of support and protest. Muhammad Yunus and Fazle Abed (2004) jointly wrote a letter titled "Poverty matters." Never published by the *New York Times*, it appeared on the Microfinance Gateway. Yunus and Abed make note of the "three decades of innovation" in Bangladesh that have made microfinance a "powerful tool" to help the very poor and that were overlooked by the article. In an interview (December 2005), Yunus registered his outrage that the letter was never published by the *New York Times*. He saw this as evidence of how his ideas were being marginalized and superseded by the authoritative knowledge produced by CGAP.

But this battle of ideas cannot be read as a struggle between a Bangladesh perspective on development and a Washington-centered apparatus of development. For in Bangladesh itself, Yunus has faced severe critique. While the Nobel Prize generated an outpouring of support, Yunus's subsequent decision to run for political office generated controversy. Shortly after the launch of his party, *Nagarik Shakti* (Citizens' Power), in February 2007, a group of Bangladeshi academics publicly challenged Yunus, arguing that microfinance was a tool for the "protection and expansion of capitalism." Microfinance loans, they noted, simply "indebted people" rather than freeing them from poverty (*Daily Star*, February 22 and 25, 2007). In a cruel irony, Yunus's ideas were now equated with the market fundamentalism of Washington-based institutions such as the World Bank and the IMF. In Bangladesh, the critiques of microfinance are not new. The Bangladesh press and academic establishment have often fiercely exposed the power wielded by microfinance organizations in collecting loans. This too seems to be a crucial part of the Bangladesh model: a vigorous auto-critique about development and its instruments. But this time the criticism was explicitly directed at Yunus, a national figure who until now had enjoyed unquestioned moral legitimacy. By May 2007, Yunus had withdrawn his political candidacy, returning to the world of microfinance. In this chapter, I take a closer look at the Bangladesh model of microfinance, its debates and its contributions.

THE BANGLADESH CONSENSUS

Bringing Bangladesh to Washington DC

While microfinance evangelism was being critiqued in Bangladesh for entrapping the poor in cycles of debt, the Bangladesh model of microfinance was being aggressively promoted in Washington DC by the Microcredit Summit. A project of the Results Educational Fund (hereafter Results), a US-based grassroots advocacy organization, the first Microcredit Summit was held in 1997 to advance a poverty-focused model of microfinance with the goal of reaching 100 million households by 2005. Since then, the Microcredit Summit Campaign, led by Sam Daley-Harris, has foregrounded the role of citizens in getting educated and involved in the struggle against global poverty. Daley-Harris sees the Microcredit Summit as one that mimics the UN summits except that it is "a citizens' process." In this sense, as he explained at the 2006 Microcredit Summit, the summit can be understood as a "collective social movement." But the Microcredit Summit is perhaps better understood as a platform, one that reiterates a particular microfinance formula in its regularly held regional summits and most boldly at the 2006 "Global Microcredit Summit" held in Halifax. Here, the summit put forward two new goals: that 175 million of the world's poorest families, especially their women, receive access to credit by 2015; and that 100 million of the world's poorest families rise above the US$1 a day poverty threshold by 2015 (http://www.microcreditsummit.org/, accessed December 9, 2005).

Such goals explicitly challenge the Washington consensus on poverty, shifting the focus from financial benchmarking to human development. Firmly rooted in Washington DC, the Microcredit Summit Campaign strategically deploys the tools of this node of power—lobbying, citizen advocacy—to erode CGAP's hegemony. In doing so, it resurrects the Bangladesh model of microfinance at the very center of Washington DC. These efforts by the Microcredit Summit Campaign are most evident in microfinance legislation passed during the last decade by the US Congress and often fiercely resisted by USAID, CGAP, and their allies.

The Microenterprise for Self-Reliance Act (HR 1143, PL 106-309), passed by the US Congress in 2000, ensured a steady stream of funding for microfinance programs and also directed half of this funding to the poorest of the poor, noting that many of the extremely poor are women. The act's bipartisan co-sponsors billed microfinance as a "beautifully simple approach" derived from Bangladesh, and as "one of the best investments around" (*Seattle Times*, April 9, 1997). Benjamin Gilman, the Republican Chair of the House Committee on International Relations, hailed the "self-reliance" component of the bill: "Microenterprise institutions not only reduce poverty, but they also reduce dependency and enhance self-worth. . . . This investment, rather than a hand out, makes good sense" (http://www.gpo.gov/fdsys/pkg/CREC-2000-10-05/pdf/CREC-2000-10-05-pt1-PgH8893.pdf, accessed June 5, 2005). The act was many years in the making, with Results working since the mid-1980s to make possible such legislation. Newspaper headlines and editorials on microfinance abounded: "Bangladeshi Landless Prove Credit Worthy," "Bank Lending to Bangladesh Poor a Trail-Blazer," "Barefoot Money Management," "Banking on the People," and "Turning the Tables on Banking" (Bornstein 1996: 230). In 1987, then President Ronald Reagan signed a bill authorizing funding for microfinance. The 2000 act was thus the climax of such efforts, not their first step.

But in 2004, the US Congress, under pressure from the Microcredit Summit Campaign, was to amend the 2000 act. Titled the Microenterprise Results and Accountability Act (HR 3818, PL 108-484), this initiative reestablished a centralized office of microenterprise development within USAID and also directed USAID to develop and certify at least two poverty measurement methods for use by its partner organizations. In addition, the act sought to ensure that "more money goes directly to impoverished clients instead of expensive consultants." Introduced by Representative Christopher Smith, vice-chairman of the International Relations Committee and co-chair of the Right to Life caucus, the act had all the trademarks of "microfinance evangelism." In an interview (June 2005), George Phillips, an aide to Representative Smith, noted how microfinance was an important tool in the Christian struggle against the trafficking of women, a theme that makes itself into the committee statement of the act (http://chrissmith. house.gov/lawsandresolutions/microresultsandacctact.htm, accessed June 5, 2005).

But there is more to the act than microfinance evangelism. As self-reliance was a central ideological tenet of the 2000 act, so accountability is the key feature of the 2004 act. The main focus of the act is the workings of USAID. In a report submitted by Henry Hyde, chairman of the House Committee on International Relations (House Report 108-459, April 2, 2004), USAID was faulted for "inappropriately" contracting out large portions of the program to consulting firms and other for-profit contractors.

> USAID's own recent assessment showed that during fiscal year 2002, out of $165 million provided directly to microenterprise organizations, nearly $30 million went to consultants. . . . Numerous worthwhile established organizations that have the capacity and expertise to deliver services directly to poor clients are locked out of the process when the Agency uses "task orders" against "indefinite quantity contracts" with for-profit enterprises.
>
> (http://www.congress.gov/cgi-bin/cpquery/
> R?cp108:FLD010:@1(hr459), accessed March 19, 2005)

To this end, the act redirects USAID contracts to global microfinance networks and other non-profit private voluntary organizations, including Finca International, Freedom from Hunger, the Grameen Foundation, and World Vision. In a dissenting view, Jeff Flake, Representative of Arizona, noted that "it is ironic that ... a program intended to foster entre-preneurship and for-profit enterprises in developing and free markets around the world" limits "the participation of such enterprises in the very execution of the program" (http://www.congress.gov/cgi-bin/cpquery/R?cp 108:FLD010:@1(hr459), accessed March 19, 2005).

"The gloves are off for USAID," said Phillips, Representative Smith's aide, in an interview (June 2005): "it is time for accountability." This talk of accountability was consistent with right-wing Republican ideology, including that of many of the congressional representatives who supported the 2004 act. It promoted a "lean and mean" vision of government with a mandate for aid and welfare effectiveness; it insisted on promoting US interests not only in bilateral but also multilateral organizations such as the UN—"we should have more say in the UN" went the line; and it had the strong overtones of a US liberal imperialism out to save the world's poor from a fate of poverty, terrorism, and godlessness. From Christopher Smith to Bob Bennett, the authors and supporters of the 2004 act viewed the struggle against poverty, waged through instruments such as microfinance, as wholly in keeping with—even a necessary part of—their orthodox religious and moral positions. It is with these holy crusaders that Results has forged a pragmatic alliance—to promote the Bangladesh model of microfinance, to curb the spread of the CGAP consensus, and to hold USAID accountable for its allocation of development capital.

The various legislative acts attempt to create accountability by requiring USAID to identify and use poverty tools that would monitor the poverty outreach of microenterprise programs. A fierce debate has ensued about poverty measurement. In a 2006 testimony before the Committee on International Relations, the assistant administrator noted that USAID was unable to settle on two internationally valid poverty tools, instead choosing "country-level tools" that can "achieve significantly better accuracy" and that will be field-tested by "practitioner organizations selected on a competitive basis" (http://www.usaid.gov/press/speeches/2006/ty060727. html, accessed May 19, 2008). But the debate is not simply about the valid measurement of poverty; it is equally about the validity of poverty-focused microfinance.

Critics of the legislation, including many CGAP and USAID staffers, argue that a poverty quota will restrict and distort the growth of a global microfinance industry. In the words of CGAP, these are "at bottom private sector initiatives to develop private sector activities . . . increasing the depth of outreach will not come through legislation" (http://www.microfinance gateway.org/p/site/m//template.rc/1.9.24201, accessed December 1, 2005). At the 2005 Boulder Institute, Christen railed against the work of the Microcredit Summit saying that it had "politicized microfinance by putting it in the public arena." Microfinance will now be subject to repressive regulation, such as caps on interest rates, he argued, and this will discourage new players. "If they can't make money, the banks won't come in and this is unfortunate. We need to be under the radar."

Supporters of the legislation note that USAID microenterprise funds are after all public funds. In an unpublished 2004 letter to the *New York Times*, Chris Dunford (2004), president of Freedom from Hunger, argued: "It is a better use of public funds than most to legislate a bias toward funding microcredit for the very poor." Or, here is Alex Counts (2004), president of the Grameen Foundation USA: "Our view is that private investment is often best suited to programs that target the better off poor and non-poor; scarce government and philanthropic subsidy is appropriate for those pushing the frontiers of micro-credit outreach and impact amongst the poorest." Supporters also argued that global financial markets and development banks had already failed the poor; that such a quota—as well as the monitoring of this quota—was necessary to ensure that the poor had access to credit. Thus wrote Yunus and Abed (2004): "Without incentives, the free market doesn't cater to the world's poorest people. Instead they are the first to be left behind." Their argument rehearses familiar themes of millennial development: of market failure, of persistent poverty as a severe form of such market failure, and of the role of development interventions in mitigating market failures. But it also rehearses a geographical imagination that challenges the Washington consensus on poverty:

> If the experts in New York and Washington lived in Bangladesh, as we have done for more than 50 years, and were confronted with the same stark realities and intimate knowledge that only experience provides, perhaps they too would see what is possible and needed in the lives of the very poor.
>
> (Yunus and Abed 2004)

The microfinance legislation marks a set of victories for the Microcredit Summit Campaign. It also indicates the ways in which the Grameen Bank has made a home for itself at the very heart of Washington DC, not only through the establishment of the Grameen Foundation USA but also through a powerful alliance with US-based advocacy groups such as Results. As Yunus withdrew from CGAP and its agenda-setting work, dismayed at what he perceived as the "mission drift" of microfinance, so the target of this alliance became Capitol Hill. Deploying the tactics of representative democracy, the Grameen–Results alliance convinced US lawmakers of the continuing relevance and significance of the Grameen model, long after that model was declared backward and primitive in the circuits of truth crafted by CGAP. The legislation was inevitably bipartisan, carrying a wide appeal that ranged from empowering poor women to promoting free enterprise to curbing terrorism. It was also cast in the language of "accountability," one that had been forged in the crucible of Reagan-style neoliberalism but had considerable traction during the Clinton years of welfare reform. These appeals spoke to lawmakers ranging from Christian fundamentalists to social democrats. Together, through congressional power, they resurrected the Bangladesh model, creating new circuits of truth as well as new circuits of development capital. Thus, shortly after the 2004 legislation had passed, Sam Daley-Harris noted in an interview (October 2004) that it is imperative to engage with, and reform, donor institutions for they "provide financing and control knowledge." "When you look at the underbelly of these institutions you realize that Yunus's ideas have been lost . . . if it weren't for the legislation I would be depressed . . . Without the Microcredit Summit Campaign, I think Yunus would have lost the battle of ideas."

But it is worth asking if this has been a limited victory; had the Microcredit Summit Campaign won the battle and lost the war? For the legislative tactics could only be direct focused at USAID and its microenterprise funds—$211 million in the fiscal year 2005 according to the USAID 2006 testimony—development capital that is a tiny portion of the global microfinance industry. As one former CGAP staffer argued in an interview (May 2006), USAID funding is an ever diminishing piece of the microfinance industry. The effects of the legislation will thus be minimal, she noted. Acutely aware of this, the Microcredit Summit Campaign continues to work with lawmakers, both in the US and elsewhere, to put pressure on other development institutions—from the UNDP to the World Bank. But these multilateral institutions are not necessarily accountable to US lawmakers and their constituencies.

In 2007, in a meeting organized by the Microcredit Summit Campaign, US lawmakers met with World Bank President Robert Zoellick to double World Bank spending on microfinance (from 1 percent to 2 percent), to commit half of those funds to those living below $1 a day, and to use poverty measurement tools to ensure compliance. But as Results itself reports: "all Mr. Zoellick could promise was more meetings" (Results 2008). Zoellick's response to Results, that the poor require grants and safety nets rather than microcredit, echoes a poverty truth that is entrenched in the circuits of CGAP and Boulder. This truth, sketched by Marguerite Robinson, in that indelible line that she draws between the economically active and entrepreneurial poor and the economically inactive poor, seems impossible to challenge. It haunts the debates around the legislation, such that an unusual voice, Didier Thys (2004), serving then as executive director of MIX, asks somewhat angrily in a letter to the *New York Times*, also unpublished:

> Why should a poor woman in India, stigmatized as an "untouchable," be less worthy of investment than the landowner for whom she works? Can't fifty cents on every dollar we invest in microfinance be used to help her and her neighbors? Does it all have to go to the landowner? I thought we were beyond that.

Homegrown Institutions

The landscape of microfinance in Bangladesh is dominated by a few large players, notably the Grameen Bank, BRAC, and ASA, each of which commands a vast hinterland of clients and also has a global presence. More recently, it is ASA that is often lauded by the microfinance industry as the Bangladesh success story, making it to the top of the "MIX Global 100" lists and Forbes ranking, and hailed by the Asian Development Bank as the "Ford" of microfinance for its "efficiency" and "productivity" (Fernando and Meyer 2002). In 2008, ASA received the "Banking at the Bottom of the Pyramid" award of the International Finance Corporation and *The Financial Times*. In these global rankings, the Grameen Bank is recognized primarily for its "outreach," in other words for the millions of borrowers that it serves, but it is rarely presented as a model of innovative microfinance. Instead, such praise is reserved for BRAC, whose innovations have been circulated by CGAP and its experts. BRAC's founder Fazle Abed has received substantial global recognition—from the Conrad N. Hilton Foundation

Humanitarian Prize to the first Global Citizen Award of the Clinton Global Initiative. In presenting BRAC with the Gates Award for Global Health, Bill Gates noted that "BRAC has done what few others have—they have achieved success on a massive scale, bringing lifesaving health programs to millions of the world's poorest people" (Covington 2009). A recent book on BRAC makes note of its "remarkable success," a message endorsed by the who's who of millennial development: from Bill Clinton to George Soros to James Wolfensohn (Smillie 2009).

Since its modest inception as a small-scale relief rehabilitation project in 1972, BRAC has grown into one of the world's largest non-profit organizations with over 40,000 full-time staff and over 160,000 para-professionals, 72 percent of whom are women. BRAC's annual budget is over $430 million, 78 percent of which is self-financed. BRAC's microfinance program, with 6 million borrowers, has cumulatively disbursed $4 billion. More than 1.5 million children are currently enrolled in 52,000 BRAC schools and over 3 million have already graduated. BRAC's health program reaches over 100 million people in Bangladesh with basic healthcare services and programs for tuberculosis, malaria, and HIV/AIDS (http://www.brac. net/, accessed August 3, 2008). ASA too is of substantial size, serving 5.7 million borrowers through its microfinance program (http://www.asa.org. bd/, accessed August 3, 2008).

These global rankings and statistics tell us little about how these institutions function and how together they are part of what may be understood as a "Bangladesh consensus on poverty." As development organizations, the Grameen Bank, BRAC, and ASA are indeed impressive in their sheer size and scale serving millions of households. Established in the 1970s, in the wake of Bangladesh's struggle for national independence, these civil society institutions represent an apparatus of development that far outpaces and exceeds the reach of the state. In the skyline of Dhaka, the Grameen and BRAC buildings loom large, as if to declare, as does Abed: "If you want to do significant work, you have to be large. Otherwise we'd be tinkering around on the periphery" (Armstrong 2008).

Size and scale are only elements of a distinctive ensemble of develop-ment ideas and practices. Led by charismatic men, these are "homegrown institutions" (Bornstein, 1996: 249) that while different in methodology are united in an ideology of poverty alleviation and institutional practice. I call this ideology the "Bangladesh consensus on poverty." Its hallmark is the non-profit delivery of a wide range of services, including microfinance, to the poor. It is explicitly opposed to the CGAP consensus and its emphasis on market infrastructure, rejecting it as a "commercialization" that distorts "values" and "governance structures." Such critiques emanate not only from the Grameen Bank, but also from ASA. In a set of interviews (July 2004), the program director of ASA insisted that ASA is a "grassroots" organization that serves the poor and that it cannot accept the types of commercialization that are being imposed in top-down fashion by CGAP. This, he argued, has a focus on "profits" rather than poverty; it is a "banking" model rather than a "NGO" model.

Most surprising is that the work of the World Bank office in Dhaka bears closer resemblance to the ideas and practices of the Grameen Bank and BRAC than to those of CGAP. During an interview (August 2004), one top-ranking World Bank official drew a sketch of different segments of the poor that was an echo of Marguerite Robinson's diagram separating the bankable poor from the unbankable. Yet, against prevailing CGAP wisdom, he drew his arrows past the ultra-poverty line indicating how World Bank programs in Bangladesh are targeting the ultra-poor and seeking to harness their "entrepreneurial skills." His talk of the need for "flexible credit delivery mechanisms" for the bottom 10 percent of the poor was almost identical to the second incarnation of Grameen lending, or Grameen II. Similarly, the argument that the ultra-poor may need more than credit—that a combination of grants and training may be necessary—was once again a weak echo of BRAC's celebrated ultra-poverty program. These resemblances do not necessarily mean that the World Bank office in Dhaka is busy replicating Grameen or BRAC programs. Rather, it indicates the consolidation of a Bangladesh consensus marked by a certain "common sense" about poverty alleviation.

I use the term, "consensus" deliberately. It is meant to evoke what has been identified as a "latent Southern consensus," one that does "not exist as a political reality" and that is not "articulated analytically" (Gore 2000: 795). While in the previous chapter I documented a Washington consensus on poverty, in this chapter I argue that there is a rival consensus, produced in Bangladesh and disseminated globally. It is a viable and vital, rather than latent, Southern consensus. Indeed, a striking feature of the Bangladesh consensus on poverty is a keen and self-conscious sense, among the leading institutions, of the existence of a unified Bangladesh model of microfinance.

When I used the term "Bangladesh consensus" with interlocutors in these institutions they instantly knew what I meant, often detailing what they saw as the key characteristics of the consensus. Such a narrative asserts the homegrown qualities of this model, of its coming to maturity in the crucible of dense and extreme poverty, of a unique history of development where the emergence of poverty-focused institutions was embedded in the more ambitious enterprise of nation-building. In such a context, the CGAP principles and mandates seem irrelevant and strangely out of place. Imran Matin, director of BRAC's Research and Evaluation Division, and who had worked at CGAP for a short stint, noted in an interview (July 2004) that in Bangladesh

> microfinance is driven by our own analysis. Some in Washington DC have the power to say what is appropriate and what is not. They insist that one has to first build financial institutions and then do social development. But that is not our history. We did not start out as financial institutions. We are development institutions and we won't blink an eye to do this development work.

The poverty focus in Bangladesh emanates not from donor mandates or global best practices but rather, in Matin's words from a "moral urgency" that is immediate and proximate.

The Bangladesh consensus is more than an alternative to the Washington consensus on poverty. It is a parochialization of the Washington consensus on poverty, for it presents CGAP's ideas as derivative of the Latin American experience and thus irrelevant to the vast swaths of microfinance that is "Asia." For example, Salahuddin Ahmed, then director of Palli Karma-Sahayak Foundation (PKSF), an apex microfinance institution established by the World Bank, in an interview (August 2004), dismissed CGAP ideas as hopelessly limited:

> These highlight the Latin American model, but that model is derivative of high finance. It starts with a financial norms and standards. And its main success story, BancoSol, was in fact a disaster. In Bangladesh, our model is that of the grassroots; we start with practice and from this emerges new norms . . . It is time to unlearn everything that Boulder teaches about best-practice microfinance.

It is thus that the Bangladesh consensus transforms the peripheries of globalization into a powerful centrality. For some of the key agents of development in Bangladesh, the struggle for the control of microfinance is an indication of the hierarchies of the world system itself. As one senior Grameen Bank official put it during an interview (December 2005):

> You have to think about this geopolitically. There are the vast resources of the world occupied and controlled by white people. We brown people are stuck in our part of the world. Capital can move. But we cannot. So how do we transform our own countries and how do we do so despite bad leaders?

The Bangladesh consensus does not imply that there is a consensus on the value of microfinance in Bangladesh. Indeed, a key element of the Bangladesh consensus is that it is shaped by a set of sharp and often public critiques of microfinance. The Bangladesh press repeatedly presents microfinance organizations as predatory lenders, charging high interests and enforcing repayment even in the face of natural disaster. After each flood or cyclone in Bangladesh, the headline story is as much that of devastation and destruction as it is of microfinance loan officers making the rounds of poor households, insisting on loan collection. Bangladesh's politicians—from finance ministers to prime ministers—put forward similar critiques, framing microfinance as a sector that exploits rather than helps the poor. It is thus that in Bangladesh a common label for microfinance institutions is that of the *kabuliwallah*, the stereotyped figure of the professional, itinerant moneylender who historically hails from Afghanistan, serves communities by providing lines of credit, and yet who is seen to charge exorbitant interest. It is this stereotypical figure that is humanized in a Bengali literary classic, Rabindranath Tagore's touching short story of the friendship between a *kabuliwallah* and a young girl. The stereotype is that of itinerant commerce, of moneylenders and vendors, of those that cannot be trusted. But it is also that of foreignness, of practices and norms that hail from the mysterious geographies of Kabul. This taint is an irony, for the Bangladesh microfinance institutions are, if nothing else, homegrown. And in a curious reversal, it is Bangladesh's premier microfinance institution, BRAC, a so-called *kabuliwallah*, that has now set up shop in Kabul, Afghanistan.

The existence of a Bangladesh consensus should also not be taken to mean that the field of microfinance in Bangladesh is centralized and fully coordinated. Indeed, in the words of one Bangladeshi interlocutor, this field is characterized by "multiple sovereignties." While there is a striking consensus on the ideology of poverty, there is not always a consensus on practical methodologies. For example, a debate that exposed the splinters and fractures in the field of microfinance in Bangladesh was around a proposed interest rate cap of 12.5 percent. A project of PKSF, a wholesale microfinance institution established by the World Bank, the interest rate cap received strong support from Yunus and the Grameen Bank. In an interview (August 2004), Yunus argued that such a cap was necessary to ensure that "a few bad NGOs" do not "ruin the lending environment" and the "public image" of microfinance. But BRAC and ASA did not support the proposal, arguing that microfinance institutions should be able to determine the interest rates at which their operations were viable.

The interest rate cap, which was ultimately abandoned, marked the effort of PKSF as an apex financial intermediary to respond to the *kabuliwallah* stereotype. But it also marked the rather bold move by PKSF to assert its independence from the very institution that established it: the World Bank. Underwritten by World Bank loans, PKSF is a wholesale microfinance intermediary that lends to microfinance NGOs (Khandker 2005). Well aware that the World Bank, and particularly CGAP, is fiercely opposed to interest rate caps, PKSF nevertheless pushed for such a cap in Bangladesh. When I interviewed the director of PKSF (August 2004), Salahuddin Ahmed (who went on to become head of the central bank in Bangladesh), he presented the interest rate cap not as a distortion of the market, as goes the World Bank argument, but rather as the correction of a market characterized by powerless borrowers and powerful lenders, "a model price." It is in this way that PKSF could claim its lineage as a "home-grown" institution. Indeed, in an angry response to a *Wall Street Journal* article that criticized the Grameen Bank, Yunus (2002b) insisted that PKSF was set up not to distribute "foreign funds" but rather "to resist donor money." Such claims are central to the Bangladesh consensus.

The Bangladesh Paradox

Bangladesh has been long vilified as an "international basket case"—Kissinger's infamous phrase—and viewed as a hopeless combination of political instability and deep poverty. Microfinance, Bangladesh style, was accordingly seen as a set of micro-interventions that could do little to address these macro-structures of underdevelopment. Yet, recently, Bangladesh has been hailed as a forerunner in human and economic development, at least among low-income countries. The World Bank, in particular, has drawn attention to this so-called "Bangladesh paradox." In a visit to Bangladesh in November 2007, during which time he met with Yunus, World Bank president, Robert Zoellick acknowledged that "Bangladesh has made significant economic and social gains since the 1990s. Its human development achievements have been remarkable in reaching a number of the Millennium Development Goals." World Bank statistics show sharp drops in poverty (from 70 percent in 1971 to 40 percent in 2005); as well as significant increases in secondary school enrollment, childhood immunization, food security, and drops in infant and child mortality and fertility. World Bank reports now forecast that Bangladesh could join the list of "middle income" countries in ten years (http://www.worldbank.org.bd/WBSITE/EXTERNAL/COUNTRIES/SOUTHASIAEXT/BANGLADESHEXTN/0,,contentMDK:20195502~menuPK:295767~pagePK:141137~piPK:141127~theSitePK:295760,00.html, accessed May 17, 2008).

Such human development impacts are a matter of pride in the development community in Bangladesh. In an interview (December 2004), Fazle Abed noted the decline of maternal mortality as one of the most important achievements of Bangladesh in recent years. As described by Covington (2009), Abed has a personal tie to such an issue, with his first wife having died in childbirth in 1981: "I thought at the time, 'My God, if my wife can die in a Dhaka hospital, it must be so much riskier for the poorest women having difficult childbirths in rural areas without any hospitals, without any support.'" But it is also a story about institutions: BRAC's maternal mortality program currently reaches 30 million people and is set to "scale up to cover the entire country" (Covington 2009). The interest in such indicators also marks the Bangladesh consensus as ineluctably different from the Washington consensus on poverty. While the latter gives place of prominence to financial indicators, the former is focused on human development and the inter-generational transmission of poverty.

Who bears the credit for these achievements? A World Bank report focused on gender transformations draws direct connections between human development achievements and the work of Bangladesh's microfinance institutions. Titled *Whispers to Voices: Gender and Social Transformation in Bangladesh*, the report "concludes that there has been a far-reaching change in gender norms in Bangladesh" which are the result of "constructive policies and programs" (Das 2008: 3). This Bangladesh paradox—strides in gender equality in a "cultural context widely believed to be repressive to women"—needs explanation. The report draws attention to a variety of unique global and national forces and conjunctures, including Bangladesh's insertion into a global garment industry fueled by female labor as well as the formation of a powerful women's movement with NGOs fighting for gender equality. But the report also credits two programs or policies that were "expressly intended to improve women's status"—the state's education policy and the "NGO-driven microcredit program." "Not only did women learn to save and get access to credit but the credit groups created a sense of solidarity that allowed for other services, such as family planning, to be delivered through them" (Das 2008: 5).

Yet another World Bank report, titled *Bangladesh: Strategy for Sustained Growth*, credits "income growth" as the "strongest engine for raising living standards and reducing poverty" but also acknowledges "innovative social programs," notably the Grameen Bank and BRAC (Mahajan 2007: xv). While the World Bank tends to present such human development outcomes as "trickle-down" effects of economic growth, this report acknowledges that, in Bangladesh, "much of the social sector progress started in the first two decades before independence, *well before* the growth acceleration" (Mahajan 2007: 4, emphasis added). Indeed, it argues that this "social development" and the "good progress on women's advancement" were "important" factors in "sustaining the higher growth" (Mahajan 2007: 12).

The hopeful and laudatory tone of the World Bank reports is previewed in the 2005 Poverty Reduction Strategy Paper, titled *Unlocking the Potential: National Strategies for Accelerated Poverty Reduction*, prepared by the Government of Bangladesh. The transformation from an "international basket case" to a development success story is presented as the "march of hope." Taken together these institutional documents seem to settle a long-standing debate about the value of microfinance and its impacts on macro-economies. However, village-level studies in Bangladesh present a more complicated picture of both poverty reduction and gender empowerment. Although I will not rehearse the arguments of these studies in detail, two points of debate are worth a closer look.

The case for the impact of microfinance on poverty is made most vigorously by Shahidur Khandker, lead economist in the World Bank

Institute's Poverty Reduction and Economic Management Division and the Development Research Group at the World Bank. In a series of studies published between 1998 and 2005 (Khandker 1998; Pitt and Khandker 1998; Khandker 2003; Khandker 2005), and conducted as a collaboration between the World Bank and the Bangladesh Institute of Development Studies, Khandker (2003: 4) finds that microfinance programs "help the poor through consumption smoothing and asset-building," "promote investment in human capital (such as schooling) and raise awareness of reproductive health issues (such as use of contraceptives) among poor families" and "help women acquire assets of their own and exercise power in household decisionmaking." These findings are borne out by other scholars who argue that "Grameen and BRAC provide credit to the core poor" and can thus "improve the incomes of the poor, even moving them above the poverty line" (Hulme and Mosley 1996: 115, 109). In a more recent study, which uses panel data from the 1990s, Khandker (2005: 23) concludes that "the results are resounding": "The net reduction in moderate poverty is about 18 percentage points in program areas, 13 percentage points in nonprogram areas, and 17 percentage points overall between 1991/92 and 1998/99."

But do such benefits accrue to all poor borrowers? Critiques of Khandker's earlier findings suggest that less poor households, those that are not necessarily the target group for microfinance, may bias the results (Morduch 1998). To this end, Khandker (2005: 4) provides reestimates "by excluding mistargeted households" and notes that the results still hold. However, other questions persist. Particularly significant is the specter of "credit-induced crisis" for poor households, one where microfinance loans increase indebtedness and ultimately reduce asset levels. At least one study calls for more research on why borrowers—an estimated 15 percent per year for Grameen and 10–15 percent for BRAC—leave such financial institutions (Hulme and Mosley 1996: 122).

A second debate has called into question the established wisdom that microfinance loans empower women. Researchers argue that although women borrowers bear the burden of repayment, they lack "managerial control" over microfinance loans, with such loans usually utilized by male relatives (Goetz and Sengupta 1996: 53). When women do retain managerial control, the credit is usually "invested in conventional women's activities," those that do not challenge "gender role ascriptions" and that may not yield "profitable expansions" of the household income (Goetz and Sengupta

1996: 53). These studies conclude that the success of microfinance institutions rests on their power to exist patriarchal control over women, a "new form of domination" (Rahman 1999: 67). Women, they note,

> are easy to locate, being much less able than men to leave a locality temporarily to evade field workers, and they are easier to intimidate into repayment than men, who can always threaten violence. In effect, the household is internalizing the high transaction costs of lending to men . . . These costs are primarily those of monitoring men's loan use and enforcing regular repayment. Women in effect offset these costs by using intrahousehold gender relations of obligation or persuasion to recover weekly loan repayments.
>
> (Goetz and Sengupta 1996: 55)

This critique—of microfinance as a patriarchal ideology that turns women into "instruments" of development—is important. It brings to light the gendered logic of millennial development, of the pro-poor development that is undertaken "in her name." These critics are correct to reject the "preoccupation with credit performance" and how women's high repayment rates have come to be seen as a "proxy indicator for control and empowerment" (Goetz and Sengupta 1996: 45). But while it is important to reject the microfinance industry's primary indicator of success, loan repayment, it is equally important to call into question what seems to have become the feminist critic's primary indicator of empowerment, managerial control of the loan. In a perceptive analysis of such feminist critique, social economist Naila Kabeer (2000) calls into question the ideas of "empowerment" that underpin the focus on managerial control. She notes that various studies (for example that by Hashemi, Schuler, and Riley 1996) demonstrate that women's ability to bring in microfinance loans greatly enhances their decision-making powers within the household. BRAC's own studies, conducted by its Research and Evaluation Division, confirm these findings, indicating that after several years of microfinance loans women were able to not only command more power within the household but also in local labor markets (Mahbub et al. 2001).

In an important intervention, Katharine Rankin (2008) highlights a set of contradictions in microfinance programs in Nepal. She shows how high repayment rates are sustained by "loan swapping," or what has been criticized as the increased debt-liability of poor households. But Rankin

(2008: 1968) notes that such practices, while they may not generate the types of entrepreneurship lauded by microfinance programs, nevertheless point to "women's skillful manipulation of a development technology to sustain debt financing of subsistence and social investment activities." Most striking is the finding that the "appearance of conformity" by poor women can be "deceptive." Thus, a microfinance borrower in Nepal states: "We recite that we will always tell the truth, we will be disciplined. But no one here is speaking the truth about these matters. Even me" (Shakya and Rankin 2008: 1223). Indeed, it seems that in this case the patriarchal design of micro-finance programs, with their elaborate conditions, sparked fierce critique among poor women, including against the rural rich who were seen to be immune from such imposed conditions.

Naila Kabeer's research (2000) also highlights the ambiguities asso-ciated with a measure often correlated with gender empowerment: physical mobility. Women's participation in microfinance programs may increase their mobility in "certain spaces, such as the NGO office and health centre" but not necessarily in the "male-dominated public sphere" (Mahmud 2004: 183–184). In fact, Kabeer notes that as women's economic conditions improved so they often chose to reduce rather than increase physical mobility, adopting "purdah," or seclusion, as a symbol of socio-economic status. Kabeer (2000: 70–71) foregrounds the paradox:

> If empowerment entails the expanded capacity for making choices then . . . the paradox is that in many cases, this leads women to opt for some form of purdah if they can afford to, both to signal their social standing within the community and to differentiate themselves from those women who do not have this choice.

Such debates cast doubt on microfinance's most prominent measure of success: loan repayment. They demonstrate the "hidden transcript" (Rahman 1999: 69) of loan repayment—from women's loss of managerial control of the loan to the patriarchal discipline that is enacted in order to ensure loan collection. But they also indicate the manner in which microfinance loans may serve as an arena for the negotiation of power and hierarchy—both within the household and beyond. Above all the debates make visible the paradoxes that attend the ambitious claims of poverty alleviation and gender empowerment. Microfinance can serve the poorest households but it may also entrap them in ever-expanding debt. Microfinance can empower women to make choices but this may in turn lead to women transferring loans to their husbands and secluding themselves from the public sphere. These too are elements of the Bangladesh paradox.

POVERTY TRUTHS

Best-practice microfinance, as defined by the Washington consensus on poverty, is meant to be both more and less than the Bangladesh model. On the one hand, the terminology of "microfinance," and now "financial services for the poor," suggests a range of inputs that exceed credit and include services such as savings and insurance. On the other hand, CGAP principles call for a minimalist microfinance, one that draws a clear line between social development and finance and between NGOs and financial institutions. The Bangladesh consensus rejects this idea of minimalist microfinance, instead asserting the norms and values of poverty-focused development. But, while it stubbornly holds on to the term "microcredit," and while the Grameen Bank showcases "credit as a human right," the Bangladesh model in fact provides a range of financial services of which credit is only one among many. These microfinance—rather than microcredit—innovations deserve a closer look.

The Grameen Bank is often associated with a lending orthodoxy: lending groups, weekly meetings, rigid repayment schedules, and joint liability. Yet, nearly a decade ago, the Grameen Bank implemented a lending system that breaks with many elements of this orthodoxy. Known as the Grameen Generalized System, or Grameen II, this recalibration of the Grameen Bank, allows borrowers considerable repayment flexibility with loan rescheduling, customized loans, and even a "flexi-loan detour," a way of "exiting the loan highway" and returning several months later in the case of repayment difficulties (Yunus 2002a: 8). While the lending group is still maintained, Grameen II dismantles the "group fund" and other instruments of joint liability. Instead, it relies on "obligatory savings," a deposit equal to 2.5 percent of the loan value that is deducted from the loan, placed in a special savings account, and that cannot be withdrawn for three years. Another 2.5 percent of the loan value is placed in a personal savings account. For loans over 8,000 taka there is also a mandatory pension deposit. While the Grameen Bank continues to state that it "does not, cannot, and will not accept physical collateral of any kind," the obligatory savings scheme in effect acts as a form of loan security. It is not surprising then that Dowla and Barua (2006) title their account of Grameen II with the microfinance cliché: "the poor always pay back."

Grameen II marks an important moment of auto-critique and reflexivity within the Grameen Bank. While the devastating floods of 1998 are often blamed for high default rates in Bangladesh—and thus the formulation of flexible repayment schemes—Yunus (2002a: 3) himself notes that the floods only revealed long-standing, structural problems with repayment:

> In 1995, a large number of our borrowers stayed away from centre meetings and stopped paying loan installments. Husbands of the borrowers, inspired and supported by local politicians, organized this, demanding a change in Grameen Bank rules to allow withdrawal of "group tax" component of "group fund" at the time of leaving the bank . . . At the end we resolved the problem by creating some opening in our rules, but Grameen's repayment rate had gone down in the meantime . . . When the repayment situation did not improve as desired, we thought this would be a good opportunity to be bold, and to dare to design a new Grameen methodology.

Grameen II can be credited for having resolved these issues of repayment and default. But these problems had already garnered the Grameen Bank a certain amount of international notoriety. A 2001 *Wall Street Journal* article presented microcredit as a "great idea with a problem" (Pearl and Phillips 2001). That problem was the Grameen Bank, its high default rates, increasingly rebellious borrowers, and lack of financial transparency. The article reported:

> In two northern districts of Bangladesh that have been used to highlight Grameen's success, half the loan portfolio is overdue by at least a year, according to monthly figures supplied by Grameen. For the whole bank, 19% of loans are one year overdue.

The article was not sympathetic to the Grameen II overhaul, arguing that since the "bank is converting many overdue loans into new 'flexible' loans . . . the situation may be worse than it appears." In his response to the article, and in particular to its lead author, Daniel Pearl, then Asia Bureau chief of the paper, Yunus (2002b) argued that while the Grameen Bank was often faulted for not following the "industry standard," it was important to recognize that it was creating a "banking counter-culture of its own." In 2008, amidst the financial collapse of US lending markets, the *Wall Street Journal* ran another article on the Grameen Bank, an interview with Yunus, this time billing him as the "subprime lender," marveling at how and why this brand of subprime lending had turned out to be successful (Parker 2008). I will return to this theme in the closing chapter.

Microfinance Multiplied

While the 2001 *Wall Street Journal* article draws the lines in the battle of ideas between the Washington consensus and the Bangladesh consensus, it also distracts from some of the innovations of the Bangladesh model that can be glimpsed in Grameen II. Central to these innovations is savings, which can be understood as a form of asset-building (Dowla and Barua 2006). This is in keeping with a new and broadly held wisdom about the value of savings. "Financial services for the poor are essentially a matter of helping the poor turn their savings into sums large enough to satisfy a wide range of business, consumption, personal, social and asset-building needs" (Matin, Hulme, and Rutherford 2002: 273). If we think of poverty as the "tyranny of emergency" (Appadurai 2001: 30), then the value of savings becomes apparent.

In addition to allowing the poor to manage risk, saving is also being celebrated as a business opportunity, since poor people are willing to pay to save. For example, a 2007 CGAP article makes this point with considerable vigor, noting that in 2006 there were "1.3 billion low-average balance deposit accounts versus 190 million loan accounts in developing and transitioning economies." Stuart Rutherford (Rutherford et al. 2004: 38), the founder of the innovative and highly regarded SafeSave, thus concludes that the Bangladesh model has shifted from microcredit to microfinance: "The microfinance revolution in Bangladesh was a micro*credit* revolution, led by Grameen. It is astonishing but fitting that it is Grameen who is leading the massification, if not the introduction, of contractual savings products like the Grameen Pension Scheme."

Savings also allow microfinance institutions to manage risk. During the 2004 floods in Bangladesh, Grameen II was tested. This time, "borrowers used their savings to withstand the flood and the bank used the cushion of large amounts of internal savings to deal with the flood" (Dowla and Barua 2006: 123). Such a "cushion" is particularly important at a time when joint liability, an icon of the microcredit mythology, seems to be bankrupt. Imran Matin (1997: 261), director of BRAC's Research and Evaluation Division, thus quotes a Grameen Bank borrower: "They (referring to a group credit lending institution) do not need police to compel repayment: we (centre members) have been doing it so . . . It can't be done any longer." This "unzipping of joint liability," as Matin puts it, necessitates the turn to a different instrument of loan security, in this case savings. Matin (1997: 265) thus concludes:

> I find the concept of advances against future savings a much more realistic lens in understanding the repayment game where the credit taken is a lump sum advance (expensive though) against the ability of the household to save in small quantities which principally make up the kisti (repayment) . . . The weekly repayment schedule allows the borrowers to make use of their small savings with the centre and group structures acting as a "disciplinary mechanism" required to "force" the household to save in a sustained way.

Such innovations in risk and discipline undergird the transformation in Bangladesh of microcredit into microfinance. Framed as a primitive and backward model of credit by the knowledge-producing institutions of Washington DC, the Bangladesh model turns out after all to be a frontier of finance.

The Bangladesh model is also an experiment in social development. While the Washington consensus valorizes a minimalist model of microfinance, the Bangladesh model is best understood, in the words of Fazle Abed, founder of BRAC, as "microfinance multiplied" (Microfinance Gateway 2008). Of the many innovations, let me highlight three: "opportunity ladders" for the ultra-poor; social enterprises and value chains; and building economic and political assets.

There is, as I have noted earlier, an uncanny convergence between the neoliberal mandates of CGAP and the leftist critique of microfinance: both warn that credit runs the risk of indebting, rather than helping, the ultra-poor. The CGAP consensus, in particular, draws an indelible line between the economically active poor and the economically inactive poor, a distinction that one interlocutor of the Bangladesh consensus rejected as "a caste system." From the Grameen Bank's beggars program to ASA's hardcore poor program, the Bangladesh institutions have insisted on extending credit to the ultra-poor. The most complex experiments have been sustained by BRAC, first through its Income Generation for Vulnerable Group Development (IGVGD) program and more recently through its CFPR/TUP (Challenging the Frontiers of Poverty Reduction/ Targeting the Ultra Poor) program. Explicitly targeting the poorest of the poor, mainly female-headed, landless households, this program combines safety nets (in the form of food aid, guaranteed employment, and healthcare) with employment and skills training and compulsory savings, and ultimately with microfinance, thereby creating what Imran Matin (2004) calls "opportunity ladders." It is important to note that the program is subsidized and that BRAC does not seek to recuperate its financial and administrative costs (Hashemi and Rosenberg 2006: 5). The subsidies work out to about $135 per woman, a "deal" in the world of development (Hashemi 2001).

BRAC's innovation has come to be celebrated by CGAP (Hashemi 2001; Hashemi and Rosenberg 2006). At the 2005 Boulder Institute, Robert Christen showcased BRAC's program, especially its combination and sequence of safety nets, asset-building, savings, and credit. In her course, Marguerite Robinson cited the program as an example of BRAC's "extraordinary achievements." "Rather than take the banking industry to the starving," she noted, "we need institutions like BRAC to bring these starving people up." Indeed, BRAC's ultra-poor program has become a poverty truth, the rare case of a truth that emerges from the Bangladesh model and is taken up by the Washington consensus. Yet, it is within BRAC that there is constant examination and critique of the program. This is the work of its Research and Evaluation Division, an impressive apparatus of both knowledge production and auto-critique. Here, researchers often voice an explicit "dissatisfaction" with the first round of ultra-poor programs, with how they often fail to serve "the poorest and most vulnerable" (Matin 2004: 6), and with how the poorest participants cannot easily "graduate" and often need continuing support from safety net programs (Hashemi 2001: 7; Halder and Mosley 2002). Of these, the most radical auto-critique is perhaps the acknowledgement by Imran Matin, in an interview (July 2004), that "not all poor people can be developmentalized," that even the best designed programs exclude the most vulnerable. In BRAC, such internal debates about program design drive constant experimentation and innovation.

BRAC's concept of "opportunity ladders" for the ultra-poor is embedded in a broader context of development, one in which BRAC actively initiates and manages "value chain projects." These provide human development infrastructure such as health clinics and schools, thereby seeking to create "well-functioning, pro-poor health systems at the village level." The numbers are staggering, with BRAC covering an estimated "110 million people with services in microfinance, health, education, social development, human rights and legal services, and microenterprise support" (Microfinance Gateway 2008). Other value chain projects are related to economic development. From poultry hatcheries to dairy plants to silk production, these BRAC projects link the microenterprises of the poor to national and global markets. They seek to transform subsistence economies into those that can generate economic value. While separate from the microfinance programs, these value chain projects nevertheless have a direct, and possibly dramatic, impact on the livelihoods of microfinance clients. It is estimated that BRAC's commercial enterprises account for $90 million in revenue each year (Armstrong 2008). They are rivaled by Grameen's sprawling empire of enterprises, which include both profit-making enterprises such as Grameenphone and "social enterprises" such as Grameen Telecom and most recently the Grameen–Danone Food company.

Equally ambitious is the idea of "asset-ing" the poor (Matin and Begum 2002), of ensuring that microfinance borrowers not only smooth consumption and manage risk but also build up assets. Particularly noteworthy here is Grameen's housing program. A recipient of the Aga Khan Award (1989) and the World Habitat Award (1998), this program makes available housing loans, viewing them "as investment rather than consumption" (Diacon 1988). The award-winning house design focuses on simple but sturdy structural components—brick foundations, reinforced concrete pillars, bamboo tie beams, wooden rafters, corrugated iron roofing sheets. But the key to the program is that it mandates that the homestead land be registered in the name of the microfinance borrower, in other words, women. In an interview (August 2004), Dipal Barua, Grameen's second-in-command admits that such a practice is "revolutionary," providing great security for women in a patriarchal context. The program is one of the few that pass the muster of feminist critiques of the Grameen Bank, for the registration requirement ensures that women remain in control of housing resources (Goetz and Sengupta 1996: 50).

BRAC expands the scope of assets to include social and political power. Fazle Abed and Imran Matin (2007: 4) argue that the "greatest power of microfinance lies in the process through which it is provided" and how it thus creates "new forms of engagements, relations, and capacities" through "social intermediation." They call this "process capital." BRAC's village organizations, each with 30–40 women members, are a key institutional arena for the creation and circulation of such process capital. Established by BRAC, the village organizations are federations of the poor that achieve autonomy and that manage various aspects of development—from loan repayment to what Matin, in an interview (December 2005), described as "pressing claims at the local level for resources." The village organizations are both an institution that facilitates "one of the world's largest nongovernmental financial intermediation programs" as well as a way of organizing the poor through practices of conscientization (Lovell 1992: 1). As in the case of its ultra-poor programs, BRAC is acutely reflexive about its village organizations. In an interview (December 2005), Matin speculated on whether they serve as pathways for poor women to enter into the public life of the village and even political life beyond. Others in BRAC seek to understand whether such village organizations can be relied upon to ensure that the benefits of development reach the ultra-poor and thereby resist the "elite capture" of such benefits (Hossain and Matin 2004: 7). These are radical considerations that speak directly to structures of power. Could it be that the very field of action, microfinance, which has been accused of "stalling the revolution" in Bangladesh, can engender revolutionary change?

The Conditions of Protection

The critics of the Bangladesh model have argued that its "public transcript" of poverty alleviation and gender empowerment is at odds with a "hidden transcript," which is the patriarchal exploitation of poor women (Rahman 1999). I suggest that a quite different "hidden transcript" is at work. The "public transcript" of microfinance in Bangladesh, especially that advanced by the Grameen Bank has exalted credit, insisting that credit is a human right. It has also exalted the entrepreneurial talents and capacities of the poor, especially poor women. However, a closer look at the Grameen Bank, as well as at BRAC and ASA, suggests a logic of development to which neither credit nor entrepreneurship are key. It is my contention that the poverty truths of the Bangladesh consensus fit much more comfortably in the "social protection" family of programs and policies than in the "micro-enterprises" family. Such forms of social protection are greatly enhanced and deepened by the human development infrastructure and value chains created by these institutions.

The *Chronic Poverty Report 2008–09* (2008: 39), recently issued by the UK-based Chronic Poverty Research Centre, defines social protection as "a broad concept, describing all interventions . . . to support communities, households and individuals, in their efforts to manage and overcome vulnerability." In recent years, the theme of social protection has gained considerable traction. Particularly popular are social protection programs that are designed as minimum income grants or conditional cash transfers, such as Brazil's Bolsa Familia and Mexico's Oportunidades. Earlier known as Progresa, the Oportunidades program makes small payments to poor households, aiming primarily at women, but with conditions that mandate various human development outcomes, such as sending children to school and visits to health clinics. The program uses both geographic and income targeting to reach the poor but does not allow any local discretion, central-izing the allocation of cash transfers in order to bypass systems of patronage that may benefit elites. Such conditional cash transfer programs are being lauded for "raising consumption, schooling, and health status among beneficiary households" (Chronic Poverty Research Centre 2008: 44). Nancy Birdsall, president of the Center for Global Development, has declared these programs to be "as close as you can come to a magic bullet in development." Although these programs may not be this, they can be seen as a new social contract that protects the poor (de Janvry and Sadoulet 2004: 9).

Studies of poverty alleviation make a distinction between "protectional" and "promotional" strategies (Hulme and Mosley 1996: 107). The latter, characterized by microenterprise programs, primarily serve prosperous borrowers, those who can manage more risk (Hulme and Mosley 1996: 103, 113). Protectional strategies target poor households, providing services such as voluntary savings and emergency consumption loans (Hulme and Mosley 1996: 107). Despite the rhetoric of credit and entrepreneurship, the Bangladesh institutions seem to be engaged in forms of social protection. On the development spectrum, this places them closer to conditional cash transfer programs such as Oportunidades than to those in the commercial microfinance family, such as Bank Rakyat Indonesia (BRI) or BancoSol, that serve substantially less poor borrowers. Although Grameen Bank-style microfinance is often praised by free-market enthusiasts, such as former US Senator Tom Campbell (at the 2004 microfinance conference at the Clausen

Center)—as an example of a development intervention that is "simple," that is "not charity," and that "without conditions creates opportunity"—it is in fact a complex social protection program that deploys a framework of conditions.

The Bangladesh model is an intricate system of incentives, sanctions, and conditions—for borrowers and field workers. For all its advertised flexibility, Grameen II maintains significant disincentives for borrowers to utilize flexi-loans: "the moment she exits from the basic loan highway, her loan ceiling, that she has built over years, gets wiped out" (Yunus 2002a: 8). Indeed, it gives Grameen staff new tools of discipline in order to ensure that such flexi-loans are minimized:

> The main device is the imposition of what could be called "*meeting-day joint liability*": the refusal to end the meeting and allow members to return to their homes, and the refusal to conduct other bank business—such as processing loan applications or authorising savings withdrawals—until all repayments due are collected, or at least until there are firm promises of paying them before the close of the day's business. This puts effective pressure on members to lend each other enough to cover the day's dues.
>
> (Rutherford et al. 2004: 30)

Similarly, the *ASAs Manual* (ASA 2001: 39) lays out detailed procedures on how staff can minimize the risk of default—from trying to "recover the loan with the help of the local elite" or by creating a "vigilance team" or by "staying overnight until the default loan is collected" or by filing a petition case at the police station. Such mechanisms constitute what Fuglesang and Chandler (1988: 95) term "pragmatic discipline." Critics argue that these are forms of "dominance and violence" (Rahman 1999: 151). In an echo of the Ohio School orthodoxy, other critics see the enactment of pragmatic discipline as a cost borne by the poor:

> The costs of lending through solidarity groups are high. Groups are not a forum for contractual exchange, but are costly institutions built on social capital. The costs of group formation and interaction outweigh the benefits of high repayment rates associated with group control . . . Borrowers in micro-lending programmes are low-margin customers, and personal service is essentially a luxury for which they cannot pay.
>
> (Reinke 1998: 553)

Such too is CGAP's argument about the need to treat the poor "just like us," to move away from forms of microfinance that subject the poor to weekly meetings, social conditions, and other rituals of development.

The achievement of human development goals also requires conditions and control. The carefully sequenced choreography of BRAC's ultra-poverty program and the Grameen Bank's formal framework of conditions, known as the 16 Decisions, all ensure and enforce discipline. Grameen Bank staff are evaluated not only on their performance in yielding high repayment rates but also in meeting human development goals, such as the enrollment of children in primary schools.

However, I suggest that the Bangladesh model is unique because it involves much more than discipline, conditions, and social protection. The success of social protection programs, especially those that impose conditions, depends on the existence of an accessible human development infrastructure. For what good is it to mandate that the poor send their children to school if there are no functioning schools in a region? It is thus that the Chronic Poverty Report (Chronic Poverty Research Centre 2008: x) insists not only on social protection programs but also on the provision of infrastructure, "particularly transport infrastructure; education, and information." As outlined earlier, central to the Bangladesh model is the creation of value chains and a human development infrastructure. It is this that Fazle Abed has titled "microfinance multiplied" (Microfinance Gateway 2008).

It is possible that such forms of infrastructure achieve more than the delivery of services. Naila Kabeer (2003: 107–108) argues that microfinance addresses "institutional exclusion" and thus strengthens "capabilities" and "agency." BRAC's own research, often critical and reflexive, suggests a transformation that it terms "social intermediation"—"a process in which investment is made in the building up of both human resources and institutional capital, with the aim of increasing the self-reliance of marginalized groups, and preparing them to engage in formal financial intermediation" (Zohir and Matin 2002: 202). In a thoughtful analysis, Naila Kabeer and Imran Matin (2005: 3) present lending groups not as enforcers of financial discipline and social conditions but as a new "form of association based on horizontal relationships." They argue that such groups may provide the poor with an alternative to "dominant relationships . . . which tend to be vertically organized—explicitly or implicitly—as patron–client relationships."

Such interpretations of the Bangladesh model suggest that what may be at work is more than social protection. In a recent interview, Fazle Abed noted that "at the heart of BRAC's approach to development is organizing the poor" (Microfinance Gateway 2008). Microfinance, and indeed the entire infrastructure of institutional inclusion, thus becomes an effort to halt "pauperization and marginalization in rural areas by building power at the grassroots level through the formation of landless groups" (Zafar 1988). This effort, I would argue, requires more than the work of civil society institutions. In Bangladesh, as some BRAC staffers believe, the presence of pro-poor NGOs has a demonstration effect, putting pressure on the state, through the "proof of concept" to provide infrastructure and serve the poor.

The "hidden transcript" of the Bangladesh model is a far cry from the mythologies of microfinance. It is the story of a unique and ambitious model of development about which we need to learn much more. However, it is the "public transcript" of the Bangladesh model that has come to be globalized, the "hard sell" of "microfinance evangelism" (Rogaly 1996). A recent *Financial Times* article thus sought to expose microfinance by showing that "fewer than half of microcredit borrowers invest the money in the grass-roots businesses that such loans are intended to foster" and that "micro-credit loans are used to buy food" (Chazan 2009). The critique is misplaced, for it is in fact proof of the social protection effects of microfinance that the poor use microfinance loans to smooth dips in consumption and manage vulnerability. This is an effective anti-poverty strategy, not a failure of development. But rather than claim the mantle of such social protection successes, Bangladesh's much celebrated microfinance institution, ASA, vigorously challenged the findings. In the language of microentrepreneur-ship and micro-miracles, ASA once again promoted the "public transcript" of microfinance.

GLOBALIZING THE BANGLADESH CONSENSUS

While CGAP seeks to dominate the global discourse about micro-finance, the globalization of microfinance both precedes and exceeds the Washington consensus on poverty. Only a few years after its inception, the Grameen Bank attracted international attention. Indeed, as outlined in an earlier chapter, the formation of CGAP was a testament to the global reach of Grameen's microfinance ideas. As CGAP came to focus on financialization, so the Grameen Bank turned to the creation of its own global networks. Today, various institutions that are directly or loosely affiliated with the Grameen Bank work to replicate the Grameen model in different parts of the world. Based in Bangladesh, the Grameen Trust acts as a global wholesale fund, seeding and supervising replication programs. As of September 2008, the Grameen Trust had supported 144 programs in 38 countries. These programs reach 6.18 million borrowers, 94 percent of whom are women. They boast a repayment rate of 96 percent (http://www.grameentrust.org/, accessed October 14, 2008).

The majority of Grameen Trust programs are collaborations with local NGOs seeking to establish microfinance programs modeled after the Grameen Bank. In rare cases, the Grameen Trust directly implements the program through build-operate-transfer or build-operate-own models. The Grameen Trust closely monitors all replication programs, using both "performance indicators of USAID and CGAP and project evaluations of impacts on lives of borrowers" (Latifee 2004: 26). Indeed, the Grameen Trust crosses over into Washington circles of development in interesting ways, landing grants from the World Bank, USAID, and Citigroup Foundation.

Based in Washington DC, and founded in 1997, the Grameen Foundation also works to replicate the Grameen model. It commands a global network of 55 microfinance partners in 28 countries serving a total of 6.8 million borrowers (http://www.grameenfoundation.org/, accessed October 14, 2008). In the closing chapter of this book, I discuss the ways in which the Grameen Foundation participates in, and reshapes, global circuits of capital and truth. The newest addition to the global Grameen family is Grameen America. Established in the wake of Grameen's Nobel Prize, Grameen America provides microfinance loans to the poor in America, seeking to provide an alternative to "high-interest rate predatory lenders such as payday loan corporations, pawnshops, and check cashers" for America's "unbanked" poor. In strict adherence to the Grameen model, Grameen America uses Grameen Bank staff to establish programs that lend to groups of poor women (http://www.grameenamerica.com/About-Us/Grameen-America.html, accessed March 30, 2009). It is thus that the Bangladesh model has sought to make a home for itself at the very heart of power.

More recently, both ASA and BRAC have sought to craft their own global networks. ASA has emerged as an important microfinance "consultant" providing technical assistance to other microfinance programs. BRAC's approach is quite different. Premised on the belief that BRAC cannot be replicated—that it is a unique relationship between institution and context that cannot be reduced to a blueprint—it seeks to establish and manage microfinance programs in other settings. The most famous of these is BRAC Afghanistan, which as of April 2008 had a local staff of 3,600 and served 141,698 borrowers. In an echo of its Bangladesh programs, BRAC Afghanistan currently runs schools staffed by female teachers and health centers managed by community health workers (http://www.bracafg.org/, accessed June 19, 2008).

BRAC's international success poses interesting questions about the globalization of microfinance. Unlike the Grameen Trust replications that adhere, in seemingly strict fashion, to a formula—first the Grameen Bank model and now Grameen II—BRAC's international programs seem more fluid. Thus, Fazle Abed notes that in Afghanistan, BRAC had to start with community infrastructure projects rather than with microfinance: "Organizing women into microcredit groups began as a follow-on service to tailoring centers and quickly gained acceptance." Similarly, in Africa, BRAC adjusted its lending practices: "Trading activities are more common among our African clients, so we responded to their demand for shorter duration loans" (Microfinance Gateway 2008). Will BRAC be able to hold on to this philosophy, articulated by Imran Matin in an interview (June 2004), that while it is possible to learn from its work in Bangladesh, it is impossible to replicate this work in any formulaic fashion? Will the influx of development capital—$15 million from the Gates Foundation to replicate BRAC's microfinance, agriculture, and health programs in Tanzania and $1 million from Nike to establish designated centers for teenage girls in Tanzania—transform BRAC into a "best practices" institution?

Recently, BRAC has established "non-profit resource mobilization organizations," one in London and one in New York, to "support BRAC's global expansion." Like the Grameen Foundation, these seek to create "Northern solidarity in support of Southern leadership" and to promote "South–South collaboration" (http://www.brac.net/usa/about_us.php, accessed February 16, 2009). This programmed globalization seems to be a departure for BRAC, where until recently, staffers insisted that BRAC did not seek to shape or control global discourse. They saw this as Grameen's issue: "we do not hold summits," BRAC staffers would often note. "We will accept international expertise, ideas, assistance from any organization if it turns out to be useful. Our goal is pragmatic and functional rather than ideological." However, BRAC USA and BRAC UK inevitably articulate a blueprint for a globalized BRAC: "barefoot bootstrapping" and a set of fundamental principles including this one, that "investing in women and girls has a disproportionately large return for communities." This once again seems to be the "public transcript" of the Bangladesh model, now in a globalized incarnation.

Although the globalization of the Bangladesh consensus requires the articulation and dissemination of a formula of best practices, it has the potential to present a significant challenge to the Washington consensus on poverty. The Bangladesh institutions are uniformly aware of the politics of knowledge and their marginalization in this battle of ideas. Not surprisingly, their global replication and network strategies all seek to create an alternative discourse of microfinance. "This is a knowledge industry dominated by Northern consultants," said Lamiya Morshed of the Grameen Trust (August 2004). In an interview (December 2005) Imran Matin said:

> CGAP is global and very influential, especially through its indicators and monitoring tools. Even our Grameen Trust partners often have to follow CGAP indicators in order to procure funding from donors. How do we create an alternative? . . . It is as if we are an exhibit in Ripley's Believe It or Not. . . . We have demonstrated success with these ideas in Bangladesh and yet in global forums no one wants to believe that it can be done. It is frustrating.

He and other Bangladeshi interlocutors argue that the key to winning the battle of ideas is the production of development knowledge in Bangladesh. To this end, in 2001, BRAC established BRAC University, which includes a wide range of programs—from public health to development studies. BRAC University states as its mission the promotion of a "national development process" through the training of "creative leaders" and through the "creation of knowledge" (http://www.bracuniversity.ac.bd/about/, accessed December 18, 2008).

The issue at stake though is not simply the establishment of knowledge institutions, but rather the legitimacy and authority of the knowledge that is thus produced. In an interview (July 2004), eminent Bangladeshi academic and founder of the Power and Participation Research Centre Hossain Zillur Rahman noted that there is a fundamental "knowledge asymmetry" in the global system: "We were disarmed by the initial global acceptance of microcredit and so we did not see this coming. We set up CGAP but lost the institution. Now it even refuses to acknowledge Yunus's pioneering role in microcredit." He argued that the Washington consensus on poverty has to be confronted by "practice." "Practice is our way of keeping the debate focused on evidence, and keeping it focused on poverty. Practice is our way of transforming knowledge into knowledge capital. We have to confront Washington DC through practice."

One such instance of knowledge production is the Grameen Dialogues, hosted by the Grameen Bank a few times each year in Bangladesh. Conceptualized by Grameen Trust staff as an "inversion of banking ideas and knowledge," the Dialogues are Grameen's equivalent of the Boulder Institute. Several of the key figures in the Bangladesh consensus—such as Imran Matin and Syed Hashemi—have served as rapporteurs of the Grameen Dialogues. Here, participants, many of them from the Grameen replication programs, are trained in the Grameen model and in broader ideologies of microfinance and development. Most important, the inversion of banking knowledge takes place through what Morshed calls "fieldwork," an intense ten-day stint in a village studying the life of a Grameen borrower. It is intriguing to review the "data" produced by the Grameen Dialogues, for these case-studies of poor women are as revealing of the transformations wrought in a woman's life by microfinance as they are revealing of the transformations wrought in microfinance practitioners by the Dialogues experience. Grameen Trust managers thus rightly note that only those fiercely committed to the task of poverty alleviation are able to survive and learn from a context of spartan living conditions: "It gives us at Grameen Trust a sense of who is serious about poverty and who is not and this is useful knowledge about our partners," said Morshed (January 2006).

The archives of the Grameen Trust are filled with narratives of transformation. They speak to the insistence of the Bangladesh consensus on placing priority on human development (rather than simply loan repayment or income generation). They also reinforce the argument made repeatedly by Bangladesh institutions—that what matters most is not the decrease in income poverty for microfinance borrowers but rather the impacts on their children, as noted by Fazle Abed in an interview (December 2004):

In BRAC we constantly ask how we can create the maximum impact on the next generation, especially girl children . . . There have been great improvements in Bangladesh in infant mortality and other human development indicators. I never thought I would see them in my lifetime. Grameen and BRAC have directly contributed to these achievements.

But can the stories of such achievements told by the Grameen Dialogues match the authoritative statistics put forward at the Boulder Institute? Drawn from the practices of commercial banking these minimalist gauges of financial performance—from PAR to FSS—crowd out the complex narratives and detail-laden stories of poverty and social change. Their dominance indicates what postcolonial critic, Gayatri Chakravorty Spivak (1999: 388) has noted as the tendency for the experiences of the global South to be viewed only as "the repository of an ethnographic cultural difference," as a set of dispersed stories that do not add up to a comprehensive system of knowledge. The global financial indicators make their way into the Grameen Dialogues as the Grameen Trust, bowing to global norms, reminding its members of the prevalence and power of these benchmarks. It is not surprising then that in the closing session of the forty-fifth Grameen Dialogue, held in 2003, Yunus said the following: "So the process works like this: that our indigenous ideas have to be validated by the West before we can accept them. We don't know how to sell our own ideas" (Grameen Trust 2003).

A UNIQUE HISTORY

It is impossible to make sense of the "Bangladesh paradox" or the "Bangladesh consensus" without paying attention to the unique history of development in Bangladesh. Despite pragmatic differences, the three large and renowned microfinance institutions in Bangladesh—Grameen, BRAC, and ASA—are united by a common history. In 1972, Bangladesh achieved independence from Pakistan, having been placed in this geopolitical configuration by British colonial rulers as they departed the Indian subcontinent in 1947. The war for independence exacted a heavy toll of death, suffering, and sacrifice. It is in this context that BRAC emerged as a relief organization, led by Fazle Abed with a small founding core of "young, nationalistic youth" working to resettle refugees in the remote northeastern reach of Bangladesh. After a while, Abed and his team "came to realize that reconstruction was only a stop-gap and that new approaches were needed to help poor villagers on a permanent basis" (Lovell 1992: 23; see also Chen 1983). Abed recounts the transformation as one dictated by the need to address poverty: "Poor people are poor because they are powerless." Relief work, he felt, did not address such powerlessness or challenge the distribution of wealth (Armstrong 2008). BRAC thus went from being "an almost entirely donor-funded, small-scale relief and rehabilitation project" to "an independent, virtually self-financed paradigm in sustainable human development . . . one of the largest Southern development organizations" (http://www.brac.net/, accessed July 10, 2008). ASA's transformation is even more unusual. Formed in 1978 by seven young men, including Shafiqual Haque Choudhury, "to train poor villagers to fight for their political and social rights," at its inception ASA was best understood as "a brotherhood to fight rural poverty" (Rutherford 1995: 1, 4). By the 1990s, ASA had morphed from an organization of "rural revolutionaries" to one of "village development bankers" (Rutherford 1995: 1).

There are many striking features to this institutional genealogy, such as the convergence around microfinance. Although there is considerable diversity in microfinance practice among the Bangladesh institutions, and although the "microfinance multiplied" model, as I have argued, does much more than microfinance, the "public transcript" of these institutions nevertheless emphasizes the crucial role of credit in mitigating poverty. This may be related to a history of experiments with cooperatives in South Asia (Woolcock 1999). On the one hand, in 1904, British colonial administrators passed India's first Cooperative Societies Act, thereby creating a "legal framework for village-level self-help user-managed societies." A colonial mission of "improvement" accompanied the act, for the idea was to teach peasants "thrift and cooperation": "It must be credit which shall be so obtainable that the act and effort of obtaining it shall educate, discipline, and guide the borrower" (Rutherford 1995: 26). On the other hand, the struggle for independence, especially that charted by Gandhi, sought to articulate goals and means of economic self-reliance. Cooperatives were central to such a project and played an important role in the economic policies of the new nation-states of South Asia. Yet, they remained plagued by elite capture, often with "loans monopolized by an elite minority" (Rutherford 1995: 31). In the wake of Indian independence and partition in 1947, a new development experiment was launched in what was then East Pakistan, now Bangladesh. Known as the Comilla project, it focused on rural cooperatives. It is seen to have laid the groundwork for "pioneers such as Abed and Yunus who endeavored to correct the fundamental flaws of cooperatives by purging them of political affiliations, limiting membership to the very poor, and focusing on women" (Woolcock 1999: 35). And key elements of the Comilla experiment may have survived—such as emphasis on compulsory savings as well as the "ten commandments" that dictated social goals (Rutherford 1995: 29–30).

The history of ASA provides further insights into the emergence of microfinance as a dominant institutional strategy. As Rutherford notes, in its early days, ASA was actively opposed to microfinance. Eager to "prepare the poor for conflict," Choudhury and others eschewed the strategies of BRAC and Grameen, instead contemplating "armed struggle" for the groups of poor being formed and mobilized by ASA: "We didn't understand credit at that time. Rather we criticized Grameen Bank, all banking facilities, World Bank . . . We said these people are exploiting us, ruining our economy." Such efforts received the support of international donors such as Freedom from Hunger, keen to fund "a grassroots NGO" and to promote "development as struggle" (Rutherford 1995: 66). But as BRAC shifted from relief work to poverty alleviation, so ASA shifted from development as armed struggle to "development as finance" (Rutherford 1995: 84). The shift was prompted by a set of auto-critiques, including a 1984 internal report titled "Is unity and social action enough to develop the poor?" The report noted that ASA members were more concerned with economic deprivation than with political powerlessness, that ASA was losing large numbers of these members to Grameen, and that its members were eager to take out microfinance loans (Rutherford 1995: 67). Here then is Shafiqual Haque Choudhury, ASA's founder and president:

> The basic objective was to organize the poor people, so that they could bargain for more wages, for their rights, etc. . . . By working like that, we solved a lot of problems, but we did not offer direct economic empowerment. From that time on, from 1986, people started asking how they would make a living. This was the question raised by the poor people in front of us.
>
> (*Microcapital* 2008)

Choudhury continues: "When we said to them, please come for fighting with the moneylender or with the landlord they would say no, no, why? They are helping us in some way at least. But you are not helping, you are giving only sermon or lecture" (Rutherford 1995: 61).

By 1992, ASA had remade itself, not only borrowing heavily from the Grameen template by transforming its membership into predominantly women's groups but also articulating "self-reliance" as the new motto both for its members and for itself. By 1994, ASA's groups—the cooperatives—are only mentioned as expedient devices for the recovery of loans. Yet, it is not possible to simply dismiss credit as an instrument of development and empowerment. Interlocutors of the Bangladesh consensus such as Syed Hashemi (in Khandker 2005) argue that "the credit market was the scene of the most brutal exploitation of the poor" and "also the arena where interventions were easiest for allowing the poor to break out of their cycle of poverty." Indeed, Khandker (2005: 83) suggests that Grameen loans have "a significant positive effect on the wages of men and children in the program villages," triggering complaints from the rural elite.

Another striking feature of the Bangladesh story is the social constitution of leadership. While the two iconic figures in Bangladesh's field of development—Yunus and Abed—come from quite different socioeconomic backgrounds, the former from a middle-class family and the latter from a wealthy landowning family, both gave up a life abroad to return to Bangladesh to participate in nation-building. Their paths were initially quite different, with Yunus taking up a professorship at Chittagong University and Abed pursuing a corporate career with Shell. And yet these paths converged through their individual encounters with hardship and poverty in Bangladesh. Shaken by a deadly cyclone that hit the country in 1970 and killed 500,000 people, Abed took up relief work: "It really changed the way I look at things." The war for Bangladesh's independence and its aftermath was to deepen his commitment, and in 1972, he sold his London apartment, using the proceeds to establish BRAC (Armstrong 2008). Similarly, Yunus was to encounter poverty in the villages surrounding Chittagong University. He was struck by the persistent disjuncture between the elegant economic theories he taught in his classroom and this dire poverty. How was knowledge and pedagogy useful if it could not address the sheer material reality of the Bangladesh context? Taking along a few students and with a grant from the Ford Foundation he explored anti-poverty interventions, ultimately settling on credit and the institutional form of the Grameen Bank as a solution (Bornstein 1996: 33).

Yunus and Abed are emblems of a unique conjuncture: the emergence of an educated, nationalist class actively engaged in the creation and management of massive, pro-poor service delivery organizations. The members of this class have been able to build strategic relationships both with the state and with global forces. While working outside the domain of the state, these leaders and their organizations do not necessarily challenge or diminish state power. Imran Matin (December 2005) thus noted that, in Bangladesh, these institutions have been able to "create a space of relative autonomy." This politics of development can be understood thus:

> He [Yunus] negotiated the [Grameen] Bank's progression to be a statutory organisation under authoritarian rule. This gave the Bank the freedom to escape having to lend as part of a patronage system, to set its own interest rates and to be officially regulated in ways that did not constrain the institution. Subsequently, the Bank has been able to avoid challenges from the country's various democratic governments—BNP, Awami and Coalition—by careful management. This involves closely following politics, managing a set of elite relationships and a public image so that the Bank is prominent but non-controversial and creating an image of being non-political.
>
> (Hulme and Moore 2006: 20-21)

While Yunus (2002b) has often declared that the Grameen Bank, starting in 1995, "decided not to receive any more donor funds," such support is a key element of the "conjunctural forces" of development in Bangladesh (Wood and Sharif 1997: 27). Grameen's early expansion was underwritten by IFAD (International Fund for Agricultural Development), the Ford Foundation, NORAD (Norwegian Agency for International Development), and SIDA (Swedish International Development Authority) (Bornstein 1996: 178). While Yunus has always been critical of what he perceives to be the World Bank's miserly allocation of resources toward microfinance programs, in 1993 the Grameen Bank received a $2 million grant from the World Bank (Bornstein 1996: 239). Yunus also became a founding member of CGAP, serving as chair of its Policy Advisory Group. Donor funds remain an important source of BRAC's annual income—about 20 percent—and provide "funding for innovation" (Smillie 2009: 252). The important feature of the Bangladesh model is that despite such donor support, it is not driven by donor mandates. That rather unique "space of relative autonomy" created by these institutions has ensured the formation of a development model nearly independent of donor fads and fashions. It is thus that the Bangladesh consensus has emerged as a counter-point to the Washington consensus on poverty.

Also at stake in the issue of donor support is the financial formula of the Bangladesh model. While the Grameen Bank has repeatedly made the case that its operations, all the way down to individual branches, are self-sufficient and do not rely on donor funds, a closer look indicates otherwise. As economist Jonathan Morduch (1999a: 1591) notes, between 1985 and 1996 the Grameen Bank had access to soft loans of $80.5 million at a concessional rate of 3.7 percent on borrowed capital. He calculates that "to reach full economic sustainability between 1985 and 1996, Grameen would have had to increase average interest rates by about 65% to a rate of 26% per year" (Morduch 1999b: 245). The sources of such cheap capital have shifted over the years—from grants and soft loans from donor agencies to, starting in the mid-1990s, capital from the Bangladesh Bank at discounted rates and eventually financing through bond sales guaranteed by the Government of Bangladesh (Morduch 1999b: 240). These subsidies work out to $15 per member per year (Morduch 1999b: 243). BRAC openly acknowledges its reliance on donor funds, that such funds enable the piloting of new programs and the financing of existing ones. ASA's figures show that over 30 percent of its funds comes from PKSF, the wholesale microfinance retailer that provides capital at concessional rates (Ahmed 2002).

Such calculations have provided considerable fodder for the Washington consensus on poverty. The Grameen Bank has been accused of lacking financial transparency. "Subsidy dependence" has emerged as a "new criteria of financial sustainability" and against these benchmarks "Grameen was declared less successful than Indonesia's BRI program" (Woolcock 1999). But another way of interpreting this data is to acknowledge that subsidies are central to the Bangladesh model and that such subsidies enable institutions in Bangladesh to reach the poor. Jonathan Morduch (1999b: 230) states that "microfinance programs that target the poorest borrowers generate revenues sufficient to cover just 70% of their full costs." Morduch's statement reads like a lament in a piece seeking to reject Grameen's claims about self-sufficiency. And yet this lament is also a vital conclusion, an insight into the workings of pro-poor microfinance. This may not be high finance but it is finance as development.

The distinction that the Washington consensus on poverty draws between pro-poor, subsidized microfinance and commercialized, market-driven microfinance is patently false. As starkly revealed by the financial crisis of 2008, and the subsequent bailouts, high finance itself is a heavily subsidized sector, an instance of what political economist Robert Reich (2008a) has called "socialized capitalism." If the subsidies for the Grameen Bank are in the millions, for Citigroup they are in the billions. But this is not the mantle claimed by Grameen or ASA—that of development finance done right, one where subsidies and state guarantees are in fact essential elements. Once again the "public transcript" of the Bangladesh model is at odds with its "hidden transcript." In talking the talk of self-sufficiency, Grameen unfortunately replicates the very discourse of high finance and commercial banking that it otherwise rejects.

How then should we view the Bangladesh model, its strategies, transformations, and compromises? Was the transformation of institutions such as ASA into development banking a betrayal? Here is ASA's president, Shafiqual Choudhury:

> After the 1971 struggle most of us were primed for a socialist approach. I now find that I am confused about these issues: am I a traitor? But I had no alternative. Financial services have proved to be easily the best way to help the poor. That means, easiest and cheapest to deliver on a really massive scale.
>
> (Rutherford 1995: 166)

Others in Bangladesh concur, with a local leader stating: "By extending credit to a few, the poor are becoming divided. They are also being idle. But no revolution can come about with dead men. At least the Grameen Bank is keeping the rural poor alive" (Fuglesang and Chandler 1988: 188).

The Bangladesh model also seeks to professionalize development. In an interview (June 2004), Imran Matin noted that the "pioneers" of microfinance in Bangladesh were intent on creating a "self-regulating" and "highly professional" sector. Such a professionalization sets into motion various contradictions. For example, in the process of professionalization, ASA "replaced local women with non-local men" as its staff, an irony for an organization seeking to serve poor women (Goetz 2001: 104). BRAC has sought to beat this trend by highlighting the "social pioneering role" of its female staff (Goetz 2001: 200). The debate about the professionalization of development is also a debate about the role of NGOs, a term that technically does not apply to the legal structure of the Grameen Bank but nevertheless connotes its non-governmental status. NGOs, especially those in Bangladesh, are not necessarily people's organizations or citizens' associations. They are managers and trustees of development. "From villagers' perspectives, they can seem like a hybrid of state or market . . . as new additions to the 'officer class', or . . . as a particularly lucrative type of business" (White 1999: 321). It is thus that the Bangladesh microfinance NGOs stand accused of "deradicalizing politics" (Haque 2002: 427–428).

This debate plays out within these institutions as well. The critique within BRAC is voiced eloquently and loudly by Afsan Chowdhury, the head of the advocacy division. Highly critical of BRAC's bureaucratization, in an interview (December 2004), Chowdhury called for processes of conscientization and mobilization that can allow the poor to take ownership of the groups set up by BRAC, to become political agents rather than clients. For Chowdhury the provision of credit is not a development model; it is "a coping mechanism," a "transactional choice" made by a bureaucracy that is in effect "a subsidiary government." Organized service delivery, he argues, saps social energy. Chowdhury's vision seeks to reverse this depoliticization and disenfranchisement—his terms—by empowering village associations. But, he notes that such empowerment may mean that BRAC not only will have to give up some of its power but also that it may ultimately become irrelevant. Such arguments are to be expected from the "advocacy" division of BRAC. However, there is a surprising twist to Chowdhury's vision. Dismissing the "social entrepreneurship" framework deployed by Yunus and Abed and its "rational humanist view of the market," Chowdhury insists that it is macroeconomic growth rather than microlending that will ultimately alleviate poverty in Bangladesh. While he acknowledges that microfinance institutions have had an impact on extreme poverty, he argues that macroeconomic forces—from inflation to the terms of trade—threaten to overwhelm such achievements. And he believes that it is the market that can radicalize politics, for it forces the poor to be "free" of the well-intentioned but "semi-feudal" bureaucracies of service delivery and microfinance. It is thus that this radical advocate returns us to one of the key themes of millennial development: economic freedom.

The Performance of Dissent

The 2006 Microcredit Summit, held in Halifax, Canada, was a celebration of the Bangladesh consensus. Emboldened by the awarding of the Nobel Peace Prize to Yunus and the Grameen Bank, speakers at the summit repeatedly cast doubt on CGAP best practices. The most dramatic of these performances came from Shafiqual Haque Choudhury, the founder and president of ASA. In a plenary session on institutional action plans held on November 14, 2006, Choudhury spoke after a well-received presentation by Ingrid Munro of the pro-poor Kenyan microfinance organization, Jamii Bora. Choudhury boasted of the rapid growth of ASA, claiming that his organization had achieved in 12 years what it took BRAC 24 years to build. "We are the lowest cost microfinance provider in the world," he insisted. "We are the McDonald's of microfinance. We operate through standardization and decentralization. McDonald's provides cheap and affordable models. We provide microfinance."

At first, the message seemed in keeping with the global discourse of best-practice microfinance, for which ASA has long been the low-cost darling. Repeatedly ranked as one of the top ten global MFIs by the MIX, ASA seemed to be claiming a mantle of greatness in the wake of Grameen's fall from grace. Once hailed as the "Ford motor model of microfinance" (Fernando and Meyer 2002), Choudhury's McDonald's analogy seemed to now present ASA less as an efficient assembly line churning out microloans and more as a nimble network of franchises rapidly serving up a standardized formula. At Halifax, Choudhury proudly declared that by the global standards established by CGAP—from productivity to FSS—ASA was a success.

However, Choudhury's narrative was more complex than a proclamation of CGAP-endorsed success. In just a few minutes he shifted to a bitter rant against "Western" consultants and their control of the circuits of development knowledge:

> We run our own programs. We did not get them from Harvard. We designed them . . . We don't need people educated in the US to tell us how to manage our accounts and calculate our finances. What are accounts? Debit and credit. A right side and left side. We don't need to attend long and expensive courses in Europe and America to learn how to do microfinance, or to cook or to drive . . . Consultants come from the West and they charge 800 euros a day and stay in five-star hotels and study poverty.

Turning to Sam Daley-Harris, founder and president of Results, he continued: "For you Sam, a dollar is a coin. For a Bangladeshi, it is two kilos of rice." "We do the work to serve poor families. We know who the poor are, what poverty is. But if we don't hire a few academics with Ph.D.s they won't believe that we have done the work." Choudhury's speech received wild applause from the Microcredit Summit audience. Attendees, many of them from the global South, leapt to their feet, showering him with bravos and cheers. Choudhury emerged as the folk hero of the summit, wrapping himself in the aura of the Bangladesh consensus.

Choudhury's performance of dissent at Halifax did not surprise me. I had first met him in August 2004 during a research trip to Bangladesh. During a lengthy interview, conducted in Bengali, Choudhury asserted the strength of a Bangladesh model of microfinance, rejecting the "Latin American-style commercialization that is pushed by CGAP." Although once a member of CGAP's Policy Advisory Board, he argued that CGAP ideas and mandates were irrelevant for the work being done in Bangladesh:

> The problem with CGAP, with books like the one written by Marguerite Robinson, is that they look at Bangladesh through their eyes rather than through local eyes. In this gaze, Bangladesh seems to be backward. . . . I am sorry to use a vulgar example but in the US it's ok to kiss in public. In Bangladesh, I would not even sit close to my wife in public. Not all ideas produced in the US can be imposed on us here in Bangladesh.

Indeed, Choudhury's critique of knowledge hegemonies is much more explicit and radical than those publicly voiced by Yunus or Abed:

> We need to research why microfinance has been so successful in Bangladesh. There is the pioneering work of Yunus and Abed, and it needs to be acknowledged. In Bangladesh, we do the work on the ground. In doing so we figure out issues. Western policymakers want all issues figured out first. Well, in that case no work can get done. They insist that there has to be 100% immunization and 100% clean drinking water as a precondition to having babies—but then in Bangladesh no one would be able to have babies.

As at the Halifax summit, Choudhury, in that interview, was especially critical of the knowledge produced by the Washington consensus on poverty:

> Boulder has no practitioners. I was once a faculty member there. The institute has a western tone. That's what the attendees hear for three

weeks. We should have equal time at that pulpit to present our ideas . . . You look at CGAP publications and there are no dissenting voices. It's the same people and the same ideas presented again and again. We need a counter-network.

Particularly galling to Choudhury is the knowledge industry:

I have often told Elizabeth Littlefield that the amount of money CGAP spends on each board meeting could fund microcredit in an entire poor country . . . The Asian Development Bank loves to praise ASA but they do not really believe in our approach. Their approach is lavish—they sit in their fancy building in Manila earning US$6,000 a month—for what?

In an echo, albeit much sharper, of Yunus's anxieties, Choudhury noted that the practitioners of microfinance in Bangladesh have not spent any time creating global legitimacy for their work: "We are focused on practice, not on the pen. And this has harmed us. It has marginalized us. We don't know how to speak and write in English and make our ideas known." Perhaps his most piercing critique that day in 2004 came in the form of the following anecdote, an allegory about the politics of knowledge that has stayed with me since:

The world wants to know if microfinance helps the poor. We don't turn poor people into profit-making entrepreneurs. We simply help them survive. The problem is that consultants show up, making $1,000 a day and staying in five-star hotels. They make a trip to a village and ask a poor woman if her microfinance loan has helped her. She responds hesitantly saying that there have been small changes in her life—she now has a blouse to wear underneath her sari when she once never had one, that she now has a bar of soap with which to bathe. The consultants, trained at Harvard, are unhappy. They are not convinced that this is social change.

Choudhury lays bare the passion of the Bangladesh model and presents a formidable challenge to the Washington consensus on poverty. The challenge is simultaneously moral, putting forward a responsibility to serve the poor, and pragmatic, arguing that authentic knowledge has to be forged through practice on the ground. Against the belabored efforts of the Washington consensus to find and demarcate the poor stands John Hatch's caustic statement made at the 2006

Microcredit Summit: "Poverty is like pornography: you know it when you see it." In the 2004 interview, Choudhury thus laughed at my question: How does ASA identify the poor? He laughed and said: "As you tell a man apart from a woman, so you can tell the poor apart from the non-poor . . . In Bangladesh every alternate person is poor. Why do we need to spend so much money figuring this out?"

At Halifax, the Microcredit Summit pledged "to find and implement credible methodologies and to measure progress of our clients above the US$1 a day threshold and to report these findings to the Campaign on an annual basis." Kate McKee, formerly head of USAID's Microenterprise Division and now a senior advisor at CGAP, noted that "donors and investors have to invest in this knowledge." CGAP, she announced, was going to work with the Grameen Foundation to develop such tools. Yet, as Choudhury's scathing critiques point out, such methodologies have been at work for decades in Bangladesh. The Grameen Bank's "ten indicators to assess poverty level" (Yunus 2006b) is a sophisticated and nuanced statement of human development—from access to safe water and shelter to the seasonal rhythms of vulnerability and deprivation. But such forms of practice are rendered parochial, and even marginal, amidst the push to create a global consensus on microfinance, a consensus centered in Washington DC. In the new millennium, such methodologies are being newly "discovered"—often as quaint and exotic artifacts.

Choudhury's performance of dissent did not reveal the "hidden transcript" of the Bangladesh consensus on poverty. At the summit, little was said by Choudhury—or Yunus for that matter—on the key role of local and international development finance in the making of the Bangladesh paradox or on the utilization by the poor of microfinance loans as social protection. The "public transcript" was instead omnipresent.

The question that also remained was whether or not the Bangladesh model can disrupt circuits of poverty capital, those that seek to transform microfinance into a frontier of accumulation and profit. After all, the 2006 Microcredit Summit, this site of dissent, was sponsored by various key players in the global microfinance industry, from the Omidyar Network to Citigroup. Prominent among the sponsors, its logo blazing on all conference material, was the Monsanto group, the notorious agro-business. In 1998, at the first Microcredit Summit, Grameen had announced a partnership with Monsanto. The agro-business wanted to use Grameen's networks "to distribute its seeds, collect payments, and discipline those farmers who tried to store their seeds for reproduction rather than buying Monsanto's genetically engineered, self-destructing variety" (Elyachar 2002: 498). In an open letter addressed to Yunus, South Asian ecofeminist, Vandana Shiva, declared the partnership a betrayal of the interests of poor women: "Your microcredit support to the spread of Terminator seeds or patented seeds will not liberate the poor; it will enslave them irreversibly" (Shiva 1998). The Grameen Bank withdrew from the partnership. But in 2006, at the Microcredit Summit that boldly taunted the Washington consensus on poverty, the partnership seemed to have been revived. It was the Monsanto logo that loomed large and a silence prevailed about its presence.

NOTE

1   John Hatch, speech at the Microcredit Summit, November 11, 2006, Halifax, Canada.

CHAPTER 4

The Pollution of Free Money

Debt, Discipline, and
Dependence in the Middle East

Microfinance will only become sustainable and permanent in Afghanistan when it no longer requires the presence of outsiders.

(Amjad Arbab, director of MISFA, 2008[1])

Microfinance at Empire's Frontier

On the website of the Microfinance Investment Support Facility for Afghanistan (MISFA), there is posted a picture of hope. It is an image of Enzar Gull, a

Figure 4.1 Enzar Gull, microfinance client (MISFA).

microfinance client. Enzar, who "lost both his legs, left arm and two right hand fingers due to a land mine that struck him in Gereshk way back in the year 1996 when he was still 23 years old" is presented as a "true survivor." A microfinance success story, Gull has repaid his loan in four rather than six months, working as a gardener and converting his tiny plot of land into a "flowering and ornamental plants nursery." "His customers are the rich people of Helmand including the workers of the international NGOs operating in the province." Enzar Gull is pictured in his "custom-built hand-driven tricycle," in which he travels daily, a journey "that usually takes him more than an hour to negotiate the more or less four kilometre bumpy road." On the website, Gull's story and picture are surrounded by the logos of the Western donors who have helped establish MISFA, including the World Bank, CGAP, and USAID (http://www.misfa.org.af/, accessed on February 1, 2009).

With his lost limbs, in a tricycle that must navigate an infrastructure of deprivation, Gull is quoted as saying that "the road ahead is always certain." MISFA, in turn, is similarly optimistic. It is meant to be a symbol of what development can achieve at the start of the new millennium. Established by the Government of Afghanistan in 2003, it is meant to mark the "end of the war in December 2001" and to deploy microfinance as a tool of post-war reconstruction. Heavily steeped in the rhetoric of best practice, transparency, and accountability, MISFA seeks to avoid forms of "subsidized credit" that can "severely distort the financial market." Thus, MISFA is meant to coordinate donor practices and objectives, thereby creating a "sustainable microfinance sector" that can "serve poor people throughout Afghanistan, especially women." CGAP (2008a) is bold: "The World Bank, CGAP, and the donors that followed, seized the opportunity to establish a model microfinance industry in this virgin territory—with a view toward doing things right from day one."

At first glance, microfinance in Afghanistan seems to be a new frontier of microfinance "best practice." Yet, it is also a complex development terrain, one that is characterized by fractured sovereignties and fraught with ambiguity and contradiction. Many of the programs funded by MISFA, such as those operated by BRAC, Finca International, and the Aga Khan Development Network, are rooted in the NGO rather than commercial banking model. Indeed, BRAC Afghanistan seems to be as committed to the model of "microfinance multiplied" as BRAC Bangladesh. Here, its microfinance operations work alongside five other programs—infrastructure and social development, community-based health, education, training and resource centers, and agriculture and poultry livestock. Its practices rely on familiar fundamentals of the Bangladesh model, such as community health workers.

It is tempting to see Afghanistan, the microfinance frontier, as the battleground of competing paradigms of development—on the one hand, the preemptive move of the Washington consensus on poverty to lay claim to this space, and on the other hand, the counter-incursions of the Bangladesh model. But the reality on the ground seems to be a story of entanglements rather than of a stand-off. BRAC, for instance, is the implementing partner of the Afghanistan Ministry of Public Health for its Basic Package of Health Services (BPHS), a program that is in turn supported and funded by the World Bank, USAID, and European Commission. The seemingly separate and competing ideologies of state, NGO, and donor are thus elements of a single structure of development. BRAC Afghanistan, registered as a foreign NGO since 2002, seeks to create local capacity, training Afghans to manage and implement development. While it hires large numbers of Afghans, a practice in keeping with what CGAP (2008d) calls the "Afghanization" of the microfinance sector, it is this foreign NGO that remains the implementing partner on the key development projects of the Afghan state. Its motto "A just, enlightened, healthy and democratic Afghanistan free from hunger, poverty, environmental degradation and all forms of exploitation based on age, sex, religion and ethnicity" is forged in solidarity, establishing an equivalence between the establishment of BRAC after the Bangladesh war of liberation and rehabilitation and development in post-war Afghanistan.

But this is after all BRAC's motto, one that places "women's rights and their role in Afghan society" at the center of development. It is a motto that derives quite directly from the experiences of Bangladesh (http://www.bracafg.org/about1.php, accessed November 18, 2008). Thus, Syed Hashemi, senior microfinance specialist at CGAP, notes that

> MISFA has completely defied all expectations of what one could achieve in Afghanistan . . . They said, "You can't lend to women in Afghanistan" . . . they have lent to women. They said, "You can't employ female loan officers in Afghanistan" . . . they have female loan officers. And they said, "You can't have women in management positions in Afghanistan" . . . and we are now seeing women becoming branch managers.
>
> (CGAP 2008d)

But Hashemi is also an interlocutor of the Bangladesh consensus, his frameworks of microfinance rooted in his experiences at Grameen and BRAC. From BRAC Afghanistan to MISFA, development in Afghanistan raises urgent questions about autonomy and sovereignty.

Here it is worth returning to the story of Gull. He is an icon of hope, rebuilding, and reconstruction in the wake of war. But he is also a grotesque symbol of the unending war that is Afghanistan, making a mockery of the American declaration of the end of war in 2001. His crippled body serves the gardens of the rich and of international NGOs. These glimpses of present-day Afghanistan, hidden amidst the celebratory language of microfinance and entrepreneurship, are revealing. They remind us of an Afghanistan depicted by Tariq Ali (2008: 13) as a "broken country," one that is "subjected to the combined predations of NGOs and NATO," one where a "new elite clustered around Karzai and the occupying forces . . . has specialized in creaming off foreign aid to create its own criminal networks of graft and patronage." Ali (2008: 14) argues that "little of the supposed $19 billion 'aid and reconstruction' money has reached the majority of Afghans." The NGOs and 10,000 NGO staff who "have turned Kabul into the Klondike during the gold rush . . . take orders only from some distant agency . . . but then the same goes . . . for the supposedly sovereign Afghan government." This broken country also houses a transnational population of prisoners, bodies held in the "black sites" of the war on terror, secret CIA no-law prisons with names such as Salt Pit and Dark Prison (Paglen and Thompson 2006: 126).

Microfinance in Afghanistan is thus inevitably part of a frontier of empire. Such imperial occupation and rule takes place not only through war, military might, and violence but also through humanitarianism, aid, and reconstruction. What is evident here is geopolitical dominance as well as the expansion of capitalism. USAID in Afghanistan seeks to rebuild infrastructure and systems of governance, to "invest in people." But it also seeks to privatize the Afghan economy, through a "rapid transfer of state-owned assets to the private sector" to create a "transparent, market-based economy" (http://afghanistan.usaid.gov/, accessed September 29, 2008). It is thus that the "war on terror" in sites such as Afghanistan must be understood as a "war to fill in the interstices of globalization" (Smith 2004: xv).

But what is at work in Afghanistan is not just any type of capital; it is development capital. Microfinance is a chip or microprocessor in these circuits of capital, facilitating investment in sectors such as telecom and in worthy causes such as poor women. There are also important circuits of truth that are associated with these circuits of capital. The American occupation of Afghanistan was conducted not simply as retaliation for 9/11, but rather in the name of democracy and rule of law. Supporters of the occupation, such as Max Boot, former editor at the *Wall Street Journal*, argued that it was time to provide "anarchic" countries such as Afghanistan with "the sort of enlightened foreign administration once provided by self-confident Englishmen in jodhpurs and pith helmets" (in Ferguson 2002: xii). Gull's maimed body must be located in this historical context. It is at once a testament to the entrepreneurial promise of a now-liberated Afghanistan and evocative of the violences of the "enlightened foreign administration" that makes such liberation and entrepreneurship possible.

Gereshk, the site at which Gull lost his limbs in a land mine explosion in 1996, at the age of 23, is a town on the Helmand river in central Afghanistan. Since 2002, Helmand Province itself is both the recipient of considerable foreign aid and the site of extensive poppy culture. But there is also an older history. Gereshk bears witness to the long history of colonialism and occupation in Afghanistan. The Gereshk fort was captured by the British in the first Anglo-Afghan war of 1839–1842. Gereshk is located on Highway 1, the transportation corridor built during the Soviet occupation of Afghanistan that lasted from 1979 to 1989. At such moments, as at many others, Afghanistan was the frontier of rival interests and aspirations—a nineteenth-century possession to be claimed by an expanding British empire that was to outflank the Persian and Russian empires; a twentieth-century battleground of brutal war between Soviet communism on the one hand and the alliance of the religious mujahidin, the American CIA, and a Saudi monarchy on the other hand. It is this latter context that was to spawn the nativist fundamentalism that took shape in the form of the Taliban, the regime against which a post-9/11 USAID presents its liberal agenda of combating terrorism and poverty. It is also this latter context—with its unholy mix of a transnational Islamic militancy and American geopolitics—that was to produce the Al-Qaeda and Osama bin Laden of the twenty-first century. Gull's maimed body, crippled at Gereshk, stands at the crossroads of such millennial histories.

"Weapons of Mass Salvation"

Afghanistan does not lie in the territory named, imagined, and managed as the "Middle East." That colonial construction identifies not so much a geographical location—for example, South Asia—as it does a geopolitical logic, the distance from a center of power and hegemony. It is worth asking: Middle of where? East of what? Central to such geopolitics is what Edward Said (1979), in his seminal analysis of colonialism, identified as "orientalism"—discursive and imaginative practices that create an image of the orient that in turn becomes reality. After the attacks of 9/11, as the US launched a retaliatory war on Afghanistan, the borders of the Middle East once again seemed to stretch. Afghanistan, along with Iraq, became the latest sites of military intervention, linked by a new imperialism and orientalism concerned with the "Muslim world." There are certain key features of millennial imperialism. It advances, as I have already noted, an argument about anarchic, rogue, and backward societies, which must be conquered and civilized through imperial occupation. Civilization itself is cast in terms of both democracy and economic globalization. Niall Ferguson (2002: xix), proponent of a Pax Americana for the new millennium, thus asks: "Can you have globalization without gunboats?" Such economic globalization has been an unabashed privatization of the economies of Iraq and Afghanistan, often through imperial means and wartime mercenaries such as Halliburton Inc. and Blackwater Inc. Activist Arundhati Roy (2003) thus states that "Iraq is no longer a country. It's an asset." How does this asset make possible the capitalization of another asset, microfinance?

While 9/11 became the occasion for occupation in Iraq and Afghanistan, it also brought the merchants of economic globalization and imperial power face to face with what was perceived to be rage on the "Arab street." In a Senate testimony, USAID staff quoted President Bush to articulate this link between the war on poverty and the war on terror: "We fight against poverty because hope is an answer to terror" (Chamberlin 2003). It is in this way that 9/11 leads us back to poverty alleviation, to microfinance, and to Enzar Gull.

The discourse of terror and poverty is not unique to the Bush administration and the imperial administrators of Iraq and Afghanistan. In an essay titled "Weapons of mass salvation," Jeffrey Sachs (2002: 217) made the case that "one cannot fight a war against weapons of mass destruction through military means alone." As the search for the so-called "weapons of mass destruction" justified the military occupation of Iraq and Afghanistan, so Sachs highlighted "weapons of mass salvation"—"anti-AIDS drugs, antimalarial bed nets, borewells for safe drinking water, and the like." These, he argued, "can save millions of lives and also be a bulwark for global security." The war on terror, it seemed, could not avoid a war on poverty. "There is no wall," declared then World Bank President, James Wolfensohn, "between security and poverty" (Mallaby 2004: 12). Here once again is Sachs (2005: 1):

Since September 11, 2001, the United States has launched a war on terror but has neglected the deeper causes of global instability. The $450 billion that the

United States will spend this year on the military will never buy peace if it continues to spend around one thirtieth of that, just $15 billion, to address the plight of the world's poorest of the poor, whose societies are destabilized by extreme poverty and thereby become havens of unrest, violence, and even global terrorism.

Microfinance is seen as "one of the most effective, cost-efficient weapons in the fight against poverty"; a "down payment on building stronger economies and more stable societies"; an approach that is both "good development policy" and "good security policy" (Hochberg 2002). A few months after 9/11, newspapers ranging from the *Houston Chronicle* (March 18, 2002) to the *Boston Globe* (March 18, 2002), thus concluded that microfinance could be a way to fight poverty and terrorism "in small bites." "This is sound foreign aid," the *Boston Globe* argued. "It is not a handout. The money goes to people, not governments, so its benefits are easy to see . . . One place to spend more money is Afghanistan, where terrorism breeds and people are smothered by poverty." A few years later the enthusiasm had not waned, with former Secretary of State Madeline Albright noting the "macro-benefits" of microfinance, that it is "a proven tool for transforming suffering into hope, one individual at a time" (Albright and Doerr 2004).

As microfinance is a preferred weapon of mass salvation, so the Middle East is the site at which the war on terror and the war on poverty are conjoined. Launched in 2002, by the US Department of State, the Middle East Partnership Initiative (MEPI) directs resources to the Middle East in order "to create educational opportunity at a grassroots level, promote economic opportunity and help foster private sector development, and to strengthen civil society and the rule of law throughout the region" (http://mepi.state.gov/, accessed October 13, 2008). With its twin goals of economic and democratic reform, the MEPI is one example of a "kinder and gentler" imperialism that seeks to use instruments such as microfinance. Here then is a confluence of various forces and energies: millennial development and its mandate of poverty reduction; an imperial expansion in the Middle East animated by a war on terror; and the global popularity of microfinance as a tool of entrepreneurship and empowerment.

This confluence can be glimpsed in an initiative launched by then President Bush: the "USA Freedom Corps." Described in his 2002 State of the Union address (Bush 2002), the USA Freedom Corps is meant to "build on the countless acts of service, sacrifice, and generosity that followed September 11." A year later Bush was to announce a special initiative of the USA Freedom Corps: "Volunteers for Prosperity," meant to "give America's highly skilled professionals new opportunities to serve abroad" and to "show the world the energy and idealism of the United States of America" (http://www.volunteersforprosperity.gov/about/, accessed October 13, 2008). The MEPI is a partner of the Volunteers for Prosperity. The MEPI also partners with a "not-for-profit, public–private" volunteer network, the Financial Services Volunteer Corps, which "seeks to build capital markets." Established in 1990 "at US Presidential request" by a former US Secretary of State and a former chairman of Goldman Sachs, its motto: "building strong financial systems to achieve a better quality of life" (http://www.fsvc. org/, accessed October 13, 2008) sounds like a line out of CGAP. MEPI projects in Egypt include funding of the activities of the Financial Services Volunteer Corps. Here then at the intersection of the war on poverty and the war on terror are some key elements of the composition that is the new millennium: freedom, prosperity, and financial services.

Yet there are important contradictions in this composition of the Middle East and microfinance. One is the seeming clash between Islam and usury. But this may turn out to be the simplest of all dilemmas, for microfinance thrives in many Muslim contexts—from the villages of Bangladesh to the southern suburbs of Beirut. Indeed, there is the emergence of a new type of globalized "Islamic finance," sustained by petrodollars and fueled by a "new quest for purity on the part of wealthy Middle East Muslims" (Maurer 2005: 9). This world of Islamic finance nimbly manages the matter of interest income. Thus, a CGAP (2008a) publication bills Islamic microfinance as a "new market niche."

But a more persistent contradiction, one that is often discussed by USAID staff, concerns the target of microfinance. Microfinance, as it emerges from the context of Bangladesh, is a technology of lending to poor, married women who are embedded in patriarchal households in the densely populated villages of South Asia. In the wake of 9/11, microfinance is being deployed in the Middle East as a technology of development meant to target America's most visible Muslim: the angry young man on the Arab street. USAID bureaucrats are acutely aware of this challenge. "We are under pressure," as one high-level USAID official put it (June 2005), "to give loans to young men." "We are being told that either these young men will utilize these loans and start their own businesses selling falafel, or they will all become suicide bombers." Microfinance, in the words of yet another USAID official (March 2004), has become "the safety-valve for the anger of young men in moderate Muslim countries."

The problem of "disaffected youth"—as the euphemism goes—is a severe one in the region. Each year, the Millennium Development Goal Report shows that the rates of educated, unemployed youth are the highest in the countries of the Middle East and North Africa. These numbers have barely budged and they speak to the entrenchment of structures of economic marginality and the retrenchment of public employment. These numbers also generate an anxious discourse about youth and terrorism, as if the choices facing young men (and women) in the Middle East are that clearly defined: be an entrepreneur and sell falafel or become a suicide bomber. Can microfinance, that technology for lending to South Asian poor, rural women, be effective as a tool to solve the unemployment of young, educated men in the cities of the Middle East? Such questions will become front and center as, later in this chapter, I discuss the discourse and practice of microfinance in Egypt and Lebanon. But they are also at odds with a key goal of the MEPI and other US incursions in the Middle East: the empowerment of women.

As there is the rather frantic effort to target young men, so there is also pervasive talk of transforming Middle East societies by "promoting women entrepreneurs" (Husseini 1997). Such a mandate is in keeping with the general theme of microfinance, of a form of development that is undertaken in the name of the Third World, poor woman. Millennial empire is also "in her name." The democratization of Iraq and Afghanistan, achieved through military occupation, was meant to be a liberation of women. This was starkly evident during the early stages of the American occupation in Afghanistan:

> Once the Northern Alliance had chased the last of the Taliban from Kabul, First Lady Laura Bush took over her husband's weekly radio address to comment on the success of the campaign. "Because of our recent military gains in much of Afghanistan," she said, "women are no longer imprisoned in their homes." U.S. newspapers ran front-page photographs of women tossing off their burkas; magazines ran triumphant articles on girls returning to school. In his first State of the Union address after the victory, the president declared, "Today women are free."

> (Sevcik 2003)

A *New York Times* editorial (November 24, 2001) declared that the "reclaimed freedom of Afghan women is a collateral benefit that Americans can celebrate." In predictable fashion, the editorial touted microfinance for women as one of the most "efficient" ways to reduce poverty. "Operation Enduring Freedom," as the military campaign is called, seems to be about both economic freedom and the freedom of women. Microfinance promises both.

Freedom is a key theme in the Arab Human Development Reports, which contain a Human Development Index specially modified for the Arab world with a "freedom score" (Hasso 2009). The 2005 Arab Human Development Report bears the title *Towards the Rise of Women in the Arab World* and is concerned with "the deficit in gender equality" in the Arab world (Abu-Lughod 2009). It is a text that continues to be vigorously debated. Feminist scholars have interpreted the report as producing "an Arab world that is the negative foil for an enlightened and allegedly noncultural modern West" (Abu-Lughod 2009: 86), as presenting Arab women as "victimized women" (Hasso 2009: 63). But Islah Jad (2009: 61), one of the co-authors of the report, reveals the struggles that went into the making of the text. She presents the report as a stand against imperialism, refuting "categorically any use of women's rights by the occupying powers in the region (Americans and Israelis) trying to cast themselves as 'women's liberators' or as a development power." But she also notes that the report fails to comment on the many different types of privileges and inequalities that shape women's lives in the Arab world: "This lacuna was related to 'internal' views shared by some of the authors who were strongly driven by a neoliberal and women's liberal rights approach and 'confident' in their beliefs about what is 'good' for women" (Jad 2009: 62). Jad's commentary reveals an important tension: that the rejection of imperialism can go hand in hand with the adoption of neoliberalism and its theme of economic freedom. Such reconciliations and contradictions are not simply imposed on the Muslim and Arab world by the West; rather they are actively produced in various sovereign sites.

DISCIPLINE AND DEBT

In the winter of 2005, Egypt launched its "National Strategy for Microfinance." The event, which I had the opportunity to attend, was held in the ballroom of the Marriott Hotel. It showcased the main players in the microfinance sector of Egypt: USAID, UNDP, the Social Fund for Development, and national and international commercial banks. EQI, the main development consulting firm in Egypt, did much of the event organization and planning. The event also served as the occasion for the "Global Microentrepreneurship Award," sponsored by the Citigroup Foundation and meant "to celebrate entrepreneurship and promote micro-finance in the Arab region." The room was strikingly divided between the "experts" of the microfinance industry—bankers, bureaucrats, consultants, development brokers, ministers—and the recipients of development—the poor women who are microfinance borrowers. It is rare to find these women, in their *galabeyas* and head scarves, in the corridors and ballroom of the Marriott Hotel, a palatial structure built by a nineteenth-century Egyptian ruler eager to impress the Empress Eugenie of France, and more generally Europe, at the ceremonies marking the opening of the Suez Canal. This lavish and ostentatious remaking of Cairo was to bankrupt the country and set the stage for colonial occupation by the British and the French. Over a century later, in this palace, a new exhibition of development was on display. Poor women from Bulaq, Dahb-al-Amar, Miniya—Cairo's impover-ished neighborhoods—were vital elements of the exhibition. They embodied both entrepreneurship and empowerment. A representative of the Citigroup Foundation gave out awards to the women who had been deemed the most successful "microentrepreneurs." As the development industry politely clapped in applause, the women ululated, filling the ballroom with a "native" enthusiasm.

The awards themselves were part of a growing circuit of "micro-entrepreneurship" awards, an intricate variation of region, scale, and jurisdiction—from those run by PlaNet Finance to those run by the Sanabel Network, the Arab world's main microfinance network. These awards make visible the lives touched by microfinance. There is for example the "Afghan mother," Zainab Barat Painda Khan, a "mother of six" and carpet-weaver who was at first hesitant to take on a microfinance loan and yet did so, thereby "increasing her income by 70%" and who now encourages "other women in the village to apply for loans" (http://www.chfinternational.org/node/28374, accessed January 17, 2009). There is Zeinab, who is celebrated in a Grameen Foundation mass email (February 27, 2009) as the "good news from the Arab world." Billed as "this week's story," Zeinab's success in launching a business selling wooden kitchen utensils with a $45 loan is celebrated. "As her business grew, so did the loans she was able to obtain. Today, three of her children have jobs, working with Zeinab to run the business. She owns her own workshop and an inventory of raw materials. Her last loan payment was £4,000 EGP ($700). "This is more than any government officer gets in two months," she says with a smile and laugh.

The work that goes into making and giving such awards is little discussed—the tireless work of microfinance organizations to submit the applications that have to prove a transformation wrought by microfinance, from a life of misery to one of hope. It is truth-making work. It is complicated work, as in the case of award winners who must hide such awards from their own households, for the award gives away what may be the secret practice of a woman seeking to eke out an autonomous livelihood amidst staunch patriarchy. Such was the story of one of the Sanabel microentrepreneurship award winners, told to me by Reham Farouk, director of Al-Tadamun, a microfinance organization in Egypt (January 2006). She was unable to make the trip to Morocco to accept the award since she had hidden the microfinance loans from her husband. Was this woman a symbol of the failure of gender empowerment via microfinance in the Arab world? Or was her stealth precisely proof of such empowerment?

Questions about autonomy and sovereignty also haunt Egypt's National Strategy for Microfinance. It was meant to symbolize an alliance between "forward-thinking" donors on the other hand and a "skeptical" Social Fund for Development, the main government entity responsible for microfinance. To whom then did this National Strategy belong? Was it owned by the Egyptian government or by the bilateral and multilateral donors who establish global best practices of microfinance? This debate, playing out in the shadows of the gala event, was itself a performance—of the distinction between national autonomy and donor-driven development. The Social Fund for Development is after all at once a government entity and a creature of donor agendas, giving the lie to the idea of Egyptian sovereignty. It is a state bureaucracy created and underwritten by donors to mitigate the social devastation unleashed by the forced liberalization of the state economy, one mandated by donors through regimes of structural adjustment and austerity. The Social Fund is thus a paradoxical combination of neoliberalism and state-led social protection. Microfinance, it seems, is a particularly useful way of performing the paradox.

Egypt's National Strategy for Microfinance not only knitted together the seemingly separate worlds of international donors and the Egyptian government, but also deftly crafted a consensus where free-market principles could be reconciled with the alleviation of poverty. The strategy listed three core principles: that

> poor people will be best served when they have access to a wide range of services, for the best price, with choice between different financial services and different providers ... this is most likely to happen when a free market for microfinance exists in Egypt ... and only through the mobilization of commercial capital.
>
> (Waly 2005)

Such a strategy can be read as a blatant rehearsal of the Washington consensus on poverty, "placing the commercialization of microfinance at the heart of Egypt's development agenda" (Government of Egypt 2005: 1). The talk of "best-practice" microfinance looms large in the pages of the Strategy, carefully targeting the "economically active poor" on the first page and including CGAP's Key Principles of Microfinance in its entirety in the appendix. Yet, the Strategy is more than a mere copy of the CGAP consensus; it is also the articulation of a distinctively Egyptian conjuncture, one where development must negotiate various paradoxes. There is the paradox of insisting upon "sustainable financial services" in the face of "the fact that most of Egypt's microfinance initiatives, namely financing of working capital, have been donor-driven, subsidized" (Government of Egypt 2005: 14, 10). There is also the paradox of making microfinance in the image of the "free market" but relying on the state to "facilitate the use of a broader range of mechanisms to secure credit," specifically forms of "alternative collateral" that include "informal housing and properties, moveable assets, commercial papers, social/peer pressure or unconventional collateral mechanisms" (Government of Egypt 2005: 3). These paradoxes speak to the conundrum of debt, discipline, and dependence that today lie at the heart of development in Egypt.

An Ecology of Dependence

To state that microfinance in Egypt is primarily a USAID project is not an exaggeration. The birth of microfinance in Egypt can be traced to a USAID grant, made in 1988, to the Alexandria Business Association (ABA). An association of businessmen, the ABA functioned as a community service organization since 1983, deploying the Islamic idea of *zakat*, or the giving of alms to the poor. The USAID grant transformed the ABA into a microfinance organization, underwriting a shift from philanthropy to professionalized development. With the funds provided by USAID, the ABA could now provide loans to finance enterprises and entrepreneurship. The "engineering" was managed by EQI, one of the largest development consulting firms in Egypt. As detailed by a top-ranking EQI staffer (May 2006), the firm successfully bid on the contract to establish ABA as a microfinance entity. In doing so, it sought to create a Latin American-style institution that could facilitate access to credit and serve as an alternative to Egyptian informal credit associations or the *gammayat* that were the primary mode of credit for small and medium enterprises. Through contracts to EQI, USAID was to replicate this technique several times, ultimately creating an ecology of microfinance spread out across the various governorates of Egypt and made up of non-profit business associations and community development associations acting as brokers of microfinance funds.

It is an ecology closely controlled by USAID. Acknowledged worldwide as the "market leader" of Egyptian microfinance, ABA itself is the direct outcome of changing USAID agendas. Initially focused on lending to small and medium enterprises, by 2001 ABA was to launch a new program entirely focused on poor women. Named "Blossoms," the program utilizes a group lending model and was once again engineered by EQI (Brandsma and Burjrjee 2004: 42). It was described by ABA staff as the result of "USAID conditions." While registering high repayment rates and a fast growth in clients, Blossoms was nevertheless seen by the ABA director as a difficult program to run (July 2005):

> Should I worry about satisfying USAID or worry about satisfying my community? Loans to women are problematic and we faced a lot of opposition. There was even opposition in the government. Finally Mrs. Mubarak had to facilitate the idea by asking: Is it hurting you to help your daughter, your wife, your granddaughter, your sister? But let us be clear: we were compelled by USAID to start this program.

Blossoms must be understood in the context of American interests in the process of so-called Arab democratization. The liberation and empowerment of Arab women is a central icon in such a process. But Blossoms also has to be understood in light of the conditions imposed by the US Congress on USAID. Poverty lending is one such important standard: "The number of loans going towards poverty lending (less than $350) was expected to increase to reach 50% of the loan portfolio" (EQI/NCBA 2005: 4). These conditions are the result of the lobbying efforts of the Microcredit Summit, which were described in a previous chapter. In Egypt, such poverty targeting has been implemented through group lending programs such as Blossoms that lend primarily to women. Entrepreneurial men are seen as unlikely candidates for transactions that bear such high costs: small loans, group meetings, and the social stigma of poverty targeting.

By 2006, when I was conducting a second round of interviews at ABA, the mood had shifted again. While all of ABA's funding still came from USAID, it was now under pressure to "become independent," mainly by raising commercial funds. Critical of this new direction where donors seek to "build capacity" through training but do not fund programs, staff expressed anxiety that even being a "market leader" may not be enough to guarantee ABA access to sufficient commercial funds. ABA and other Egyptian microfinance institutions saw themselves caught in an impossible situation: that on the one hand USAID dominated the microfinance scene but was now refusing to release more funds and on the other hand because of the presence of USAID no other donor or investor was likely to enter the scene. Yet, ABA staff remained convinced by other elements of the Washington consensus on poverty, especially the forms of authoritative knowledge produced at Boulder. The ABA vice-director talked proudly of his attendance of the Boulder workshop and of his credentials as a "trainer of trainers" (June 2006). He, and other ABA staff, insisted on the need for "best-practice" microfinance and argued that the most effective model of microfinance was presented by BancoSol in Bolivia, a highly commercialized entity. Unlike their complaints about USAID conditions, they presented this model as one that they had freely chosen in a world of development muddied by shoddy practice and political manoeveurs. Against the Social Fund for Development, which they repeatedly dismissed as the "political fund," these foot soldiers of "best-practice microfinance" proudly claimed for themselves a development expertise and professionalism.

153

USAID's ecology of microfinance in Egypt presents a dilemma. The Washington consensus on poverty advocates "sustainable microfinance" and valorizes measures of sustainability such as OSS and FSS. Its rejection of the Bangladesh model of microfinance is framed in the language of subsidy indices and other registers of dependence. Yet, in Egypt, the microfinance industry remains overwhelmingly dependent on USAID for both financial and technical assistance. Such dependence not only runs counter to the "best practices" globalized by CGAP but also contradicts the goals of the USAID mission in Egypt: to support "financial privatization." In recent years, reports generated by the Washington DC development establishment have thus started to lament the state of microfinance in Egypt. They note that USAID has allocated $141 million to Egypt's microfinance sector since 1989 but that in doing so it has "created institutions that are highly reliant on it for vision and growth." Such donor-dependence is seen as the sign of a larger malaise: "Many of USAID's partners have limited institutional vision, lack sound governance, and are highly inefficient . . . Their focus on the donor as opposed to their clients makes them more supply-driven and not market-oriented" (AVID Consulting Corporation 2004: 1). The *Benchmarking Arab Microfinance* reports produced by the MIX (2003: 4) generalize thus: "Arab microfinance institutions remain almost completely dependent on donor funding."

It is a discourse of failed institutions put forward by the very forces of development that established such an ecology of dependence. Firmly ensconced at USAID headquarters in Cairo, a top USAID official (August 2004) could thus declare to me that the dependence of microfinance institutions on USAID was standing in the way of the "decentralized programming of development and the full ownership of development by recipient countries." "It is time for this sector," he argued, "to have a business model rather than to rely on grants from us." He noted that in doing so Egyptian microfinance institutions may have to stop focusing on poverty alleviation. Only a few years after USAID itself had compelled organizations such as ABA to target poor women, this USAID official declared that such a focus was "distracting" and was not in line with "CGAP best practices." But most troubling, he noted, was a context of development wholly dependent on USAID funds. "This," he boldly stated, "is the pollution of free money." His Egyptian deputy, the main liaison with the microfinance institutions that until now have been closely controlled and supervised by USAID strongly concurred, repeating, "yes, it is the pollution of free money."

The worry about the "pollution of free money" is widespread. As USAID seeks to discipline the very microfinance organizations it has created, so these microfinance organizations themselves seek to discipline their staff and borrowers. This chain of debt, discipline, and dependence stretches from international development organizations through NGOs to the poor. As USAID must struggle to discipline its NGOs, so the NGOs themselves struggle to discipline the poor. "Structural Adjustment Programs discipline naughty states. When infused with NGO-mediated finance, social networks can serve as a mechanism for ensuring that the poor discipline themselves" (Elyachar 2002: 509). It is this constant work, the repetitive rituals of discipline, and the ruptures of such discipline, that make up the politics of microfinance in Egypt. And it is this anxiety that manifests itself in the statement: the pollution of free money.

While global microfinance seems to have solved the vexing problems of collateral, guarantees, and repayment, thereby opening up a new frontier of accumulation—what may be understood as "poverty capital"—microfinance in Egypt continues to wrestle with fraud and delinquency. I had initially thought that the distinction lay between individual lending programs and group lending programs such as Blossoms. Surely the latter with their proven formula of joint liability or at least peer pressure, enacted through women's groups, would be able to easily ensure loan repayment? Yet, the workings of the two microfinance NGOs affiliated with the Grameen Foundation, Al-Tadamun and RADE, both located outside the USAID ecology and each staunchly committed to the Grameen model of microfinance, gives the lie to such a distinction.

Established in 1996 as a project of Save the Children USA, Al-Tadamun, a Grameen Foundation partner, works in poor urban neighborhoods in Cairo. RADE, also a Grameen Foundation partner and established in 1997 by Catholic Relief Services, is based in Sohag, an impoverished rural region. While both Al-Tadamun and RADE are consistent with the logic of microfinance in Egypt—where the prominent NGOs have all been set up by international development organizations or by international NGOs—they are strikingly different from those established by USAID. Espousing an explicit poverty-alleviation goal, they primarily serve poor women using a group lending methodology and peer guarantees. While the USAID microfinance organizations remain thoroughly convinced by the Washington consensus on poverty and its expertise, Al-Tadamun and RADE are immersed in the circuits of knowledge and capital crafted by the Grameen Bank. Staff attend the Grameen Dialogue in Bangladesh, the organizations receive grants from the Grameen–Jameel Initiative and rely on the experts of the Grameen network. When they attend the Boulder Institute, as did the top staff of Al-Tadamun, it is a trip sponsored by the Grameen Foundation to train its partners in the language of financial sustainability. It is Grameen, they believe, that gave them the "chance" to make a difference. They are well-versed in the workings of the Bangladesh model, its reliance on savings, and how such a model is difficult to implement in Egypt where NGOs cannot mobilize savings. Written out of the discussions leading up to the National Strategy for Microfinance, both Al-Tadamun and RADE directors commented that rather than a focus on commercialized finance, such a strategy should have been more concerned with social development. "I did not realize this until I started working in microfinance," said Reham Al-Farouk during an interview (January 2006), "but this is about collecting good deeds. It is about helping poor clients and being able to face God at the end of one's life."

Yet one issue consumed Al-Tadamun and RADE: fraud and delinquency. When I met with the director of RADE (August 2005), she was in Cairo to meet with lawyers to discuss action on two fronts. The first was the enforcement of loan repayment: women had to pay back their loans. She asked:

> How does an organization such as the Grameen Bank maintain such high repayment rates without turning to the courts? Is it more severe than the courts? How has it succeeded in scaring women such, even more than the courts could achieve? After all, people are not angels. In fact, people + money always spells trouble.

The questions took me by surprise for she had only recently attended the Grameen Dialogue in Bangladesh. But her questions indicated a real and persistent struggle in Egypt with loan repayment. To solve the problem, Egyptian microfinance organizations, even those such as Al-Tadamun and RADE that adhere to a Grameen methodology, require a "security check"—signed by the client or a third party guarantor—as collateral. The check is important not for the funds that it guarantees but instead for the threat of criminal action that is contained within it. That check places the microfinance transaction within the broader apparatus of Egypt's criminal courts and bankruptcy laws. Anthropologist Julia Elyachar (2006: 199) explains that microfinance in Egypt was constructed in a manner that made

> nonpayment fall under criminal rather than civil law . . . NGOs could draw on the state's repressive apparatus when they needed to collect back interest. They held, moreover, a kind of undated personal check from each borrower that could be deposited at any time. If funds were not there to back up the check, criminal legal procedures would be instituted, i.e. in Egypt the police was the culture to be used for repayment.

Such a system, Elyachar argues was devised by "former Egyptian bankers" who acted as consultants to the microenterprise sector and who sought to avoid the problems of the civil courts in Egypt. It was the full force of the criminal law that was to be used to ensure repayment of microloans.

This is a stunning technique of discipline: a fingerprint by a poor and illiterate woman on a blank check that seals the threat that she will be hauled away to jail in the event of a missed loan payment, a threat greatly compounded for those women who may take out microfinance loans without the knowledge of their husbands and households. Al-Tadamun's staff (August 2005) noted that such a threat is often levied not only against individual women but against the entire group if a member misses payment:

> We do not implement the threat, but in Egypt this is the way it works. We have no collateral and so we must use this threat. We had to build the reputation that we collect loans, that Al-Tadamun will not tolerate any delays, not even for a day. This is essential for a lending culture where people do not default on loans. And if they are borrowing from other institutions then we want to make sure they pay us back first.

Is this microfinance at its crudest, a primitive mixture of state-guaranteed violence and patriarchal shame held together by the performance of threat? Or is it microfinance at an advanced stage, a logical evolution of the techniques of discipline used in seemingly kinder and gentler models?

As Al-Tadamun and RADE saw its women borrowers as sources of fraud—as defrauding the organizations by refusing to pay back their loans—so they were also worried about fraud committed by their staff. My interviews with RADE staff took place as the organization sought to overhaul its "operational and financial risk management model" and to mitigate fraud committed by its loan officers. The director explained that corrupt loan officers had issued multiple loans to poor clients, creating false records and taking a 50 percent cut on each loan. Loan repayment fell to 85 percent and the internal audit system collapsed. RADE filed criminal charges against the women borrowers and four loan officers, seeking to recover these loans. But more important, it had to create a new system of staff discipline. Al-Tadamun's managers thus noted that they check PAR on a daily rather than monthly basis. They do so not in adherence with CGAP best practices but rather as a technique of surveillance. "We have incentive schemes for our promoters and loans officers," noted Reham Al-Farouk (January 2006), "the bonus is determined by the number of clients and by their PAR figures. If the PAR is off a single day then they lose their monthly bonus." "It is not just us," she argued. "ABA's Blossoms program, the one that is always being celebrated, was shut down four times because of rumors that loan officers were taking bribes; a methodology had been imposed on them by USAID but they did not know how to run the program." Al-Tadamun's daily checks on PAR are embedded in an explicitly hierarchical organization. Although it is an organization whose top managers are women, Al-Farouk herself noted that the rest of the hierarchy was dominated by men. Loan managers were overwhelmingly male, while promoters were women. "Grameen's model," she argued, is "based on good will and good intentions. This doesn't apply in Egypt. We have to ensure discipline." Such struggles with fraud and delinquency may be seen as a failure of microfinance in Egypt, an instance of an alien development methodology imposed by USAID or borrowed from Bangladesh. Yet, such struggles lie at the very heart of microfinance. They reveal the performance of discipline that is essential for the workings of microfinance.

The Pollution of Free Money

The performance of discipline must be understood in a broader context, one that can be characterized as the performance of development. Nowhere is this more apparent than in the Social Fund for Development. It is here that the dilemmas and anxieties associated with the "pollution of free money" are crystallized.

Established in 1991, the Social Fund for Development presents itself as "a social safety net associated with the government of Egypt's agreement to undertake its extensive Economic Reform and Structural Adjustment Program (ERASP) . . . to minimize risks of social exclusion, help alleviate poverty and combat unemployment" (http://www.sfdegypt.org/about.asp, accessed August 18, 2008). As liberalization was enacted in Egypt, so USAID warned of "deteriorating social conditions in Egypt" (Bayat 2002: 4). Egypt's Social Fund belongs to a species of institutions established as "essential" components of structural adjustment in various countries. They were meant to serve as the "shock therapy" of liberalization, the "highly visible action" that "was to make the 'bitter pill' of adjustment easier to swallow" (Cornia and Reddy 2001: 10). By 1996, the World Bank had approved 51 Social Funds in 32 countries (Weber 2006: 48). These Social Funds enable donors to "ease the adoption of austerity packages" and also allow governments to "selectively court groups of voters" by distributing funds "in a discretionary manner . . . for patronage purposes" (Tendler 2000: 121). If the first phase of Social Funds were established on an emergency basis, meant to target the "adjustment poor," then in a second phase the work of Social Funds was extended to the "chronic poor." A more ambitious third phase created "promotive" rather than "compensatory" Social Funds that were to be "longer-term service delivery mechanisms" (Cornia and Reddy 2001: 8). Egypt's Social Fund belongs to this third phase.

Social Funds represent an interesting paradox. Creatures of neoliberalism they nevertheless embody mandates of state intervention in the economy to generate employment and deliver services. They are also donor projects, funded for the most part by external funds. Egypt's Social Fund was set up through $572 million of funding from various sources ranging from the World Bank, UNDP, the European Union, and the Arab Fund. As Elyachar notes (2002: 501), it was thus a "new agency positioned at once inside and outside the state."

The research on Social Funds overwhelmingly concludes that they only play a "minor role" in alleviating poverty (Cornia and Reddy 2001: 1). Yet, they remain the instrument of choice for donors seeking to supplement the harshness of structural adjustment with poverty-alleviation interventions. Scholars explain the popularity of Social Funds by noting that they are seen as a new model of development and service delivery—decentralized, privatized, demand-driven—as "efficient providers of economic and social infrastructure" (Tendler and Serrano 1999: 25). Social Funds are thus cast in opposition to traditional models of public service delivery and human development bureaucracy. While located in the state, they are meant to work as an exception, bypassing the regulations of the state, enjoying a "special autonomy" with "exemptions from civil service salary regulations and exemptions from the government's usual procurement and disbursement procedures" (Narayan and Ebbe 1997: 2). They are also meant to be tangible examples of a new model of development, a "training ground in the democratic process," an institutional form that can link "a neoliberal, market-based model of social provisioning to the formerly 'alternative' approaches of participation and empowerment" (Vivian 1995: 4, 19).

Yet, most Social Funds have turned out to be "the opposite of real decentralization" (Tendler 2000: 115). They are development "intermediaries," (Vivian 1995: 5) administered by entities attached to central governments, funded by donor agencies, and distributing development capital to communities, NGOs, and private contractors. In the case of Egypt, the donors underwriting the Social Fund also wrote the agenda of development, choosing the target groups—"women, new graduates, those laid off from public enterprises, those with low income, migrant workers forced back to Egypt during the Gulf War"—that were to be assisted through the Social Fund (Elyachar 2002: 501) and choosing the instruments—microfinance, for example—through which the Social Fund was to perform development.

The Egyptian Social Fund runs two distinct operations: poverty alleviation and employment generation. In interviews, the staff of the Social Fund took great care to separate these two worlds of development. On the one hand, there is the Small Enterprise Development Organization (SEDO), a world of small and medium enterprises, meant to target unemployed youth, to "promote entrepreneurship" through business development services, e-commerce, and various other services, and to thereby generate "macroeconomic growth." On the other hand, there is the world of microfinance, located within the Human and Community Development Group. It is meant to target poor women in deprived areas and to engender empowerment and generate income. The line between these two worlds had been drawn by the Law of Small Enterprise Development passed in June 2004 that demarcated microfinance by loan size, under L.E. 10,000. But it was also actively maintained and policed by the Social Fund staff. A loan portfolio manager thus argued (May 2005) that microfinance was delivered mainly through NGOs while small and medium enterprises were served by banks and business associations. The latter was presented as a world of rational transactions while the former was depicted as operating through the logic of "social pressure and cultural belief," one where women often had to submit "security checks" but that such checks counted on the "manhood" of poor men who would never let their wives be taken to a police station on account of a missed payment. There was little discussion of default rates or subsidies with regard to small and medium enterprises. Expressing concern about high default rates in microfinance, the Social Fund staff claimed that it was necessary to carefully monitor NGOs and NGO clients, often on a weekly basis. Such practices were confirmed by microfinance institutions such as Al-Tadamun that receive funds from the Social Fund and that are thus subject to regular audits. Yet, the Social Fund staff noted that it was also necessary to make allowances for "humanitarian cases" and to write off or reschedule loans.

A similar ambiguity attended the issue of subsidies. Social Fund staff were eager to present the work of the microfinance division as an example of global best practice, one that advocates against the subsidization of interest rates. A 2006 Social Fund report thus boldly states:

> The microfinance sector is committed to the promotion of internationally accepted microfinance best practices and will therefore no longer provide subsidized credit to its NGO intermediaries. Furthermore, the microfinance sector will only work with NGOs which charge market interest rates thereby ensuring their long-term sustainability.
>
> (Badr El-Din 2006: 5)

Yet, in interviews Social Fund staff repeatedly made note of the myriad "political pressures"—within Egypt and from donors such as the Islamic Fund, the Arab Fund, and the Kuwait Fund—to subsidize interest rates, especially in poverty-alleviation programs such as microfinance. In turn, microfinance practitioners, especially those lodged in the USAID ecology of microfinance, lamented how the Social Fund's practices of subsidies were polluting the culture of lending and diluting standards of discipline through "free money." Perhaps most striking was the statement by one of the top managers at ABA (January 2006) that by allowing defaults and distributing subsidies, the Social Fund had "failed to educate the people of Egypt for the realities of the free market."

The work of the Social Fund has to be situated in the broader context of Egypt's development. The Social Fund's SEDO bears the promise of macroeconomic growth and employment, a world where formal jobs can be generated. Yet, as Elyachar (2006: 30) notes, "economic liberalization 'freed' Egyptians into the space dubbed the 'informal economy.'" Most important it eroded a staple of middle-class Egyptian life: public-sector employment. After all, Egypt is an economy where, by the end of the 1960s, one out of every four Egyptians was directly or indirectly on the government's payroll (Luciani 1990: xx). The hollowing out of the Egyptian state, through liberalization, was thus less a story about the diminution of public services (which were always meager) and much more an issue of the contraction of public-sector employment. Today, formal employment is but a dream, the promise that is kept alive through the carefully tended distinction between SEDO and microfinance. That promise can never be fulfilled in the hollowed-out economy that is Egypt.

But the distinction matters; it takes on a life of its own. In an important treatise on colonial Egypt, Timothy Mitchell (1988: 163) notes that colonialism divided the city into two: "one part becoming an exhibition and the other, in the same spirit, a museum." The latter was a preserved, picturesque, indigenous disorder while the former was an ordered, rational, efficient, modernized space. "The identity of the modern city," writes Mitchell (1988: 165) is "created by what it keeps out. Its modernity is something contingent upon the exclusion of its own opposite." In contemporary times, microfinance is the "museum" of cultural practice, the realm of NGOs who lend to women and deploy cultural shame and social pressure in order to recover loans. The "exhibition" is SEDO, the future that cannot ever be achieved but that must be performed. It is thus that Elyachar (2005: 2) makes note of the Exhibition of the Products of the Youth Micro Industries funded by the Social Fund. Such exhibitions were lauded by Social Fund administrators as crucial tools in the work of SEDO. What is on display here is a "performance of labor" (Elyachar 2002: 503). Such exhibitions perform the distinction between an advanced economy where successful small and medium enterprises generate formal-sector jobs for educated youth and an informal economy where poor households survive through social networks and microenterprises. Yet, it is perhaps the informal economy, fueled by microfinance, that presents to Egypt an image of its own future. And perhaps the most significant performance is this: that the Social Fund, a sprawling public-sector bureaucracy, subsidized by donors and dispensing subsidized loans, is meant to oversee Egypt's new economy, one populated by free-market entrepreneurs.

These performances are embedded in a performance of development. The Social Fund, underwritten by donors and closely managed by the Egyptian state, is meant to disseminate and implement a decentralized, privatized, and market-driven model of development. It is a performance of sovereignty, at once a reward to Egypt for having made what one USAID official (December 2005) called the "good choice of an open door policy," and a tool for managing such an economy in keeping with the dictates of donors. It is also a performance of the "social contract," one where the state remains visible as a locus of development capital, one where there are persistent expectations that the educated youth will find permanent, formal-sector desk jobs, and yet where there is a "relocation of public welfare to the private sector, to NGOs, and to other civil associations" (Ismail 2006: 67). Such performances point to key structural features of millennial development in Egypt. Two, in particular, are worth noting: the militarization of aid and the privatization of development.

Next to Israel, Egypt is America's most important geopolitical partner in the Middle East. The USAID 2005 annual report on Egypt thus states that the two countries "share strategic interests that include combating terrorism." This partnership was cemented in the Camp David Accords signed by Egyptian President Anwar Sadat and Israeli Prime Minister Menachem Begin in 1978 and brokered by the US President Jimmy Carter. The Camp David Accords set the stage for the 1979 Egypt–Israel peace treaty, the withdrawal of Israel from the Sinai peninsula, and a commitment by the US to several billion dollars of annual grants and aid to both Egypt and Israel. USAID thus notes that in the last three decades, it has channeled $28 billion in aid to Egypt, "by far the largest amount of development aid given to any country in the world by the United States" (http://www.usaid.gov/ our_work/features/egypt/, accessed January 16, 2009).

The flows of funds via USAID are only a part of the story. It is estimated that since 1975 Egypt has received over $50 billion in "US largesse" (Levinson 2004). In the context of the Cold War, the unceasing Arab–Israeli hostilities, and now the "war on terror," it seems that "Egypt was worth every penny of the billions of dollars in U.S. aid that it received" (Alterman 2006). But commentators lament that these billions have "engendered little goodwill on Egypt's streets" (Alterman 2006). It is therefore worth taking a closer look at the structure of such aid. Of the $50 billion channeled to Egypt in the three decades between 1975 and 2005, $1.3 billion annually or a total of approximately $39 billion is military aid, a sum which amounts to 80 percent of Egypt's military budget and that is seen as propping up a "dictatorial regime" (Kelly 2006). The US State Department justifies such aid as helping a "strategic partnership with Egypt," which is "a cornerstone of our foreign policy in the Middle East." Such military aid quite literally buys the US military access to Egypt's airspace, priority passage for American navy vessels through the Suez Canal, and the utilization of Egyptian security forces for "extraordinary rendition" and torture programs that have become a key part of the "war on terror" (Kelly 2006). These deals provide the answer to the question posed by a *Washington Post* editorial (May 4, 2006): "Why does the administration continue to give nearly $2 billion each year to a government that mocks President Bush's democracy initiative?" In 2008, the US renewed its commitments, unveiling a ten-year $13 billion military aid promise to Egypt and a $30 billion military aid promise to Israel (Yom 2008).

The term "aid" deserves closer scrutiny. Military aid from the US to Egypt is made up almost exclusively of Foreign Military Financing (FMF) grants or "Congressionally appropriated funds that have bankrolled purchases of such advanced combat hardware . . . By law, FMF monies must be spent on American-made weaponry" (Yom 2008). Indeed, at any talk of cutting military aid to Egypt, large defense companies lobby against such a move. Egypt's FMF aid comes with another feature: cash-flow financing. Such an arrangement allows Egypt to buy weaponry on credit, in excess of its FMF allocation (Yom 2008). What seems to be aid turns out to not only be a purchase of American commodities but also a purchase financed through credit. This is also the "pollution of free money," this time in the corridors of lobbying in Washington DC.

Such a logic is not unique to military aid. It also pervades economic assistance to Egypt. In a stunning calculation, Timothy Mitchell (2006: 238) demonstrates that much of USAID's economic assistance to Egypt was allocated to American corporations. Through mechanisms such as the

Commodity Import Program, Egypt purchased grain, agricultural commodities, and agricultural and industrial equipment such that 58 percent of the economic assistance was spent in the US rather than on development projects in Egypt. Of the remaining 42 percent, Mitchell argues, a substantial chunk was also spent in the US or on American contractors in Egypt for services ranging from construction to consulting. In other words, the economic assistance provided by USAID to Egypt served as a "form of state support to the American corporate sector, while working in Egypt to dismantle state supports" (Mitchell 2006: 240). It also created a "crippling dependence" of Egypt on "imports of American food, machinery, and technology" (Mitchell 2006: 240). Thus, while USAID proudly lists the billions of dollars it has allocated to Egypt, it is evident that this too is a performance of development. The aid that seems to flow to Egypt turns out to flow back to the US, thereby sealing the Washington consensus on poverty.

Another crucial element of development in Egypt is the rise of religiosity, an issue that rarely came up in the interviews that I conducted or in the reports and institutional presentations, conferences, and data that I mined. Economic liberalization in Egypt not only set into motion a process of informalization and economic insecurity but also activated a "religious register of charity" (Ismail 2006: 74). Egyptian Islamism can be understood as "a complex web of dispersed and heterogeneous organizations, activities, and sympathies around a distinct core embodied in the reformist Muslim Brotherhood, which aimed to Islamicize the society at the grassroots" (Bayat 2007: 137). It has led to the formation of religious welfare associations, those that do the work that the state no longer does. In other words, the privatization of development has also been an Islamicization of development. Thus, in poor Cairene neighborhoods such as Bulaq-al-Dakrur where microfinance NGOs such as Al-Tadamun recruit poor women as clients and where liberalization eroded formal-sector jobs, there is a thick network of Islamist organizations that seek to provide "poverty relief," "social welfare," and "charity" (Ismail 2006: xiiii). It is important to note that, in Egypt, such forms of Islamist charity cannot be read as a religious counterpoint to neoliberal discourse and practice. Indeed, it can be argued that "militant Islamism, a middle-class movement preoccupied with moral politics and ideological struggles, fails to act as the social movement of the urban disenfranchised who may lend support to Islamists only contingently" (Bayat 2007: 580).

Rather than a social movement or federation of the poor, it is thus more appropriate to view the Islamicization of development as a privatized network that casts poverty in quite neoliberal frameworks. Islamic charity targets the "deserving poor," insisting that the poor have to present themselves as entrepreneurial and disciplined (Ismail 2006; Atia 2008). Here too the fear of the "pollution of free money" pervades. As a USAID administrator boldly declared during an interview (December 2005), microfinance could only be for the "economically active poor" and not for the "lazy, poor Egyptian on the street." Islamic charity also seeks out its appropriate subjects of development, celebrating traits of entrepreneurship, discipline, and personal responsibility and rejecting appearances of laziness, dependence, and sloth.

Such judgments about character and culture have an extensive genealogy: they can be traced to late nineteenth-century colonial ethnographies such as Edward Lane's widely circulated *Manners and Customs of the Modern Egyptians*, a text that was particularly concerned with the "indolence" and "sensuality" of Egyptians (Mitchell 1988: 106). But it can also be traced, as Timothy Mitchell (1988: 107) brilliantly notes, to late nineteenth-century Egyptian interlocutors of liberalism, scholars such as Tahtawi, who were to take on issues of industriousness, self-help, and productive labor as key themes in their work. Such Egyptian elites were to equate national progress with the "habit of industry," to translate books on self-help, and to form the "Self-Help Society" in Alexandria in 1886. The inheritors of a colonial liberalism, these elites were to forge an Egyptian nationalism in this language of self-help (Mitchell 1988: 108). Their discourses and practices haunt the business associations and Islamist charities of contemporary Egypt.

The Social Fund for Development presents itself as a vehicle of decentralization and privatization. Yet, a large proportion of private voluntary organizations, NGOs, and welfare associations in Egypt today are Islamic. A UNDP (2003b: 109) report notes that in many "slum areas" of Cairo, "all NGOs belonged to mosque based associations." How is the secular state, that important node of geopolitical forces, to manage such an entanglement? It is possible to read the authoritarian regime that the Egyptian state visits on NGOs—the mandatory registration with the Ministry of Social Affairs, the scrutiny and surveillance, the NGO laws, the censorship and arrests—as an anxiety about human rights and democratization (see Fouad et al. 2005). It is also possible to argue that USAID and other donors can "encourage incremental democratization by relying on service-oriented NGOs" (Denoux 2005: 94). But civil society in Egypt today is saturated with Islamism. The Egyptian state's performance of secular development, enacted through microfinance and through institutions such as the Social Fund, is perhaps meant to tackle the Islamist challenge. Not because the challenge is Islamist, but because it is the most sustained political challenge to the regime. Yet the state surely knows, as do its sponsors of military aid and economic assistance, that this Islamism is ultimately the face of both democratization and privatization in Egypt.

In my analysis of microfinance and development in Egypt, I have repeatedly used the term "performance." I do not mean to imply that development in Egypt is somehow less real, less authentic than it is in other places. Instead, I submit that the performance of development is a reality. It is so not only because it comes to be accepted and legitimized as common sense, but also because there are "rents" to be had on such a performance. In short, the performance of development also generates capital.

The concept of "rentierism" is well established in the study of Middle East political economy. Rent is a "reward for ownership of all natural resources" (Beblawi 1990: 85). Most often associated with natural resources such as oil, a rentier economy is one "which relies on substantial external rent"; a rentier state is one where the "government is the principal recipient of the external rent" (Beblawi 1990: 87–88). The long history of development and dependence in Egypt can be interpreted as one of a rentier economy, one reliant on abundant aid from the US (Luciani 1990: 81). Such American aid has created a new rentier class, a "flourishing consultancy—legal, technical, economic, etc.—business to prepare proposals for aid consideration. A new social class—lawyers, consultants, financial analysts, lobbyists, brokers etc.—is on the rise everywhere" (Beblawi 1990: 97–98). This is a "hard currency market" where "bilingual intellectuals" are able to capitalize on the implementation of the development agenda, what may be understood as a form of "NGO rent seeking" (Carapico 2000).

Rents are often seen as signs of corruption or as evidence of an unproductive economy. This, critics argue, is how USAID has "polluted" the field of development with "free money." I believe it would be a mistake to see Egypt's development rentierism solely in this light. As the performance of development is a reality, so the rents on development are productive of social class, capital accumulation, and even that rare thing in contemporary Egypt: salaried desk jobs. Elyachar (2006: 417) notes that the young microentrepeneurs who are the targets of development policy, came to realize this as well and "aspired to transform themselves from the objects of research into the subjects and producers of research . . . to retain control over artifacts that could, given the right conditions, be exchanged for money." It turns out that the production of development knowledge can be a profitable enterprise. For the Egyptian state itself, the performance of development ensures the flow of development capital. It is an instance of what may be called "spectacular accumulation," the "self-conscious making of a spectacle as a necessary aid to gathering investment funds" (Tsing 2004: 57). This is the productivity rather than pollution of free money.

THE BENEVOLENT LOAN

Every year, as part of its omniscient view of microfinance, the MIX, based in Washington DC and founded by CGAP, produces a *Benchmarking Arab Microfinance* report. Such reports, with their outline of "profitability and sustainability," are circulated and taken up as authoritative guides to the microfinance industry. The latest report, *Benchmarking Arab Microfinance 2006*, released in 2008 and co-produced by the Sanabel network, an Arab microfinance network also established by CGAP, presents data on 37 Arab microfinance institutions from nine different Arab countries. It provides an overview of best practices and success stories. It also outlines the limited outreach of Egyptian microfinance institutions, who together serve only 2 percent of the poor in a country where over 40 percent of the population lives under the international poverty line. The report concludes that Arab microfinance institutions do not fare well in comparison to global standards of performance, recording "negative returns in 2006, as a result of low revenues" and thus being "outshone by the more mature Asian and Latin American regions, but also by its equally young Eastern European/Central Asian counterpart" (MIX 2008: 7). The loss-making Arab microfinance institutions were found to have "a much greater share of the portfolio at risk of default (5.7%) . . . than global norms (1.4%)." The MIX attributes such problems to increased loan defaults, a result of "conflicts in Lebanon and Palestine," as well as to the high cost of money in countries such as Egypt where microfinance institutions struggled to access commercial funds (MIX

2008: 8). The latter must of course be understood against the backdrop of a changing development agenda, where USAID seeks to "set free" its Egyptian microfinance institutions and reduces the flow of subsidized capital to such institutions.

The trends outlined in the report are borne out in Lebanon. Here, as in Bangladesh, civil society organizations seeking to reconstruct the country and provide humanitarian assistance in the wake of war (in this case the long civil war and the Israeli invasion of 1983–1984) shifted, by the early 1990s, to "development." These include Caritas, a Catholic charity, AEP (Association d'entraide Professionelle), a mutual-aid association, and the Makhzoumi Foundation, a philanthropic organization. Inspired by the Grameen Bank, many of these organizations adopted microfinance as a strategy of development. But unlike Bangladesh, the prominent microfinance institutions in Lebanon are those that were established by US NGOs—Al-Majmoua by Save the Children, and Ameen by Cooperative Housing Foundation (CHF), now known as CHF International—each underwritten by a USAID grant.

Such a pattern bears striking resemblance to Egypt. While Lebanese microfinance institutions were never fully products of USAID, they nevertheless depended on USAID funding. In an interview (May 2006), a top official at USAID Lebanon talked proudly of having stopped grants and loans to microfinance institutions in 2002. "Our aim is to ensure sustainability. It is time for the microfinance institutions to access commercial funds. Money has a cost and the microfinance institutions have to now bear the cost." Indeed, during the summer of 2006, when I conducted interviews with the staff of Lebanese microfinance institutions, the quest for funds was fully underway in Lebanon. Take for example Al-Majmoua. Established in 1998 through a USAID grant and as a spin-off from Save the Children, the organization is now a partner of the Grameen Foundation. By 2006, unable to rely any longer on USAID funds, Al-Majmoua was seeking new sources of capital. "We are in an overbanked economy," noted Dr Youssef Fawaz, director (May 2006). "There are 800 branches of commercial banks in this tiny country and yet there is very little money for us. Lebanon is overflowing in cash but its banks and capital markets are risk averse."

But there is another landscape of development capital: super-institutions established within the Lebanese state by international donors. These include the $20 million Community Development Program (CDP), established by the World Bank and the $31 million Economic and Social Fund for Development (ESFD) established by the European Union ($25 million from European Union and $6 million from the Government of Lebanon) both in 2002. While the CDP made it clear that it would not fund microfinance, the ESFD stated that it would divide its efforts between community development and job creation, with microfinance as an important component of the latter. As in the case of other Social Funds, including that of Egypt, the ESFD exists both within and outside the state. It was "established to mitigate the negative effects of globalization and privatization" and to provide, as one of its top administrators put it (July 2006), a "soft landing for Lebanon as it achieves ascension to the World Trade Organization." He noted:

> We are cutting and pasting from Egypt using both a microfinance and a small and medium enterprises strategy to create jobs. This is a highly entrepreneurial culture but there is a shortage of capital. The SFD [Social Fund for Development] can remedy this by lending cheap money to banks and ensuring that banks lend to entrepreneurs.

The ESFD decided to disburse 1.2 million euros of "cheap money" through a bidding process. "Those microfinance institutions that bid with the lowest interest rate for the final borrower—while showing at the same time that the rate would cover all operational and financial costs—would win access to the EU funds to be used for onlending" (Brandsma and Burjrjee 2004: 54). Al-Majmoua put in the winning bid. But the bid soon turned out to be what Al-Majmoua director, Dr Youssef Fawaz, called (June 2006) a "financial disaster." The low interest rates demanded by the ESFD not only had to be cross-subsidized by other programs of Al-Majmoua but also came with expensive bank guarantees and cumbersome conditionalities including monthly monitoring and audits. This was neither cheap money nor a benevolent loan. In an interview (June 2006), a top-ranking ESFD official, shouldered some of the blame, saying that he and others had failed to "educate" European Union legislators about microfinance:

> The European Union wanted a bank guarantee for the loan to microfinance institutions and yet the point of microfinance is that there is no such guarantee or collateral—not between the microfinance client and the microfinance

institution, and not between the microfinance institution and the donor. We lost the trust of microfinance institutions by asking for such a guarantee.

Here again is a composition of debt, discipline, and dependence. Microfinance organizations such as Al-Majmoua are compelled by USAID to be profitable and sustainable; their performance is benchmarked by MIX in relation to such global norms; and yet they must bid, below cost, for development capital such that the European Union can claim that it is supporting civil society organizations that lend to poor women at low interest rates. "How can you call yourself a donor," asked Ziad Halaby, director of Ameen (June 2006), of the ESFD, "when you impose such conditions that are contrary to best practice and common sense?" But ESFD officials also expressed considerable doubt about the microfinance sector in Lebanon. One of them stated:

> CGAP argues for high interest rates and that is fine. It's proven by demand and often the only other alternative the poor have is moneylenders. But I think the microfinance institutions can charge lower interest rates. If they are frugal, attend fewer international conferences, buy economy class tickets, and move their offices out of fancy neighborhoods like Ras Beirut . . . Our work with Al-Majmoua tells us that the microfinance institutions can charge low interest rates but they are not willing to do so in Lebanon.

The doubt was extended further:

> Donors make the mistake of measuring the performance of microfinance institutions by outreach and default. But what we need to watch is how microfinance clients are using these loans—for televisions, school fees, consumption—microfinance institutions turn a blind eye to all of this. If we are interested in job creation, how can such loans create jobs?

It is not surprising that such circulation of doubt would in turn impede the circulation of development capital. In the face of persistent capital shortages, microfinance institutions in Lebanon have devised new ways of operating. Initially operating with a group lending methodology, with loans ranging between $200–$1,800, Al-Majmoua has recently expanded into individual lending, with loans ranging between $500–$7,500. These loans serve clients that are less poor. By the end of 2006, 75 percent of Al-Majmoua's active clients were in the Individual Loan program. By 2003, Ameen had transformed itself into a for-profit company, servicing the "microloan portfolios of commercial banks on a fee-for-service basis" (Brandsma and Burjrjee 2004: 54). Halaby, director of Ameen, thus presented his organization as a "promoter," recruiting clients and assessing risk for the more financially conservative banks. But he still asked why USAID was no longer supporting microfinance in Lebanon. "Why is this the case if microfinance is the miracle of development?" As if in response to his own question, he noted the sharp contradictions that mark the discourses and practices of donors: "they want us to attract commercial investment, to have a first-rate loan portfolio, they want us to be sustainable, and they also want us to serve the poor." By 2006, the ESFD itself seemed to be turning away from microfinance organizations with administrators noting in interviews that more important work in job creation may lie in "changing the culture of banks," of encouraging them to see the "virgin markets" that exist in the informal sector and small enterprises.

The year 2006 was of course also the summer of war in Lebanon. The MIX report is eerily silent on such matters, barely noting "conflicts" in Lebanon. The Grameen Foundation USA, of which Al-Majmoua is a partner, reports that in July 2006, the organization's PAR "skyrocketed to nearly 70%" as "business halted for many of its clients" (http://www.grameenfoundation. org/where_we_work/middle_east_north_africa/lebanon/al_majmoua/, accessed March 11, 2009). The "conflict" makes an appearance in USAID narratives of Lebanon, which highlight the $230 million in "humanitarian reconstruction and security assistance" promised by the Bush government to Lebanon. The aid comes draped in the language of benevolence and freedom: "America is making a long-term commitment to help the people of Lebanon because we believe every person deserves to live in a free, open society that respects the rights of all" (http://www.usaid.gov/lb/, accessed January 30, 2008). It is language that elides the complexity of the 2006 war between Israel and Hezbollah, one where a militia force rather than a nation-state was to declare victory.

Indeed, the most striking absence in the MIX reports on Arab microfinance is Hezbollah. It is a well-established fact that Hezbollah's microfinance program is the largest in Lebanon and possibly in the entire Middle East. Serving approximately 40,000 clients in 2006, it garners high praise from all other microfinance institutions and development organizations. In an interview (June 2006), officials of the Christian charity Caritas noted that while Hezbollah exerts hegemony in many areas of Lebanon it does not interfere with the projects of other organizations and, most important, it does good work. ESFD administrators were open in their admiration, noting that they had tried to strike a partnership with Hezbollah but could not agree on the terms of interest. The directors of Ameen and Al-Majmoua respectively admitted that their operations were overshadowed by the size and reach of that of Hezbollah. It is only USAID that remained mostly silent on the matter, with top officials claiming that they had not heard of Hezbollah's microfinance program. Yet it is the fear of Hezbollah, the memory of the 1983 bombing of US marine barracks, that casts a shadow on the existence of USAID in Beirut. Located on a hill in Dbeyih, in Christian Beirut, at a far distance from the Shiite neighborhoods of Hezbollah, the USAID compound is a military camp, complete with machine gunners, watchtowers, and armored vehicles. It is a space that constantly anticipates terror. It is less able, I argue, to anticipate Hezbollah's complex repertoire of development strategies, to create a "counterweight to Hezbollah's social and economic activities in South Lebanon and Bekaa Valley" (USAID 2002: 8). After all, it is Hezbollah's microfinance organization, Al-Qard al-Hassan, that bears the title "The Benevolent Loan."

In the summer of 2006, the world was transfixed by a new round of war between Israel and Lebanon. But the war was in fact between Israel and Hezbollah. The war provided a crucial glimpse into the ways in which Hezbollah has emerged as the de facto state in southern Lebanon and the southern suburbs of Beirut. Founded in 1984, Hezbollah, the "party of God," is the maturation of a religious militia. High on the US's list of terrorist organizations, Hezbollah is a military force but it is also a political party with representation in the Lebanese government. In addition, Hezbollah manages a vast social welfare and development apparatus whose work on behalf of poor and displaced Shiites is recognized as "radical planning" (Saliba 2000). In the wake of the 2006 war, the global media was abuzz with stories of Hezbollah's swift and efficient "charity," a response that easily outflanked the Lebanese state and overseas aid and assistance. Worth and Fattah (2006) reported that Hezbollah was handing out "grants of $12,000 in stacks of American dollars as part of its vigorous campaign to help families whose houses were destroyed over the past month."

173

Hundreds of volunteers had been deployed to embark on a swift reconstruction (Worth and Fattah 2006). It turned out that Hezbollah is as much an apparatus of development as it is an apparatus of war.

Since its inception, Hezbollah has operated two sets of development institutions: those that provide services to targeted beneficiaries (widows, families of martyrs, wounded guerrillas), and those that have a broader scope of service provision. Among the latter are Jihad al-Binaa (Jihad for Construction); Al-Imdad (The Resource); Islamic Society for Health; and Al-Qard al-Hassan (The Benevolent Loan) (Harb and Leenders 2005). Al-Qard al-Hassan, Hezbollah's microfinance program, is reputed to have over 40,000 clients and is thus easily the largest microfinance organization in Lebanon and possibly in the entire Middle East. For example, a *Wall Street Journal* article marvels at the efficiency and scope of this finance operation (Higgins 2006). It features Hussein Al-Shami, noting that while he has been named by the US Treasury Department as "Specially Designated Global Terrorist," he is also the "microcredit czar, "running an enterprise the US normally supports: making microloans to nurture a culture of self-help capitalism."

Hezbollah's work can be seen as a legacy of the political economy of civil war in Lebanon where competing militias, from those of the Druze to those of the Maronites, created systems of "para-legal public and social services" (Harik 1994: 28; Sawalha 2001), those that replaced infrastructure provided by the state. All of Hezbollah's services have outlasted the war. Today, Hezbollah's charity and development work continues to be embedded in its ideological and military struggles, in the creation of what it sees as a "resistance society" (Harb and Leenders 2005). To this end, Hezbollah conceptualizes its development work as a foundational element of resistance, a continuation of its open letter to the *umma*, or global Muslim community, in 1985 that was a "declaration of the downtrodden in Lebanon and in the World" (Norton 1999: 12). The general manager of Hezbollah's Jihad al-Binaa (Jihad for Construction) thus notes that Hezbollah fights Israel through the "development of Lebanon." Jihad al-Binaa, with its construction of housing and infrastructure, is a "weapon in the struggle" (Sachs 2000). The relationship between Hezbollah and the "people" is key. A car mechanic in southern Lebanon, when asked about Hezbollah, argues that there can be no line drawn between Hezbollah and communities: "The trees in the south say, We are Hezbollah. The stones say, We are Hezbollah.

If the people cannot talk, the stones will say it" (Tavernise 2006). Indeed, such a relationship may be more expansive than has been imagined, for while Hezbollah is a Shiite organization functioning in neighborhoods and communities that are overwhelming Shiite, the empirical research on Hezbollah indicates that Hezbollah's services are available to all who exist in a neighborhood, be they Christian or Muslim (Norton 1999).

In a regional context where development NGOs are for the most part artifacts of foreign aid, Hezbollah seems to be the genuinely native and local institution of development. In an interview (June 2006), top Hezbollah official Ali Fayyad insisted that Hezbollah's role as a "social provider" spoke to how it is "inside communities": "we are part of the community, we know and understand the needs of the people." In this sense, its loans can be understood as truly "good loans," free of the geopolitical conditionalities that remain attached to the flows of development capital that saturate Egypt and seek to penetrate Lebanon. Yet, Hezbollah's military, charity, and development activities rely on Syria and Iran for funding. Lebanon itself is a puppet of numerous geopolitical forces and the seemingly autonomous and radical Hezbollah may not be any different. After all, the various NGOs established and operated by Hezbollah "grew out of Iranian foreign policy in Lebanon." Each "depended entirely on Iranian funding and was created by a mother or model NGO based in Iran" (Fawaz 2000: 23). In other words, while Hezbollah's NGOs may have evolved "from their foreign-run, top-down, locally unpopular origins into organizations involving residents' participation, in the conception, design, and implementation of service delivery," their "foreign" origins are undisputed (Fawaz 1998: 18). Hezbollah's "good loan" then also turns out to be a composition of debt, discipline, and dependence.

In previous work (Roy 2009), I have argued that Hezbollah must be understood as an "infrastructure of populist mediation," one that is able to govern subjects and govern spaces through various technologies and norms. A crucial technology of governing is the production of knowledge. Acutely aware of the mutual constitution of power and knowledge, Hezbollah produces and maintains fine-grained knowledge of its communities. After the 2006 war, when Hezbollah set about rebuilding the southern suburbs of Beirut and southern Lebanon, it became apparent that the organization had the interest and capacity in relation to producing quick and efficient surveys of damage, in creating systems to compensate war victims, and ultimately in launching an ambitious "reconstruction" agenda. In producing such knowledge, Hezbollah actively deploys a cadre of experts—architects, engineers, researchers, doctors. Its Center for Contemporary Society and Development (CCSD), established in 1988 and located in the Shiite southern suburbs of Beirut, documents and diagnoses poverty and exclusion and also articulates an intellectual agenda for alternative forms of development. Its director, Dr Ali Fayyad, is a public figure and intellectual in the Middle East, and his ideas circulate in a web of discourses that extend well beyond Lebanon and even connect up with the public intellectuals of the Muslim Brotherhood in Egypt. In an interview (June 2006), Fayyad diagnosed poverty and underdevelopment in Lebanon as a symptom of the country's dependence on "foreign entities." Lebanon is assailed by those "with interests in the region," by "so much capital circulating through it," but these entities are "not interested in removing unemployment or poverty." And so, he argued, "it falls to NGOs, community organizations, and civil society to make a difference."

What is particularly striking about Hezbollah's apparatus of charity and development is its cultivation of an "ethics of the self," ways of being that mandate and foster discipline, including financial discipline. This is particularly apparent in how Hezbollah conceptualizes and manages its microfinance program, Al-Qard al-Hassan. Started in 1982, by what its director described (June 2006) as "a group of community leaders who wanted, in keeping with Islamic principles, to help the poor and needy," the program was transformed from a focus on charity to development. Al-Qard al-Hassan is as interested in the repayment and recovery of loans as any other microfinance organization. Serving approximately 40,000 clients and disbursing about 25,000 loans per year with an average loan size of $1,000, Al-Qard al-Hassan uses various techniques to enact discipline. Clients, both men and women, must enlist in the organization, paying a "subscription fee" for membership. This in turn serves as a guarantee for the loan. While the director of Al-Qard al-Hassan insisted that this was the only form of loan guarantee, staff at other Lebanese microfinance organizations noted that Al-Qard al-Hassan regularly holds the jewelry of women as collateral for loans. It is thus that Al-Qard al-Hassan can claim to serve poor and needy women and also claim to have "very few repayment problems." Such forms of discipline are reinforced by a network of "volunteer sisters," Hezbollah cadres who are not part of the overwhelmingly male ranks of professional, salaried development staff but whose "volunteer" work is a crucial element of the functioning of the apparatus. Initially resisted by the Iranian "mother institutions," these women visit beneficiary families on a weekly basis to "learn of their problems" (Fawaz 1998: 56–59). When the director of Al-Qard al-Hassan declares that "we have the trust of the people," it is a trust that is created and enforced by an elaborate apparatus—of guarantees, collateral, and volunteer sisters. It is also a trust that makes a sharp distinction between charity and development. The poorest of the poor are explicitly excluded from Al-Qard al-Hassan and their cases are transferred to Hezbollah's charity organizations such as Takaful (Mutual Support) and Al-Imdad (The Resource). Such organizations operate quite differently. While still encouraging self-sufficiency and entrepreneurship, Al-Imdad tolerates default rates that are as high as 80 percent (Fawaz 1998: 40), a lack of discipline that has no place in Al-Qard al-Hassan.

Hezbollah presents itself as an Islamic counter-force to American empire and Zionism. Thus, the streets of the southern suburbs of Beirut, where the CCSD, Al-Qard al-Hassan, and many other Hezbollah organizations have their offices, are lined with images of Hezbollah's "martyrs"—the fighters who have sacrificed their lives for the resistance society. These are real wars—from that waged by Hezbollah against the Israeli Defense Forces to the American "war on terror" waged against entities such as Hezbollah. One of the weapons of the latter is the criminalization of flows of money to Islamic charities and Fayyad claimed that such restrictions have impeded Hezbollah's ability to fund its charity and development work. Yet, it is not possible to interpret Hezbollah as an Islamic alternative to neoliberalism. Hezbollah's microfinance program sounds precisely the same themes as the Washington consensus on poverty. It constructs a "dataspace" that renders transparent poor neighborhoods and communities, thereby constructing financial clients. It valorizes an ethics of the self, founded on the values of entrepreneurship, personal responsibility, and self-sufficiency. It uses women as instruments of development, deploying them as "volunteer sisters" but limiting their participation in the "legitimate space" of a "culture of motherhood" (Zaatari 2006: 58). It seeks to professionalize microfinance, painstakingly policing the distinction between charity and such forms of development.

At first glance, such themes seem to reinforce the ideologies of neoliberalism. Yet, it is not sufficient to extend such a label to Hezbollah, for the internal struggles are more complex. Hezbollah's development programs seek to combat *takhalluf*, or backwardness, but in doing so they worry about "creating *takhalluf* in the form of dependency" (Deeb 2006: 183). Thus the distinction between charity and development is made. Such concerns with dependence can be traced to how Hezbollah conceptualizes the fate of the Shiite ghetto, or al-Dahiya, the southern suburbs of Beiruit. Hezbollah has shifted the framing of the Shia question from that of being disinherited (*mahrumin*) to that of being disempowered (*mustada'afin*). "The nuance is essential, as the latter invokes an opportunity for transformation and change, whereas the former involves stagnation" (Harb and Leenders 2005: 189). Microfinance is an important strategy for Hezbollah, for it promises to foster economic independence and transformation.

Scholars remain divided in their assessment of Hezbollah's approach to development. Some argue that Hezbollah's division of the world into "oppressors (*mustakbirin*) and oppressed (*mustada'afin*)" is an "Islamicization of class analysis," one that unites the Shia as a "community class" of "peasants and farmers, the laborers and the poor, the oppressed and deprived, the workers and homeless" (Saad-Ghorayeb 2002: 16–18). Others argue that the main message is not that of class conflict but rather of "moral behavior." To ensure such morality, Hezbollah creates an Islamic order of "clerical supremacy" (Hamzeh 2004: 42, 134). Indeed, it would be difficult to sustain the idea of an impoverished Shia community class with the reality of Shiite wealth both within and beyond Lebanon. This wealthy Shiite diaspora underwrites quite a bit of Hezbollah's development and charity work (Harik 1996; Fawaz 2000).

The resistance inscribed in Hezbollah's resistance society does not extend then to the mechanisms of capital accumulation that are at work in Lebanon. Indeed, while Hezbollah is often seen as the voice of the dispossessed, urbanist Mona Harb's (2001) research shows that Hezbollah has not been interested in resisting urban redevelopment even when it entails the displacement of the poor. Instead, Hezbollah has sought to shape the terms of resettlement and compensation, thus maintaining power and control over its Shiite territories in Beirut. The urban poor enter into such negotiations, represented by Hezbollah. Such negotiations rarely challenge the idea of progress that is written into such development plans. Harb (2001: 118) notes that Hezbollah has argued that urban renewal is in the national interest, and that the poor must therefore make way for the modernization projects that are necessary to transform Beirut into a world-class city. It is worth noting the language used by Hezbollah in such discourses, for it is that of *tamaddun*. While Harb translates *tamaddun* as modernization, the term is perhaps more appropriately translated as "civilization" (see Deeb 2006: 17). It derives from the term *"medina,"* which in Arabic means both city and civilization. It signifies a way of being modern. Here, *takhalluf,* or backwardness, is overcome by "two parallel notions of progress—increased modernization and increased piety" (Deeb 2006: 30).

Can modernization and piety be thus reconciled? What are we to make of Hezbollah's entanglement with the norms and practices of capitalism? Writing in the context of a "politics of piety" in Egypt, anthropologist Saba Mahmood (2005: 192) notes that such engagements

> cannot be analyzed in terms of a conflict between two historically distinct opponents . . . While contemporary Islamist activities identify secular liberalism as a powerful corrosive force within Muslim societies, the discourses in which they do so . . . are indebted to the extension of the secular-liberal project itself.

It is in this light that we can interpret the emergent global phenomenon of "Islamic finance." Such a project seeks to reconcile capitalism with Sharia or Islamic law. It is thus that Islamic bonds, or *sukuk*, are financing the wild, wild west of twenty-first-century capitalism—the off-shore "island" developments of Manama and Dubai. Seeking to attract Muslim investors, governments from Indonesia to Great Britain to France are also issuing *sukuks*, seeking a share of a new finance market that "seems virtuous as well as vigorous." A new industry has crystallized around "Islamic finance," with consultancies such as "Shariah Capital" that partnered with Barclays Capital to create a new hedge-fund platform that is sharia-compliant. It has its own accounting and auditing practices, those that reconcile piety with profit. It relies on the instruments of high finance, such as securitization, claiming them as "authentically Islamic"—in this case because securitization is financing backed by tangible assets rather than exotic derivatives in intangibles (Blease 2008). Take for example the "Islamic Solidarity Fund," a $10 billion Waqf Fund created by the Islamic Development Bank to tackle poverty (AME Info 2008). Microfinance is an important strategy of the Fund, thereby transforming the endowments created by the religious

179

practice of the *waqf* into the seemingly secular and liberal practices of entrepreneurship, economic development, and social progress.

Hezbollah is even more ambitious, seeking to reconcile the vision of a global *umma* animated by the voices of the downtrodden Shia with the vision of a cosmopolitan, capitalist economy. At the close of my interview with him, Ali Fayyad began to talk proudly of what may be understood as *tamaddun*—a civilizing impulse that is manifested in the modernization of the city. He described at some length a new space that had emerged in al-Dahiya: the "Assaha" traditional village (http://www.assahavillage.com, accessed September 15, 2006). A popular restaurant and entertainment complex, Assaha is a project of the al-Mabarrat charity and associated with Fadlallah, rather than directly with Hezbollah (Khechen 2007). But Fayyad claimed it as a key element of Hezbollah's mission of modernization, a marker of its urban cosmopolitanism: "Beirut has had its downtown; we have only had the suburbs and we never felt comfortable in downtown; now we too have our downtown; and everyone will soon come to our downtown. This will be the downtown for all." He expressed admiration for, rather than discomfort with, this urban sensibility of recreation and entertainment, leisure and consumption—good food but no alcohol, *ghazal* readings, the mixing of genders, the mixing of those with "Islamic chador and those with western clothes," massive screens for soccer matches, wireless connectivity, Disneyesque kitsch including Nasrallah memorabilia. Fayyad's words echoed an interview he had given the previous year "We are still a country of 'us' and 'them,' this is a reality. But we do not like it, we do not want it, and we want to move past it" (Ignatius 2005). For Fayyad, the Assaha entertainment complex with an architectural mix of styles and heritages that evokes Lebanon's national past, is meant to show that the Shiia "bear allegiance to the nation." "Everyone thinks that we are more patriotic to religion than to the nation but that is not true. Assaha is a symbol of cultural reconciliation." Assaha survived the bombs that rained down on Al-Dahiya in the summer of 2006. Hezbollah emerged from the war a victorious protector of not only the Shiite ghetto but also Lebanon itself.

The Camps

Lebanon has long been imagined and managed as a geography of territorial enclaves. It is a nation-state that is tenuously held together by a confessional political system such that political power and public office are divided along sectarian lines. On the ground, political parties not only represent different religious groups, but also govern distinct territories, be it the mountainous Chouf governed by the Druze or the southern suburbs of Beirut, al-Dahiya, governed by the Shiite Hezbollah. Such a system of governance and territoriality is disrupted by Palestinian refugees. Numbering over 400,000, or approximately 10 percent of the Lebanese population, more than half live in 12 refugee camps dispersed across Lebanon. Mainly Sunni Muslims, these refugees are seen as a threat to Lebanon's confessional system of political representation. Their marginalization includes "confinement to bounded, well-defined, and surveilled camps" (Peteet 1996: 27). In these camps, Palestinian refugees are dependent on the United Nations Relief and Works Agency for Palestine Refugees (UNRWA), which is the "main provider of education, health and relief and social service" (http://www.un.org/unrwa/ overview/, accessed November 11, 2008). Zoned as spaces of exception, the camps are meant to be self-governing spaces, run by "popular committees." These popular committees in turn "reflect the strength of third-party interests, in particular those of Syria, to which the Lebanese authorities as well as Palestinian political groups remain subservient" (Knudsen 2005: 219). But they are also subject to the sovereignty of the Lebanese state, falling within rather than beyond its ambit of law (Suleiman 1999: 72). The camps then are a space of multiple sovereignties.

Entrapped in the enclaves that are the camps, Palestinian refugees in Lebanon lack access to the fundamental elements of formal and substantive citizenship in that they

> do not have social and civil rights, and have very limited access to the government's public health or educational facilities and no access to public social services . . . Considered as foreigners, Palestine refugees are prohibited by law from working in more than 70 trades and professions.
>
> (http://www.un.org/unrwa/refugees/lebanon.html,
> accessed February 10, 2009)

The latter restriction is particularly important. While the 1969 Cairo Accords gave Palestinians in camps in Lebanon the right to employment, as well as to form local committees, and to engage in armed struggle, it was repealed in 1987, and since then the Ministry of Labor and Social Affairs has strictly enforced employment restrictions demarcating entire occupations, "from barbering to banking," that are closed to "foreigners" (Peteet 1996: 30). Palestinian refugees have thus had to resort to the "most menial and low-paid jobs" (Peteet 1996: 30). While some of these labor laws were modified in 1999, work permits issued to Palestinians fall far short of those issued to foreign laborers, such as those from Egypt (Knudsen 2007: 8).

Above all, Palestinian refugees in Lebanon face a critical "protection gap" (Knudsen 2007: 2). Seen to be the force that catalyzed the Israeli invasion of 1982, and massacred by the Lebanese Phalange, a Christian militia, in the notorious refugee camps of Shabra and Shatila, the Palestinians have been explicitly excluded from naturalization. The Taif Agreement (section I, h), marking the end of the Lebanese civil war, stated that "there shall be no fragmentation, partition, or settlement of non-Lebanese in Lebanon." It is not surprising then that the Palestinian refugee camps in Lebanon suffer from high rates of poverty and unemployment, higher than those in Palestinian refugee camps elsewhere. Thus, in 1995, UNRWA estimated the unemployment rate among Palestinian refugees in Lebanon at 40 percent, compared to 15 percent in Syria, and 19 percent in Jordan (Suleiman 1997: 399). Indeed, UNRWA states that of its various field offices— Jordan, Syria, West Bank, and Gaza Strip—Lebanon "has the highest percentage of Palestine refugees who are living in abject poverty and who are registered with the Agency's 'special hardship' programme" (http://www.un.org/unrwa/refugees/lebanon.html, accessed February 10, 2009). Such vulnerability is exacerbated by the multiple displacements that Palestinian refugees in Lebanon have experienced.

UNRWA seeks to serve refugees in Lebanon and its other fields of operation through both emergency relief and human development. Since 1991, microfinance has been a key part of UNRWA's activities. Initially launched in the wake of the Gulf War and the first *intifadah*, the program was geared towards the formation of small and medium enterprises. In 1994, the focus shifted to "microfinance inter-mediation" and "informal sector lending" with the "establishment of a new solidarity group-lending product" which targeted women microentrepreneurs (UNRWA 2003: 4). Piloted in the Gaza Strip, the program was eventually extended to other UNRWA sites. In Lebanon, UNRWA officials noted during interviews (May 2006) that their microfinance program was modeled after that of the Grameen Bank with a group lending methodology (without savings) that targeted women in "families with special hardship." "The Microfinance and Microenterprises Programme (MMP) can make Palestinians independent," they argued.

Yet, in Lebanon as in Egypt, the Bangladesh model seems to break down. UNRWA officials shared in considerable detail problems of loan default and their efforts to devise systems of enforcement: "The problem is that the camps are enclaves; the government's reach does not extend to them. They are exceptions to the legal system. Without such law and order how can we enforce promissory notes and take legal action against borrowers?" This too is another conjuncture of debt, discipline, and dependence. In Gaza, microfinance NGOs require borrowers to sign contracts that stipulate "that borrowers who were late with payments more than a specified period of time would be immediately taken to jail by the Palestinian security police." As anthropologist Julia Elyachar (2002: 511) notes, "the security apparatus of a nonstate . . . worked directly for NGOs to ensure that finance originating in International Organizations was collected for the banks."

In the refugee camps of Lebanon, UNRWA has installed a different system. Here, loan guarantees are provided by UNRWA staff, the bulk of whom are Palestinian refugees themselves: "We have access to the salaries of staff and so when a loan is not paid back in time we can simply deduct the amount from the salary. It's a foolproof system." UNRWA accounts indicate that the Lebanese microfinance program runs a default rate of about 10 percent, the risk of which is fully covered by deductions from staff salaries. It is a unique system, one where "UNRWA does not shoulder any risk." While UNRWA's loan portfolio remains intact because of the compensations provided by staff salaries, UNRWA staff must then expend time and energy to recuperate payments. In the words of one UNRWA microfinance administrator:

> There are other means of providing guarantees. We can do it through the NGOs and community based organizations but they write off so many loans that this is no longer microfinance . . . We can also take borrowers to court but we would not go to court as UNRWA. We would sell the debt to banks and then they would collect by going to court. The group model by itself is clearly not enough. We need strong guarantees, blacklists to enforce the group model. Staff salaries are the most effective and efficient as such guarantees.

The camps of Lebanon represent an unmediated negotiation of debt and discipline. I had anticipated a complex structure of negotiation, one managed by the "popular committees" of the camps or by NGOs. This was not the case. The logic was more simple, much more stark: the body of the refugee doubling as borrower and loan collector. In a context of severe economic impoverishment and political disenfranchisement, this double role must be understood as self-exploitation—albeit masked in the language and rhetoric of development. With the fragmentation of political and territorial power in the Palestinian territories, Palestinian refugees including those in the Lebanese camps have lost access to resources, particularly to the salaries and pensions that once flowed to functionaries of the Palestinian Liberation Organization (PLO). And Israel's military siege has literally brought economic activity to a halt in the West Bank and Gaza, a crisis acknowledged by UNRWA as "economic repression" (UNRWA 2003). Amidst this general freeze, the only flow of capital seems to be UNRWA's microfinance loans, made liquid in Gaza by police power and in the Lebanese camps by a "foolproof" system of guarantees.

Yet, UNRWA celebrates its microfinance program as sustainable and self-reliant, "in conformity with the new standards and best practices of the emerging microfinance industry that were being formalised by institutions such as CGAP and USAID" (UNRWA 2003: 5). It states with pride that the program has grown with "no external financing of institutional development or capacity building. This was . . . enhanced by training key staff in the world's foremost microfinance training programme in Boulder" (UNRWA 2003: 4). This too is the frontier of millennial development, one where the bloody horror that is today Gaza is imagined as a "product testing ground . . . an ideal environment for designing and developing various financial products to serve the needs of the poorest" (UNRWA 2003: 5). It is the most poignant performance of development in the Middle East, a heartbreaking conjuncture of debt, discipline, and dependence.

But it is also a deferral of social, economic, and political justice. UNRWA itself is a proxy for a real solution to the transnational problem of Palestinian refugees. Established in 1949, in the wake of the formation of the state of Israel and the displacement of Palestinians, UNRWA was the temporary, stop-gap measure that has now become the permanent development agency providing services and aid to over 4.5 million Palestinian refugees scattered across the Middle East. Today, it is the largest UN agency in the Middle East. At sites such as Lebanon, its microfinance and microenterprise program is a proxy for a solution to the structural marginalization of Palestinian refugees. The rehearsal of best-practice development and "sustainable microfinance" elides the fundamental issue at hand: the denial of citizenship to Palestinians such that they are kept waiting their turn for jobs, housing, legal protection, and territory.

In Lebanon, such denial has been perversely justified as a means to maintain the Palestinian "right to return." It is a deferral of justice that maintains an impossible state of dependence. Shortly after the signing of the Taif Agreement, the so-called Charter of National Reconciliation, Lebanese Prime Minister Rafik Hariri declared that "Lebanon will never, ever integrate Palestinians. They will not receive civic or economic rights, or even work permits." He argued that "integration would take the Palestinians off the shoulder of the international agency [UNRWA] that has supported them since 1948" (Knudsen 2007: 8). And so it has come to be that UNRWA is as declared by Queen Rania of Jordan, "teacher, doctor, and food provider" to the Palestinian refugees (http://www.un.org/unrwa/english. html, accessed February 10, 2009). Only by staying within the camp boundaries do refugees keep their right to UNRWA handouts (Knudsen 2005). Yet, by "being under collective assistance from UNRWA excludes refugees from individual protection by the UNHCR" (Knudsen 2007: 15) the office of the United Nations High Commissioner for Refugees that is charged with the legal protection, asylum, and repatriation of refugees.

In 2005 Hezbollah joined the Lebanese cabinet. Labor and Agriculture Minister Trad Hamadeh issued a memorandum lifting the ban that barred Palestinians from manual and clerical jobs. The memorandum did little to change the status of Palestinian refugees in Lebanon. It did not include "high-status professions requiring membership in professional syndicates (e.g., medicine, engineering, pharmacy), which since 1964 had been reserved for Lebanese citizens" and it maintained "prohibitively high fees" and employer taxes for work permits (Knudsen 2007: 13–14). Yet it symbolically raised the question as to whether Hezbollah, long opposed to the naturalization of Palestinian refugees, was now changing its mind on the "refugee file." Indeed, it seemed that Hezbollah was going to extend its charity and development services to the Palestinian refugee camps, coordinating efforts with UNRWA (Khalili 2007: 283). Was Hezbollah's "benevolent loan" now going to be made available to the figure at the edge of humanity: the Palestinian refugee?

But as Hezbollah cannot be seen as an Islamic alternative to neoliberalism, so it cannot be seen as a native alternative to external geopolitical forces. Hezbollah is a product of these very forces, and its undertaking of development is no less instrumental. Hezbollah's efforts to integrate Palestinian refugees in Lebanon remain limited. And Hezbollah has appropriated the symbols, sites, and cause of the Palestinian refugees to craft its "resistance society." Today, at the Shabra and Shatila camps, site of the 1982 massacre of Palestinians, there is only the narrative of Hezbollah as victorious protector, erasing any memory of Palestinian victimhood and struggle (Khalili 2007: 286). Brotherly solidarity too turns out to be a performance.

The story of the camps can be taken to be an allegory for millennial development at the frontiers of empire. It is a brutal conjuncture of debt, discipline, and dependence, a terrifying performance in some of the world's most hollowed-out economies. Microfinance makes such a performance possible. This performance of development is perhaps the closest that the camps will come to development— to salaried jobs and public-sector employment, albeit with the mandate that salaries be withheld until microfinance loans are successfully collected. Here there is no "free money." Such structural and symbolic violences cannot be blamed solely on imperialism. They encompass forms of power and dominance that are homegrown, that are spun through brotherly solidarity, that craft a "resistance society," and that impose moral order and financial discipline in the name of God.

NOTE

1   Amjad Arbab, director, MISFA (CGAP 2008d).

CHAPTER 5

Subprime Markets
Making Poverty Capital

What is capitalism when there isn't access to capital?

(Alex Counts, president of the Grameen
Foundation, 2006 Microcredit Summit[1])

Dead Aid

One of the latest "stars" to appear on the development scene is Dambisa Moyo, recently anointed by *Time* as one of the world's 100 most influential people. The *New York Times* ran an interview, dubbing her "the anti-Bono" (Solomon 2009). Amidst the anticipation and then release of her book, *Dead Aid*, Moyo has been garnering considerable media attention. She argues vigorously that it is aid from the West that has held back and disenfranchised Africans. Aid, she argues, is the "silent killer of growth" (Moyo 2009: 49). By contrast, she celebrates the achieve-ments of countries that were not thus burdened by aid: "Forty years ago, China was poorer than many African countries. Yes, they have money today, but where did that money come from? They built that, they worked very hard to create a situation where they are not dependent on aid" (Solomon 2009). Her narrative, pitched against global poverty campaigners such as Sachs and Bono, is a replay of William Easterly's scathing critique about aid and development. Bono (2009), in the meantime, continues to argue that aid "is not alms, it's investment. It's not charity, it's justice." He makes aid seem akin to reparations, a righting of the wrongs of a "capitalism on trial."

Moyo's sudden popularity highlights some of the key themes of millennial development. First, the global media has positioned Moyo as an African voice speaking against aid. She is, to borrow a phrase from postcolonial critic Gayatri Chakravorty Spivak (1999: 49), a "Native Informant." In the foreword to Moyo's book, historian Niall Ferguson (2009: ix) notes that she, an "African black woman," is venturing into "a public debate about Africa's economic problems" that has been "colonized" by "non-African white men" as surely as the African continent itself was once colonized—this time by "economists (Paul Collier, William Easterly, Jeffrey Sachs) to the rock stars (Bono, Bob Geldof)." This is of course the same Niall Ferguson who authored the text *Empire* in which he argues that colonialism bestows important benefits—notably markets and democracy—on those colonized.

But Moyo's career is entangled with Wall Street and Washington DC. The *Financial Times* explains:

> Moyo, who is in her thirties, was born in Zambia. Her father, the son of a South African mineworker, is an academic and an anti-corruption campaigner; her mother, the chairwoman of the Indo-Zambian bank. Equipping herself with a rack of degrees, including a Masters from Harvard and a doctorate from Oxford, she has worked for the past eight years as a global economist at Goldman Sachs.
>
> (Wallis 2009)

Moyo also worked for the World Bank for a few years and praises the "reforms" undertaken by the World Bank and IMF but faults them for not more aggressively phasing out aid. She is a figure that cuts across the seemingly separated domains of African critics and Western development bankers. Such hybrid figures abound in the apparatus of millennial development; some are even "double agents," transforming their positions of power and privilege into terrains of contestation and negotiation.

Second, as is the case with most interlocutors of millennial development, she loves microfinance. In the *New York Times* interview, she was asked: "If people want to help out, what do you think they should do with their money if not make donations?" Moyo's answer is brief, swift, and dramatic: "Microfinance. Give people jobs." The response is an indication of the unshakeable belief that both the proponents and opponents of mainstream development hold in microfinance. Indeed, microfinance is *the* icon of millennial development, crystallizing a multitude of aspirations, agendas, interests, and desires. For Moyo, microfinance contains the magic of private enterprise and self-help. Her celebration of microfinance, from Kiva.org to the Grameen Bank, is an instance of what I have earlier designated as "neoliberal populism," a blend of free-market ideology and an interest in the bottom billion. It is thus that she praises the Grameen Bank for a "no donor money" policy (Moyo 2009: 136), ignoring the important subsidies that make possible such a model. Following Hernando de Soto, she argues that the core problem is not that the poor do not have assets or savings but rather that "inefficient" financial markets impede their use. Her phrase, "billions washing about" (Moyo 2009: 137) is reminiscent of Yunus's (2009) statement that "we live in an ocean of money" (http://knowledge.wharton.upenn.edu/article.cfm?articleid=2243, accessed May 30, 2009). Niall Ferguson (2008: 280, 2), in his own text, *The Ascent of Money*, not only celebrates Grameen "housewives," but also insists that money—financial innovation, the globalization of finance—"is the root of most progress."

Third, Moyo expresses great faith in global financial markets. As a banker at Goldman Sachs, she worked in the capital market helping mostly emerging countries to issue bonds (Solomon 2009). She argues, in an interview with the *Financial Times*, that "by making life expensive for bad debtors, the bond markets compel governments to spend money more wisely. Aid, meanwhile, since it keeps on coming, has precisely the opposite effect" (Wallis 2009). This is of course the ideology of self-help writ large, now applied not only to the entepreneurial poor but also to entire countries. Moyo vigorously sounds the themes of accountability and discipline—that bond markets instill accountability and discipline—that are prominent in the discourses of CGAP. This, she seems to suggest, is the key to making Africa work. Her narrative is similar to that of one of the "white men" identified by Ferguson, Paul Collier, whose text *The Bottom Billion* also ruminates on how Africa does and does not work. While Collier (2007) calls for decisive military intervention and some types of aid, like Moyo, he insists that the lack of economic growth is one of the main ailments of poor countries and their bottom billion. Moyo places her bet on bond markets, Collier places his on international laws and charters, those that will ensure transparency and guide investment.

Moyo's proclamations, made as Wall Street crashes around us, require closer scrutiny. Are financial markets disciplined and accountable or are they reckless and secretive? A few years ago, the activist and founder of Focus on the Global South, Walden Bello (2006), argued that "one of the reasons there is such enthusiasm for microcredit in establishment circles these days is that it is a market-based mechanism that has enjoyed some success where other market-based programs have crashed." This perhaps holds true even more now. Today, the contrast between a world of aid that is corrupt and addictive and financial markets that build character and encourage competition seems at best naive, and at worst disingenuous. After all, these global financial markets have now been exposed as extreme and destructive forms of speculation. Expressing a now growing rage, the American comedian, Jon Stewart, described the system as "two markets"—"the long-term market that Americans earnestly thought would sustain their 401(k)'s, and the fast-moving, short-term 'real market' in the back room where high-rolling insiders wagered 'giant piles of money' and brought down everyone with them" (Rich 2009). Thus, even *Financial Times* reporter William Wallis (2009) expresses his reservation about Moyo's cure for Africa: "The most cynical theory I've come across in London is that the exuberance about Africa last year was itself the surest warning that investors had overshot the mark and the great global bubble was about to burst."

In this closing chapter, I explore the strange conjuncture of double agents, microfinance, and global financial markets. The Washington consensus on poverty seeks to remake microfinance in the image of Wall Street. Such a consensus is subject to critique—not only from institutions seeking an alternative but also from "double agents" working within the Washington–Wall Street complex. In the wake of the Wall Street crash, a new understanding and practice of microfinance has to be produced. Today, microfinance is being presented by both CGAP and the Grameen Bank as a successful genre of subprime lending, one that may prove to be robust and profitable for global financial markets and that may return dignity to the poor. It is in this sense that microfinance is the millennium's "poverty capital."

The making of poverty capital raises important and urgent questions about the democratization of capital and the democratization of development. Although much of this book has been devoted to the study of such themes, in this closing chapter I use the contemporary financial crisis as the occasion to examine them in a new light. If microfinance is now a resilient subprime market, then it must be asked whether such markets work or fail for the poor. If alternative visions of microfinance are now taking center stage, eroding the hegemony of CGAP, then it must be asked whether these visions break with the Washington consensus on poverty or simply repeat and replicate them. In such investigations, I am particularly interested in the role of "double agents," individuals and institutions who are simultaneously within and outside systems of power, those who are often complicit in the status quo but also, from time to time, seek to challenge the common sense. To understand double agents, I turn to the work of postcolonial theorist, Gayatri Chakravorty Spivak (1999: 191), who outlines this ethical position thus: "the impossible 'no' to a structure that one critiques and yet intimately inhabits." This closing chapter is a closer look at these lines of critique and spaces of habitation.

Double Agents

In an essay titled "Responsibility," Spivak (1994: 53) argues in trenchant fashion that the "real interest" of the apparatus of international development, led by the World Bank, is the "generation of global capital." She thus concludes that it is not necessary to do a sophisticated and critical analysis of the World Bank: "we owe it no such responsibility." I am tempted by her proposition and yet veer away from it. The "generation of global capital" is not as easy as Spivak makes it seem. It is fraught with contradictions and marked by limits. It requires the practice of global control and the production of authoritative and universal knowledge. As I have shown in this book, such efforts are challenged by counter-paradigms and subject to contestation. While in previous chapters, I have highlighted the challenges posed by institutions that remain outside the Washington development machine, here I examine how experts located within the machine articulate and practice critique. Spivak notes that the generation of global capital takes place through the figures of the "consultant and contractor." This may indeed be the case. But I also claim that such figures can be "double agents," generating not only global capital but also dissent.

During research for this book, in the offices and cubicles that line the axis of development power in Washington DC, I came across many different types of "consultant and contractor." There were powerful women who sought to protect their domain of power by expressing complete and full allegiance with the institutional status quo. They insisted on stating the "accomplishments of truth." Rarely did they deviate from the public and published agenda of their institution; rarely did they voice a disagreement. My questions, when they sought out dissent and critique, were hastily dismissed, even seen as hostile. Of course these questions themselves indicated my own particular desire to find and tell a story of counter-hegemony and resistance. I was hurried out of offices, interviews cut short. Such interviews left me disappointed, for I knew that these women, formidable in their achievements, were obscuring their own struggles within these institutions, their own efforts to make and unmake power. Such interviews also demonstrated to me the ways in which women remain both inside and outside the project of power, able to command positions of control and yet anxious about whether such authority will endure. I was struck by the contrast between these interrupted interviews and those with powerful men, conversations that were often gregarious. As powerful women sought to shore up their legitimacy by repeating the "accomplishments of truth," unnerved by the questions of a Berkeley researcher, so powerful men sought to perform a risk-taking approach to institutional norms and truths. Such maverick performances were performances of power, possible only because the authority of powerful men was irrevocable and unquestionable.

There were also young men who were in Washington DC, fresh out of elite graduate schools and brimming with progressive ideas but eager to make peace with their new careers at USAID or on Capitol Hill. While they would present their work as strategic—for example, that the concern about poverty has to be cast in the language of terror in order for it to have traction—they negotiated and maneuvered much less than they themselves imagined. These young men had quickly settled into the offices of foreign policy and development programs. They had tamed the restlessness of their ideas and now easily accepted the "accomplishments of truth." While they continued to justify their work in terms of lofty goals—ending poverty, creating accountability in development and aid—they did not call into question the transactions, contracts, and alliances through which such goals are pursued in Washington DC. This was the system and these young men had found their niches in it. Watching them, I came to understand what Spivak (1999: 68) means by "complicity"—not as a giving in, not as loss, but rather as a "folding together." The lives of these young, brilliant men were folded together with this system. Complicity, I realized, is belonging, not betrayal. They belonged, as I do, in my own world of the university, a world also seeking to capture some capital and generate some truth.

At the "knowledge management" training workshops organized by the World Bank, there were "consultants and contractors" from the global South. Many of them were committed to careers in the field of development; most had a passion for poverty alleviation. But they were also sold on the Washington consensus on poverty, proud that they had been trained by the World Bank. While they were often required to attend such training workshops, the distinction between compulsion and choice was negligent. They wanted the certificate from the Boulder Institute; it is what made possible their careers. They reminded me of the important argument that "the persuasive influence of the IMF and the World Bank is at its height when dealing with able and willing interlocutors in borrowing governments" (Woods 2006: 6). It was also this work that made it possible for them to travel abroad, to attend workshops and conferences, and more generally to consolidate a class status. While critical of elite wealth from which they were at a distance, they also distanced themselves from the poor whom they served through microfinance. It is thus that the director of a microfinance institution in the Philippines railed against "squatting," arguing that while her middle-class family could barely find housing, the urban poor had "stolen" the land of Manila. A sympathetic colleague from Pakistan lamented that the urban poor were now present in the "best neighborhoods" of Karachi. She admitted that they were needed for their "cheap labor." After all she herself required three domestic workers to maintain her household. "They simply do not work as hard as they should; I feel I am doing charity by hiring them," noted the microfinance director from the Philippines. The Pakistani development executive gave an example: "My gardener has two wives. And so I have to support both families." Such ruminations were not common, but they are insightful. They reveal patterns of habitation, of how a middle-class identity is constituted through "cultures of servitude" (Ray and Qayum 2009). In these reflections, wage-earning labor is presented as servitude and wages as charity. It is in this way that the poor are folded into the structure of microfinance—not as laboring bodies but rather as moral subjects, as either bootstrapping entrepreneurs or as lazy encroachers.

The negotiation by poverty experts of their own middle-class status has often reminded me of a poignant passage from V.S. Naipaul's 1961 novel, *A House for Mr. Biswas*. It is worth sharing at length. Desperately seeking a middle-class job, one that will serve as a buffer against poverty and social disdain, Mr. Biswas finally finds a post at the *Trinidad Sentinel*, a sensationalist newspaper that had settled upon stories of poverty as the new sensation. Mr. Biswas was appointed investigator for a newly launched "Deserving Destitutes Fund":

> It was his duty to read the applications from destitutes, reject the undeserving, visit the others to see how deserving or desperate they were, and then, if the circumstances warranted it, to write harrowing accounts of their plight, harrowing enough to encourage contributions for the fund. He had to find one deserving destitute a day . . . Deserving Destitute number one, he told his wife, M. Biswas. Occupation: Investigator of Deserving Destitutes. But that would not do . . . day after day he visited the mutilated, the defeated, the futile . . . he came upon people so broken, so listless, it would have required the

devotion of a lifetime to restore them. But he could only lift his trouser turn-ups, pick his way through the mud and slime, investigate, write, move on . . . But sometimes a destitute turned sullen and, suddenly annoyed by Mr. Biswas's probings, refused to divulge the harrowing details Mr. Biswas needed for his copy. On these occasions Mr. Biswas was accused of being in league with the rich, the laughing, the government. Sometimes he was threatened with violence. Then forgetting shoes and trouser turn-ups, he retreated hastily to the street, pursued by words . . . Deserving Destitute turns Desperate, he thought, visualizing the morning's headline. (Though that would never have done: the Sentinel wanted only the harrowing details, the groveling gratitude.)

(Naipaul 1961: 423–425)

It is this occupation as "Investigator of Deserving Destitutes" that makes it possible for Mr. Biswas to finally attain the middle-class status, complete with a house, that he had always yearned. Our truth-making work is also the making of privilege, albeit meager privilege.

But then, in the corridors of millennial development, there were a few others who were able to make something else of this belonging, this folding together, this complicity. They did not seek to unmake complicity but rather attempted to transform the terrain of belonging into a more radical project of casting doubt and even making dissent. In the MIX, that virtual marketplace of microfinance instituted by CGAP, I found a director who talked eloquently about the "politics of ideas." Located at the heart of the Washington consensus on poverty, he was able to scrutinize that consensus, tracing the marginalization of Yunus and the Grameen Bank in the formation of this consensus, and pinpointing the dominance of the World Bank in the centralization and control of knowledge production. In his narrative, the "innovations" so breathlessly described in CGAP publications and the Boulder courses were stripped of their magic, rendered mundane instruments of financialization and market-building. He described the truth-making Boulder Institute as "commercialization 101," and more important, argued that such a framework of commercialization was outdated for an era concerned with the "double bottom line." It is an irony, he noted, that the "public sector wants to be more business-like than Wall Street but in the world of business what now matters is social impacts, the impacts on poverty, the use of social metrics in investments." In one stroke, this MIX director rendered irrelevant and outdated the very marketplace that he had been charged to direct. It was an unmaking of truth in a machine committed to the "accomplishments of truth."

On Wall Street, in the highest echelons of Deutsche Bank, I found a banker who talked critically about the "hubris" of "donors." His question, "who can hold that title and what does it entail?" echoed Spivak's (1994) sophisticated rumination on the appellation, donor: Who bears that title? How is it that a Wall Street banker spoke like a postcolonial theorist? This Wall Street banker was of course less interested in reflecting upon the hubris of finance capital. Indeed, for him, the solution to poverty was access to capital and such access, he argued, could best be provided by models of microfinance supported by commercial banks such as Citigroup and Deutsche Bank. His mission was to transform microfinance into an "asset class" and to do so by creating mechanisms that would manage risk and create securitization for microfinance loans. Wall Street, rather than the World Bank, he insisted, was better able to deliver these new models of development finance. C.K. Prahalad's truth-making text, *The Fortune at the Bottom of the Pyramid*, sat prominently on his shelf. Forty stories or so above the famed Wall Street bull, this too was a bullish confidence—in how poverty can be managed and how markets can be made to work. Here was a belonging, a folding together, an intimate habitation of the structure. But here there was also a persistent disruption. Each time I thought I had made sense of this Wall Street banker, pegged him as a cog in the circuits of capital and truth, he would sound a postcolonial critique of development. He noted:

> All of these ideas that are now being celebrated have their roots in Bangladesh. These are indigenous models coming from the developing world. And these roots, these origins are important. I think it is sheer racism that we are now being made to forget that these concepts originated in Bangladesh.

Of South Asian origin, he perhaps carried with him these counter-geographies of knowledge.

In the research division of the World Bank, I found a distinguished economist whose work sought to illuminate the successes and failures of microfinance in mitigating poverty. Deeply immersed in the academic debates about methodology and evaluation, he could explain the intricacies of a survey instrument and devise innovative measurements of poverty. This world of research seemed to be a more rarefied production of truth, where the controversy was all about methodological technique rather than power or interests. It was, at first glance, a world of academic craft, removed from the sphere of politics. And yet, this World Bank economist was acutely aware of the politics of knowledge. Broadly sympathetic to the Bangladesh institutions, he issued a sharp critique of CGAP's efforts to "police" the microfinance industry. CGAP, he argued, seeks to "create rules and regulations that can be widely imposed, but they are not interested in evaluating whether these rules and regulations actually work; do they make microfinance better? Is this trend of financialization one that will improve impacts on poverty?" Yet, his critique was more complex than the drawing of lines between a financial sector approach and a poverty approach to microfinance. He argued that the paradox of microfinance was that it was simultaneously an anti-poverty instrument and a financial instrument: "This is the work that has been going on in Bangladesh, whether or not those institutions acknowledge it."

In CGAP itself, I found a most compelling double agent. Expecting to encounter only the talk of banking and technology in this outpost of the World Bank, I was surprised on my first visit to CGAP to stumble into the office of an economist who spoke a quite different language. While other CGAP staff spoke of the immediacy of microfinance, framing their work as a constant making of a better future, this CGAP double agent charted the complex intellectual and institutional history of microfinance and indeed of CGAP itself. Situating CGAP in the resurgence of neoclassical economics, he traced how the "Ohio School" had an indelible impact on the reconceptualization of development finance, on discrediting the role of the state and in celebrating the role of the market. While CGAP presents its ideas as universal, not bound by geographic particularity, this CGAP double agent mapped the geography of development ideas. He noted that many of the ideas of financial sustainability touted by CGAP derived from the Latin American experience. Above all, he insisted that there was a distinctively South Asian approach to microfinance, one that was "rooted in the struggle to empower and in the struggle to alleviate poverty." He argued: "This is a completely different type of development effort, one that seeks to wage battle against the dominance of credit markets. You can't understand them in CGAP's terms. These institutions don't see themselves as bankers." Such an analysis disrupted the universality claimed by CGAP experts. But it also cast the work of Bangladesh institutions in a new light. My CGAP double agent insisted that the Grameen Bank must be understood in the context of class struggle. In sharp contrast with Yunus's language of a reformed capitalism and social enterprises, he presented Grameen-style microfinance as an instrument of economic justice. "Class conflict rather than credit markets is the appropriate framework for understanding microfinance in Bangladesh," he argued. To this end, he saw the extension of the Grameen apparatus to Washington DC as "caricatures of the real thing." "They are important, they defend Grameen ideas, but they are very different institutions than the work being done on the ground in Bangladesh."

As was the case with other double agents, this CGAP double agent made bare the politics of microfinance and development. Central to such a revelation was his analysis of the politics of knowledge and his acute awareness of the hegemony of the Washington consensus on poverty. "Microfinance is a good example of knowledge appropriation," he noted during one of our many meetings. "How did it go from Bangladesh to Boulder? We created microfinance and then lost it." His use of the "we" was particularly significant. On that cold March late afternoon in Washington DC, he presented himself as a hybrid agent, carrying within him "the experiences of the global South." He said:

> We are good at creating snapshots and telling stories. It is like poetry. But it does not come across as technical. It seems to lack economic rationality. It lacks generalization. It cannot become universal. And so we lost it to those who can make this poetry both technical and universal.

The analysis was a familiar one, that which I had heard in Bangladesh—in Grameen, in BRAC, and even in ASA. But it had a wholly different significance when articulated at the heart of the Washington consensus on poverty, in the offices of CGAP. This CGAP double agent talked at length about returning to Bangladesh, about establishing knowledge institutions in the global South, and thus about reversing such forms of knowledge appropriation. Such imaginations dislocate the accomplishments of truth so securely lodged in Washington DC, repositioning Bangladesh as a center of development expertise.

How are such critical imaginations forged? In the case of the CGAP double agent, this is a life history that is interwoven with postcolonial struggles in Bangladesh. But it is also a life history that has taken shape not in a single location but rather through dislocations and transnational crossings. As a teenager, the CGAP double agent fought in Bangladesh's war of independence. These early years were not only steeped in anti-colonialism but also marked by the growing realization of the "thin line between civilization and barbarism." The "violence of war" was a formative experience, one that led him to leave Bangladesh for the US. The war also made apparent a set of contradictions that would become central to the life of my CGAP double agent. The Left, he notes, did not participate in the military struggle for Bangladesh's independence. Yet, in the early 1970s, in a small state college in the US, he was to soak up Leftist ideology, immerse himself in radical social movements, and find an anchor in Marxist academic analysis. On returning to Bangladesh in the early 1980s, he sought to put into practice such ideas:

> There was a lot of organizing work going on, with agricultural laborers, with dockyard workers. And there was also microcredit. It was helping poor people survive. But the Left looked down on it. The Left was made up of academics who were hoping for a massive insurrection. Their academic practice was far removed from the lives of poor people. I was not willing to tow this party line.

The CGAP double agent left Bangladesh again, this time earning a doctorate in economics from an American university. When he returned to Bangladesh, he returned also to the NGOs that had impressed him, those that the Left rejected. He joined the Grameen Bank:

> At that time Yunus seemed a strong voice that was able to define an alternative vision for Bangladesh. He challenged neoclassical economics. He challenged donors. At Grameen we would work at these thick wooden tables and we would feel pride. We would feel that it was our organization, that it was our country.

There is no easy way to make sense of this CGAP double agent, in his office overlooking the World Bank buildings, with a poster of Antonio Gramsci, the famous Marxist philosopher, behind him. Gramsci's analysis of "hegemony," which emphasizes the production of consent as a form of rule, is of course uncannily relevant for this discussion of millennial development. This CGAP economist cannot be read simply as a valiant defender of the Bangladesh consensus at the heart of the Washington consensus on poverty, for he is also convinced by the work of CGAP. He is aware of how and why he was recruited by CGAP: "It was in the late 1990s. Yunus was severely criticizing CGAP for mission drift. CGAP contacted me and my immediate reaction was no. I did not want to work for the World Bank . . . But I have learned a lot by being here. This is a very human place with people who truly care." And there is more. He was proud of the work done by CGAP and occasionally noted that "CGAP had done more than any other institution to advance the poverty agenda." This was more than an effort to give prominence to his own poverty-focused initiatives at CGAP. It was a recasting of CGAP itself:

> CGAP III is focused on dramatically expanding access to financial services, in ending the caste system in finance. To do so it feels that it must go beyond the NGO model. It has to reach scale. It has to partner with banks. And it has to think beyond credit. It has to think about savings, insurance, remittances . . . CGAP's driving interest is poverty alleviation. It is completely focused on poverty . . . There are no internal battles in CGAP about these issues.

While CEO Elizabeth Littlefield herself casts CGAP's work in the language of financial democracy, the CGAP double agent went further, presenting CGAP as tackling the very structures of financial apartheid: "as Grameen does battle against the injustices of credit markets, so does CGAP."

Such narratives mark the giving of consent—to CGAP and to the very idea of microfinance. It is the folding together that Spivak designates as complicity. This is neither false consciousness nor betrayal. Rather it speaks to the structural reality that our work acquires meaning only through the defense of the structures within which we produce that work. The significance of the CGAP double agent's practices of subversion and dissent would be greatly diminished if CGAP in particular and microfinance in general were to be discredited. The double agent cannot necessarily seek to smash, tear apart, and burn down the structure, but the double agent can occupy the structure, burrowing in, claiming territory, and marking a terrain of action.

The CGAP double agent had indeed occupied the structure. Within CGAP, his work on poverty found a home and after a while it began to circulate through the networks of the Washington consensus on poverty. A course on poverty taught by him became a regular fixture at the Boulder Institute. CGAP concept papers and focus notes appeared on poverty, the Millennium Development Goals, and social protection. The MIX expressed interest in including social performance indicators alongside financial performance indicators. Was it possible that a new "common sense" was being created within the established circuits of truth?

A New Common Sense

The most tangible form of a new common sense is the emergence of "social performance" as an important metric of measurement and evaluation in microfinance. If CGAP once gave sole prominence to financial performance indicators, then today it is also promoting social performance indicators. These indicators, such as schooling, health, women's empowerment, echo not only the priorities established by the Millennium Development Goals but also the mandates of the Bangladesh consensus. The Microfinance Gateway now has a "Social Performance Resource Center" and there is an active effort afoot to forge a network of institutions committed to the use of social performance indicators. In an alliance that seems to dissipate the stark divisions between the Washington consensus and the Bangladesh consensus, the Grameen Foundation has joined forces with the Ford Foundation and CGAP to create a social performance index. Named the "Progress Out of Poverty Index," and created as a "public good," this country-specific tool allows microfinance institutions to measure impacts on poverty and emphasizes the significance of non-financial indicators in the world of microfinance. The Social Performance Task Force, convened by CGAP and the Argidius and Ford Foundations, defines social performance as the following:

> The effective translation of an institution's social mission into practice in line with accepted social values that relate to serving larger numbers of poor and excluded people; improving the quality and appropriateness of financial services; creating benefits for clients; and improving social responsibility of an MFI.
>
> (http://www.microfinancegateway.org/p/site/ m/template.rc/1.11.48260/1.26.9228/, accessed August 15, 2008)

Such "industry innovations," as they are billed by the Grameen Foundation's Social Performance Management Center, speak to the taking hold of dissent and critique at the very heart of the Washington consensus on poverty. They possibly mark the reappropriation of microfinance by a poverty-focused South Asian paradigm of development. And yet, the story is inevitably more complex. The CGAP double agent notes that the journey has been incredibly difficult. "Just a few years ago when we presented our ideas on social performance we were attacked, almost in gladiatorial fashion, by donors. Now our task force has 150 people. But it was not easy to get here." Indeed, critics of social performance charge that the very concept of social performance remains fuzzy and that collecting such information is a costly and unfair burden for microfinance institutions (Jacquand 2005). There is also dissent within the social performance circles. At the 2006 Microcredit Summit in Halifax, John Hatch of Finca International emphasized the importance of "social audits" alongside financial audits: "In order to be a client driven industry, in order to hold firm to our mission, we must do this." Ingrid Munro from Kenya's Jamii Bora agreed. But she asked of Hatch and others in the social performance movement:

Why do we hire consultants to come to our countries to study our poverty and become rich? Organizations should do their own social performance assessments. This should not become another consulting industry. In Kenya, we have excellent young men and women. They should be doing these evaluations.

Munro's auto-critique from within the social performance movement converges with critiques from outside the movement:

One can also wonder whether these calls for reporting on the double bottom line are not an ingenuous way for scores of consultants, research organizations to justify their existence . . . Donors are often willing accomplices in the plethora of initiatives that emerge around the issue for they can also justify the significance of their work to their own constituents. Some will claim that this complicity stems from a genuine desire to gain a stronger understanding of how financial services affect poor people's lives.

(Jacquand 2005)

Indeed, it can be argued that the social performance movement works to strengthen the central role of the Washington consensus on poverty. It is thus that in my interviews with them, top USAID administrators made note of how the social performance movement is driven by a new generation of investors. This runs counter to the critique that the social performance movement may "ghettoize microfinance" and "scare investors away" (Jacquand 2005). Thus a USAID official noted (November 2006): "The donors have been more Catholic than the Pope, focused exclusively on commercialization. But socially responsible investors want to know more about impacts on poverty." In fact, as argued by the Grameen Foundation, the social performance movement takes its cues from the "global business community": "The increasing corporate acknowledgement of corporate citizenship responsibilities has led to greater acceptance of social responsibility reporting and concepts such as the social return on investment" (http://www.grameenfoundation.org/, accessed May 20, 2008).

The social performance movement marks a new effort to make "poverty capital." It is a break with the financialization of development once promoted by CGAP. But it is also an effort to integrate microfinance with global financial markets. Social performance is now institutionalized through the familiar practices of reporting, auditing, rating, benchmarking, mapping. The reality is that socially responsible investing is a massive global industry, with over $4 trillion in assets (CGAP 2008b: 1). One out of every nine professionally managed dollars in America is invested using a social screen (Tulchin 2003). The bulk of private investment in microfinance has come from these investors (CGAP 2008b). The Grameen Foundation thus presents its work on social performance as "new social investing guidelines"—those that emerged from the "Grameen Foundation's ongoing work with Oikocredit, a leading social investor in microfinance" (Grameen Foundation 2009).

At the 2006 Microcredit Summit, panelists in a session on investment and financial markets called unanimously for social performance indicators. Even Kate McKee, former head of USAID's microenterprise division, who in that role had railed against Congressional pressure to measure poverty targeting and poverty impacts, asked investors to push for more precise social performance indicators. While CGAP stalwarts had once said of financial indicators, "you tend to value what you measure," Wall Street interlocutors were now making the same statement about poverty outreach and impacts. There was a vivid sense that here was a financial frontier that was perhaps the most "transparent" of all banking sectors—after all as a member of the audience asked at that panel, "how many banks release information on how many women they can count among their clients?" CGAP thus presents social performance measurement as "truth in advertising." (Hashemi 2007: 1).

Securitization

As it is possible to interpret some development professionals as double agents, so it is possible to conceptualize development organizations, such as NGOs, as having a double role. Here it is worth returning to the Bangladesh consensus. Although it is tempting to read the work of these institutions as an oppositional force to Washington-style development and Wall Street-type capitalism, in recent years they have sought to insert themselves into such circuits of capital. This is evident in the striking trend of microfinance securitizations. The first of these, launched in 2006, provided BRAC with 12.6 billion taka or approximately $180 million of financing. Structured by RSA Capital, Citigroup, FMO (Netherlands Development Finance Company), and KfW development bank, the deal "involves a securitisation of receivables arising from the microcredits extended by BRAC . . . and the creation of a special purpose trust which purchases the receivables from BRAC and issues certificates to investors representing beneficial interest in such receivables." Fazle Abed, founder and chairman of BRAC, celebrated the securitization as "a landmark for the microfinance industry . . . We have brought the global financial markets to the doorsteps of nearly 1.2 million households in Bangladesh" (http://www.brac.net/, accessed December 17, 2006).

Securitizations can be seen as a new strategy of the Bangladesh consensus. In 2008, ASA International, ASA's global network, with operations in China, Cambodia, Ghana, India, Indonesia, Nigeria, Pakistan, the Philippines, and Sri Lanka, secured an equity capital commitment of $125 million from Catalyst Microfinance Investors, a private equity investment fund managed by ASA and Sequoia, a corporate investment firm (*Business Wire* 2008). These securitizations are meant to create access to cheap capital for microfinance institutions, thereby, as BRAC argues, "reducing dependency on volatile donor financing." They seek to recalibrate the asymmetries of global–local transactions by conferring financial power on microfinance institutions. For example, in the case of the BRAC securitization, the "entire currency risk for the transaction is borne by global investors" (http://www.brac.net/, accessed December 17, 2006). Indeed, like microfinance itself, securitizations place their faith in access to capital as the key to development.

Such is the strategy of the Grameen Foundation. Through its Growth Guarantee Program, which is a collaboration with Citigroup, it has mobilized venture capital and made equity investments in microfinance institutions. Led by a former private equity investor and fund manager, the Grameen Foundation's Capital Markets Group aggressively seeks out capital for microfinance. The idea is to leverage private capital in order to allow microfinance institutions to grow and thus, in the words of Alex Counts, president of Grameen Foundation, to "leverage microfinance as a platform for social change" (Grameen Foundation 2007b). The first of such investments took place in successful Grameen Foundation partners in India such as CASPOR and SKS. In 2007, there was a "breakthrough securitization deal" between ICICI Bank and Share Microfin, a Grameen partner, which generated $4.3 million in new loan capital (http://grameen capital.in/, accessed February 1, 2008). Since then, there has been a flurry of transactions, each with a well-regarded microfinance institution: the Kashf Foundation in Pakistan, CARD in the Philippines, LAPO in Nigeria, Pro Mujer in Peru, Fondation Zakoura and FONDEP in Morocco (http://www.grameenfoundation.org/, accessed May 20, 2008).

Extensive work on this front is taking place in the Middle East. Here, the Grameen-Jameel Initiative, a collaboration between the Grameen Foundation and the Abdul Latif Jameel Group, a business group based in Saudi Arabia, serves to secure and guarantee investments by commercial banks in microfinance institutions. It is thus that Egypt's Dakahlya Businessmen Association for Community Development (DBACD) was able to secure a local currency loan of $2.5 million from BNP Paribas. Guaranteed by the Grameen–Jameel Initiative, Citibank, and Banque Saudi Fransi, the deal allowed the microfinance organization to expand its lending to 16,000 new clients. Alex Counts hailed the transaction as opening "a new era in microfinance in Egypt, with commercial banks playing an increasingly important role in bridging the vast gap between supply and demand for microfinance in Egypt" (*CSRwire* 2006). Today, Grameen–Jameel is a joint venture company modeled after Yunus's idea of social business enterprises, a "for-profit company with a social purpose." The Grameen Foundation has established a similar entity in India, Grameen Capital India Private Limited to initiate and manage securitization transactions. By December 2007, the

Grameen Foundation announced that it had generated $112.6 million in local currency financing for microfinance institutions, from Pakistan to Peru, leveraging $20.5 million in guarantees (http://www.grameen foundation.org/, accessed May 20, 2008).

Headquartered in Beirut, Lebanon, Grameen–Jameel can be seen as a significant intervention in the ecology of development in the Middle East. It breaks the dependence of microfinance institutions on USAID and constructs alternative forms of access to capital. In an interview (June 2006), one Grameen–Jameel staffer described the situation as "financial slavery," one where NGOs remain bound by the conditions imposed by donors. In a statement that echoed the theme of the "pollution of free money," this staffer noted that "USAID had polluted the market." "Donors such as USAID are fickle. All of this time USAID fed these NGOs money but now it is pulling out. How does it expect these institutions to be suddenly independent?" Grameen–Jameel's intention is to construct autonomous circuits of capital and in particular to support institutions committed to a Grameen model of microfinance. For example, in countries such as Egypt where Grameen's partners remain on the margins of USAID circles, Grameen–Jameel seeks to support microfinance institutions with a "documented poverty focus," in other words those that are in keeping with "Grameen values" (http://www.grameen-jameel.com/, accessed May 20, 2008). Similarly, in an interview (June 2006), Heather Henyon, director of Grameen–Jameel, emphatically stated that the "double bottom line" is used to provide growth guarantees: "We have an explicit poverty focus. One of our strategic goals is to ensure that the microfinance borrowers served by our partners cross the poverty line." To this end, Grameen–Jameel funds staff from such NGOs to attend the Grameen Dialogue held in Bangladesh and even organizes, each year, an "Arab Dialogue" held at the Grameen Bank. "This type of networking cannot happen at CGAP or even Sanabel," noted Henyon. Underwritten by a powerful Saudi business group, the Grameen–Jameel Initiative is an interesting lesson in the formulation of counter-hegemonic strategy. The strategy bears striking resemblance to the tenets of microfinance, where borrowers locked out of mainstream banking are able to gain access to capital through an alternative institutional structure. This too is a democratization of capital.

However, Grameen–Jameel with its reliance on financial instruments is almost indistinguishable from the best practices and norms circulated by

CGAP. The investment seminars hosted by Grameen–Jameel showcase commercial funding and capital markets. They train microfinance institutions to evaluate deal structures and manage foreign exchange risk. Grameen–Jameel, like CGAP, is focused on developing an industry, one where entrepreneurial institutions serve microentrepreneurs. Grameen–Jameel, in keeping with the broader discourses of millennial development, seeks to restore the discipline of the market, including the discipline enacted by financial markets, to a world polluted by donor funds. This is not unlike the "capital solution" advocated by Dambisa Moyo.

Such work is buttressed by that of the Grameen Technology Center, which is based in Seattle. Here, the Grameen Foundation is seeking to deploy technological innovations and partner with technology companies such as IBM and Cisco Systems in order to create information systems for microfinance. One such system is Mifos, an open source microfinance software platform, which was financed by a grant from the Omidyar Network. In interviews (October 2005), senior staff at the Grameen Technology Center emphasized that technology can assist the microfinance industry on two urgent fronts. First, information systems can improve the management of financial systems, thereby allowing microfinance institutions to connect with capital markets. Second, such information systems can ensure global standards, or a "meta-language," in management and reporting, thereby creating "transparency." The work of the Grameen Technology Center is in keeping with the vision promoted by CGAP and MIX for a microfinance industry, to use the "microfinance institution's portfolio as a readily priced asset class" (Dailey 2005: 40). The Global Markets Institute at Goldman Sachs lent its technology professionals to help build Mifos. Suzanne Nora Johnson, chair of the institute, notes that Mifos will help "the microfinance industry advance by improving loan portfolio management, customer data analytics, and access to capital markets" (Grameen Foundation 2007a). In short, such information systems seek to create an industry of capital transactions where both poor borrowers and microfinance institutions can be mapped and tracked through information and financial technologies.

Yet, a struggle, a doubleness, pervades these efforts. As noted by Alex Counts in an interview (October 2004), the Grameen Foundation itself is an organization based in the US but closely linked to work in Bangladesh. Counts thus argued: "I believe that microfinance has to move beyond

Bangladesh but the role of Bangladesh's microfinance leaders has to be recognized." The Grameen Foundation presents a dramatic challenge to the idea that "anything of value has to emerge in New York and Washington DC." "They treat Grameen as if it is like PanAm: bankrupt; When I say that Bangladesh is the Wall Street of microfinance, it is the cutting-edge, then everyone is surprised." And yet of course, the Grameen Foundation is strategically positioned at the heart of this power, in Washington DC. It is here that the work done in Bangladesh can be leveraged to generate capital, to launch securitizations, and to provide AAA-rated growth guarantees. In short, it is in Washington DC that value is produced and a global industry is consolidated.

The pressing question is this: Can such an industry also serve the poor? At the launch of the Grameen–Jameel joint venture company in 2007, Mohammed Jameel, president of Abdul Latif Jameel Group, stated: "We believe that business principles can be applied to solve massive social problems like poverty, and we hope to see more examples of corporate social responsibility and social investment in the Arab World" (*CSRwire* 2006). It was a line out of the Washington consensus on poverty and its theme of financial inclusion. Each announcement of a Grameen Foundation backed securitization is accompanied by this argument about the democratization of capital. A high-ranking member of the Grameen Foundation thus noted in an interview (June 2004) that the pressing question was "how can we harness the desire of mainstream capital to make money in order to support our industry?" But, he noted, "if Yunus were here, he would say that we also have to handcuff capital in order to serve the poor . . . How do we do both is the challenge."

The questions apply not only to the issue of reaching the bottom billion but also to that of reaching microfinance institutions themselves. Can such access to capital be made available to all microfinance institutions? Or, in this benchmarked industry, can only the high-growth, high-ranked NGOs enter into securitizations and leverage growth guarantees? The Grameen Foundation's publicity material repeatedly emphasizes that it seeks to link capital markets with "high-performing" and "high-growth" microfinance institutions. After all, microfinance portfolios, to repeat that line from the Grameen Technology Center, are meant to be a "readily priced asset class." Inevitably, such forms of capitalization seek out frontiers of profit.

Thus, a $125 million private equity deal recently secured by ASA was narrated in different ways. Shafiqual Haque Choudhury, founder and CEO of ASA International, declared:

> This large pool of equity capital will enable us to . . . provide the non-bankable poor in these regions with first-time access to credit and other basic financial services, which will help free them from exploitation, unleash their entrepreneurial drive, and improve family's livelihoods.

But Dirk Brouwer, executive director of CMI and managing director of Sequoia, made note of "ASA's powerful, highly efficient model of microfinance" and that such a deal thus gave these investment funds "a true competitive edge as an owner and operator of microfinance institutions." Investments by some of the world's largest pension funds, including ABP and TIAA-CREF, lay at the heart of the deal. The ABP representative noted that such investments in microfinance allowed pension funds to diversify their risk. The managing director of social and community investing for TIAA-CREF similarly noted the attractiveness of investments in microfinance. The attraction, he argued, came both from the double bottom line of the industry and from the fact that the sector had "many institutions still profitable and growing" (*Business Wire* 2008). In fact, in 2006, TIAA-CREF created a $100 million Global Microfinance Investment Program (GMIP) to invest in selected microfinance institutions worldwide. It is in keeping with CREF's "Social Choice" Account, which is the largest comprehensively screened investment vehicle for individual investors in the US (Reuters 2009). This is the double promise of microfinance: that it can extend opportunity to the "non-banked poor" and that it can yield profits for investors.

The securitization deals represent an interesting new strategy on the part of Grameen, BRAC, and ASA, Bangladesh's leading microfinance institutions. They mark an engagement with global financial markets, but on terms—at least until now—controlled by these institutions. It is the generation of poverty capital to end "financial slavery," both that of microfinance borrowers and of NGOs in the global South enmeshed in an ecology of dependence. The question that must be asked is this: Can such a revolution take place through finance?

A FINANCIAL KATRINA

Hurricane Katrina, that fierce storm of 2005, also unleashed, at least for a moment, a political storm. It starkly revealed the racialized poverty that exists in the midst of American prosperity and the cruel antipathy of the government to such deprivations. Katrina was also a storm whose effects were unusually visible. The deaths, the abandonment, the warehousing of the poor in disaster management centers, were widely broadcast by the media, turning Katrina into an iconic moment and condemning the Bush administration for its callous incompetence. By the time of the 2008 US presidential election, another storm was brewing. While Hurricane Katrina still remained a cloud that darkened the fate of the Republican Party, the new storm was a growing financial crisis, and more significant, a populist fury about the management of this crisis. What had started out seemingly as a problem in the subprime housing market, with delinquencies in subprime mortgages, turned out to be much more than a convulsion. It was shaping up to be what George Soros (2008) has called the worst financial crisis since the Great Depression. Drawing on a letter to the editor published in the *New York Times*, columnist Frank Rich (2009) noted that this new storm may just be President Obama's "Katrina moment," one marked by the "full depth of Americans' anger."

This financial crisis has important consequences for millennial development. The UN has issued the dire warning that millions will be pushed "into deeper poverty"; that this in turn will lead to "the deaths of thousands of children," and that reduced growth will lead to a loss of "20% of the per capita income of Africa's poor" (Watkins and Montjourides 2009). The World Bank noted that in 2008, food and fuel prices had already added 130–155 million people to the ranks of the poor; now the financial crisis was most likely going to add another 46 million to these numbers. World Bank President Robert Zoellick thus warned that "the global economic crisis threatens to become a human crisis" (World Bank 2009). Indeed, the first financial crisis of the new millennium seems to be unraveling the Millennium Development Goals—both the progress that was made in the last decade as well as the global social contract that is embodied in this framework.

The World Bank has proposed a variety of interventions, including the establishment of a "vulnerability fund," with three priority areas: "safety net programs, infrastructure investments, and, support for small and medium-sized enterprises and microfinance institutions" (World Bank 2009). At the London summit in April 2009, G-20 leaders pledged to allocate $1.1 trillion in increased resources through the IMF and other international bodies. Such interventions raise many questions. *The Economist* (2009) noted that the figures were exaggerated, "more an aspiration than a done deal." In particular, it argued that the IMF itself had to undergo reform in order to "provide collective insurance for the prudent and conditional assistance for the profligate." And microfinance, listed as one of the World Bank's priority areas, may itself be on shaky ground. A CGAP (2008c) report notes that the ramifications of the financial crisis are multiple—from microfinance clients "hurt by inflation" and "struggling with high food and fuel prices," to "dwindling remittances." The report emphasizes that such "stresses on customers usually translate into higher portfolio at risk for microfinance institutions." Microfinance institutions also face a greater threat: "a global liquidity contraction" that may sharply increase the cost, and restrict the availability, of capital to microfinance institutions. Such worries return us to Alex Counts's provocative question, posed at the 2006 Microcredit Summit in Halifax, Canada: "What is capitalism without access to capital?"

Bad Money in the Age of Responsibility

The financial crisis as human crisis has engendered a new millennial discourse, one that foregrounds issues of inequality rather than simply those of absolute poverty. Thus, one of the authors of the recent UN report compares the "US$380 billion in public money injected into banking systems in last quarter of 2009," with the meager "$7 billion needed in increased aid for low income countries to meet key education goals." He uses such a comparison to make the case that "aid donors could clearly do far more to protect the world's poorest people from a crisis manufactured by the world's richest financiers and regulatory failure in rich countries" (UNESCO 2009). The vulnerability fund proposed by World Bank President Robert Zoellick calls on developed countries to devote 0.7 percent—a figure from Goal 8 of the Millennium Development Goals—of their stimulus packages to this fund. In a sharply worded *Financial Times* editorial, Zoellick (2009) insists that this must be "the age of responsibility": of "responsible globalization," "responsible stewardship of the global environment," "financial responsibility," and "responsible multilateralism." Such an age of responsibility, he notes, "must be a global not just a western one," a system of governance widely owned by "responsible stakeholders." Here once again is the theme of the democratization of development.

It is worth noting that in his previous incarnation as US Trade Representative, Zoellick took quite a different approach to the issue of development, democracy, and responsibility. At the 2003 WTO meeting in Cancun, as countries of the global South rejected the stubborn insistence of rich countries to continue subsidies for their agricultural sectors, Zoellick (2003) railed against the rebellion, labeling it the "politics of protest" of "won't do countries." His heavy-handed dismissal of calls for fair trade made a mockery of the democratization of development. It showed that America was still in charge of systems of global governance and global trade. In the midst of the current financial crisis, Zoellick's plea for "responsible globalization" seems to reflect a change of heart.

In America, the financial crisis is increasingly described as capitalist greed or "bad money." Key to this diagnosis is the notion of "reckless finance," of "a mixed fireworks of dishonesty, incompetence and quantitative negligence" (Phillips 2008b). Such populist fury is significant for it presents a challenge to the Washington consensus on poverty that seeks to promote the financialization of development. How can a dishonest, incompetent, and negligent Wall Street serve as the institutional model for the democratization of capital? After all, Citigroup, that poster child of Wall Street, and a key player in the commercialization of microfinance, saw its share prices plunge from $55 to $1.50. The federal government, which has repeatedly bailed out Citigroup, is now its largest shareholder (Dash and Story 2009). The company that was once worth $244 billion is at the time of writing worth $20.5 billion, riddled with "exotic financial products" such as "collateralized debt obligations" (Dash and Creswell 2008). Once exotic bundles of calculated risk, these are now toxic assets. Not surprisingly, Yunus has seized the moment to issue a stiff warning about commercialized microfinance: that "the world's biggest banks risk creating a subprime-style crisis for millions of the planet's poorest people if they continue to plough money into the booming microfinance sector" (Burgis 2008).

However, there is more at stake in the financial crisis than the discrediting of Citigroup and other Wall Street stalwarts. It is a storm that has exposed key contradictions and challenges in the structure of finance capitalism. Two in particular deserve attention: First, how can value, and therefore risk, be assessed and managed in this economy of finance? Second, how can a system that requires government bailouts be reconciled with the ideology of free markets and bootstrap entrepreneurialism? Such questions also haunt microfinance.

In his treatise, *A Brief History of Neoliberalism*, Marxist geographer David Harvey (2005: 161) argues that the 1980s saw the spread of a "strong wave of financialization . . . marked by its speculative and predatory style." Such forms of financialization were made possible by quite specific forms of state action, notably the deregulation of financial markets. Today, as this global financialization has wrought a global economic crisis, there seems to be a new consensus about the ills of such a system. Kate McKee, former director of USAID's microenterprise division and now senior advisor at CGAP, critiques this "world of 'slice and dice' finance" (CGAP 2008c). While CGAP once lauded financial innovation, McKee now casts doubt on such forms of "financial engineering," particularly the repackaging and selling of loans as securities. In language similar to Zoellick's, she calls for a "responsible finance" as well as regulation that can curb "market excesses." This recalibration of the financialization of development is interesting, for instead of promoting self-regulating financial markets, McKee notes the "limits of self-regulation." But this is a mild reform, rather than rejection, of the model. Elizabeth Littlefield, CEO of CGAP, thus warns against "activist policies," insisting that regulation must be at best "light-touch" (CGAP 2008c).

The talk of "responsible finance" skirts a more fundamental issue: the nature of value, and therefore risk, in the economy of finance. In their prescient book, *Financial Derivatives and the Globalization of Risk*, LiPuma and Lee (2004) chart a new economy that is characterized by circulation rather than production. Such an economy derives value from risk rather than only from labor (LiPuma and Lee 2004: 126). Financial products, for example derivatives, capitalize such risk, thereby generating profit through practices of speculation. While it is tempting to contrast such speculative products with real products, be it a commodity produced through labor or a housing mortgage, in this new economy such distinctions do not hold. It is the derivative that is the product. It drives the economy.

Observers thus rightly note that the diagnosis of the financial crisis as a "subprime crisis" is misplaced, for it implies that changes in the real economy, i.e. the subprime housing market, generated crisis in financial markets (Gowan 2009). Instead, the derivatives market was its own type of "fast capitalism" (Fisher and Downey 2006: 9). Central to this new economy is "a separation . . . between the underlier and the derivative" (LiPuma and Lee 2004: 98). In these financial frontiers, "securitization required that investors accept standardized ratings as substitutes for evaluating the specific risks associated with individual loan relationships" (Fisher and Downey 2006: 8). The financial markets thus became their own enclosed world of "speculative arbitrage" (Gowan 2009: 6), driven by their exotic fictions that are now the main products of contemporary capitalism.

It is in this sense that "millennial capitalism" is "magical," with the capacity to yield wealth "purely through exchange . . . as if entirely independent of human manufacture" (Comaroff and Comaroff 2000: 301). In a previous chapter, following the work of French philosopher Michel Foucault (1966), I designate such a moment as the end of "political economy," or the end of frameworks of capitalism that are concerned with the extraction of surplus value from the labor of workers. Now it is financial speculation, the management of risk, and the circulation of money, that are seen to produce value. The popular call to make the economy "more just" by making it "more real" is thus misguided. Money, as anthropologist Bill Maurer (2006, 2008) argues, is necessarily a fiction—an abstract and calculative index that can never fully represent the social, cultural, or personal. Yet, this fiction is real in that it has real effects.

The troubles of financial globalization raise important questions about the future of microfinance. The microfinance loan, and its valuation of risk, has only a tenuous connection to entrepreneurial labor and the products and profits of microenterprise. Indeed, as discussed at various points in this book, this connection—between microfinance and microenterprise—may just be an exotic fiction. The risk scoring in microfinance is thus less a valuation of the labor of the poor or the assets of the poor and much more an assessment of the capacity to enact repayment. After all, "the poor always pay back." This is the speculative arbitrage that underlies micro-finance, a calculation about the habits of the poor and the guarantees of financial discipline provided by microfinance institutions. Such practices may not be a far stretch from global financial markets. After all, financial markets, as Reich (2008b) notes, "trade in promises." But as financial innovations such as securitization now sweep through the field of micro-finance, a second separation must occur: between the risk associated with each microfinance loan and the bundle of loans, with intangible risk, that is now securitized. Can this bundled and securitized risk be managed? Or is a new financial crisis lurking here?

Markets are Planned

If this is a Katrina moment, then it reveals some key structural features of the economy of finance. The crisis, and then the bailouts, show that the "New Wall Street system" is a monopoly, "dominated by just five investment banks holding over $4 trillion of assets," "a far cry from the decentralized market with thousands of players . . . depicted by neo-classical economics" (Gowan 2009: 6). The Obama administration's efforts to regulate the financial markets and protect consumers will do little to challenge this system. Such a monopoly, as David Harvey (2005) has argued, is also a class project, with the rewards highly concentrated in the hands of a financial elite. It is this monopoly that remains obscured in the Washington consensus on poverty. The key interlocutors of this consensus put forward a seductive vision of the world system as a people's economy, of a bottom billion economic order. Cast in the rhetoric of economic freedom—rather than wealth redistribution—this vision makes the case for markets that work rather than fail. Markets work because they are free, subject at most to "light-touch" regulation. But as the economic historian, Karl Polanyi (1944: 146) had so brilliantly analyzed at a quite different historical moment, markets are planned rather than free: "the road to the free market was opened and kept open by an enormous increase in continuous, centrally organized and controlled interventionism." The Wall Street bailouts are only the most visible and recent instance of the planning of markets.

The Katrina moment makes visible the logic of a system that privatizes profit and socializes losses, what has been called "Wall Street socialism" (Phillips 2008b) or "socialized capitalism" (Reich 2008a). A far cry from Bill Gates's "creative capitalism," such markets operate through the collectivization of risk, such that the rewards of speculation are reaped by the few but the fallout of miscalculated risk is borne by a broader public. Particularly striking is how debt forgiveness programs have been extended to powerful Wall Street firms but denied to America's middle class and poor. To mitigate such a severe inequality, the Obama administration has sought to launch a housing plan that would give lenders incentives to modify the mortgages of homeowners facing foreclosure. The plan garnered critique from conservative commentators such as Rick Santelli of CNBC who argued that the plan rewarded the "bad behavior" of "losers." The Obama administration responded by noting that Santelli was a derivatives trader and that the plan was meant to benefit Main Street, not "speculators who took risky bets" or "dishonest lenders" (Stolberg 2009).

Here, Wall Street stands discredited, its once bold arbitrage now reframed as irresponsibility. The plan itself, with its call for detours, flexibility, and the rescheduling of loans, bears striking resemblance to the Grameen II model, that which was vilified by the *Wall Street Journal* as "cooking the books." Today, such loan modifications are the cornerstone of a new effort to institute fair and nimble credit systems in the American housing market. The most successful modifications have come from small mortgage companies that reschedule loans not as "acts of charity" but rather "based on calculations of whether changing loan terms are in the best interests of investors" (Bajaj and Leland 2009). Such too is the business of microfinance: a retooling rather than forgiving of debt. This too can be understood as financial innovation rather than "bad money."

Yet, leaders of the microfinance industry express concern about the retooling of debt. Elizabeth Littlefield asks policy-makers not to implement "quick fix" programs such as debt forgiveness (CGAP 2008c). It is a plea that evokes a history that haunts microfinance: of a debtors' revolt, in 1999, in Bolivia. A financial crisis of "over-indebtedness," facilitated by "quick and easy credit from consumer lenders," that led not only to high rates of delinquency but also the formation of unions and associations that demanded debt forgiveness (Rhyne 2001: 144–146). Microfinance, which was to be the social antidote to Jeffrey Sachs's "shock therapy," had set into motion a social crisis. Elizabeth Rhyne (2001: 149), now director of Accion International's Center for Financial Inclusion, laments that these debt protests "politicized microfinance," "changing attitudes about credit and damaging Bolivia's once-excellent repayment culture."

These pleas against debt forgiveness reinforce the distinction that is central to the Washington consensus on poverty: the distinction between a self-regulating, market-based microfinance and a donor-subsidized micro-finance. The former is seen to engender efficiency and promote economic freedom. The latter is seen to be unsustainable and neocolonial. This distinction, as I have argued earlier in this book, is also a normative state-ment about different regional orders of microfinance. Latin American-style microfinance is thus seen to be "a generation ahead," while Bangladesh's microfinance models are seen as picturesque and primitive. After all, Bolivia, once the site of debtor revolts, was quickly transformed into a frontier of commercialized microfinance, its NGOs rapidly transforming themselves into "formal financial institutions" such as the famed BancoSol. Littlefield's plea is instructive since it is made against the backdrop of US government bailouts of Wall Street banks, which too are debt forgiveness programs. Is this not the "pollution of free money"? William Easterly's popular mantra is the following: "the rich have markets, the poor have bureaucrats." The Wall Street bailouts, and the reluctance to extend such kindness to Main Street or to the Bottom Billion, demonstrates that his mantra can be revised to state: "the rich have state-help, the poor have self-help."

Hurricane Katrina was a searing moment in the consciousness of the American nation. But it was also a fleeting moment. By the time Katrina "refugees" had been dispersed to trailer parks, motels, and public housing around the country, the redevelopment of New Orleans was already underway. Displacement quickly became invisible again; more important it set the stage for an aggressive gentrification. Post-Katrina New Orleans was the wild, wild west: a no-law frontier where rules could be suspended in order to foster urban development. Will the current financial crisis be a similar Katrina moment—an analogy that Rich did not intend in his use of the term? Or will it prolong the searing exposure of the economy of finance, placing "English-speaking capitalism on trial" (Burns and Thomas 2009)? Observers note that the crisis may also shake up the economic, moral, and ideological hegemony of America. America's deficits are being financed by countries with saved surpluses—Japan, China, South Korea, Taiwan, and the Gulf States (Harvey 2009). Nobel Prize-winning economist, Paul Krugman (2009) thus concludes that it is "America" itself that is now "tarnished," its crisis "shockingly reminiscent of crises in places like Russia and Argentina," in the "third world."

These are bold sentiments indeed and they may in fact correctly predict the waning of the Washington consensus on poverty. But the study of microfinance allows one to pay closer attention to the fine grain of this hegemony, to notice a remaking of markets in the age of millennial development.

The Subprime Frontier

Microfinance investment funds, Jonathan Lewis of MicroCredit Enterprises notes, represent a "faith-based belief in the market." He argues that while microfinance is known for its individual borrower repayment rates, the default rates of microfinance institutions are unknown:

> Someday, people will have to cross a Rubicon, because there will be events like foreclosures . . . Will the president of Tufts and Pierre Omidyar, when they are waiting for a liquidity event, say to 27,000 women, "Sorry, we're closing down and you're going to lose your loan—so go back to feeding your kids twice a day?"

> (Bruck 2006)

Two years prior, Lewis, at the Microfinance Conference at UC Berkeley's Clausen Center, had declared that "we are in the wild west of microfinance." His frontier metaphor stayed with me, gaining rather than losing relevance as the financial crisis gathered force. For while the specter of foreclosures and catastrophic failure lurks in the shadows of microfinance, it is resilience rather than vulnerability that has been the key microfinance discourse in the context of the millennium's financial crisis.

In Mexico, the directors of Compartamos declared that it was resilient (Thomson 2009) with only a slight increase in default rates. The argument about resilience is not new. In 2003, Stanley Fischer, then vice-president of Citigroup, reminisced about the East Asian financial crisis of the previous decade: "A large Indonesian bank, suffered nearly 100% default rates in its corporate portfolio, but only 2% in its microfinance portfolio" (*New York Times* 2003). At the 2009 annual conference of Sanabel, the Arab Microfinance Network, Bob Annibale, global head of microfinance for Citigroup, once again declared that microfinance markets were resilient (Halawi 2009). At the height of the financial crisis, Citigroup ran advertisements in newspapers such as the *New York Times*, advertising its microfinance programs. They were meant to convey a message to American taxpayers that their money was well spent on the bailouts since it ultimately reached poor women with the capacity to repay loans. Microfinance seems to be "good money" in the "age of responsibility." But most important, it is a market. A CGAP report concluded that microfinance funds have been "relatively unscathed by the financial crisis," thus proving the resilience of these loan portfolios. The report shows that assets of the top ten microfinance investment funds grew by 32 percent in 2008, making "microfinance one of the few asset classes with a positive return in 2008." Such links between "microentrepreneurs and international capital markets" are being celebrated, and microfinance is seen as a market "where arbitrage possibilities remain to be exploited" (Bystrom 2008: 2110). Microfinance seems to be the new subprime frontier of millennial capitalism, where development capital and finance capital merge and collaborate such that new subjects of development are identified and new territories of investment are opened up and consolidated.

A subprime system of lending offers high-risk borrowers access to credit at interest rates that exceed those made available to "prime" borrowers. "High risk" is of course a social construction, a stigma that is placed on particular social groups—the poor, racial/ethnic minorities, and women. Their financial inclusion takes place on subprime terms. As evident in the workings of American housing mortgage markets, "exclusionary denial and inclusionary segmentation into subprime credit are two sides of the same coin" (Wyly et al. 2008: 12). It is the systematic redlining of particular social groups—defined by race, class, and gender—from financial institutions that necessitates subprime lending. They are now included, but on less than equal terms, paying much more than for the same product—a loan—than other consumers. This is the peculiar logic of subprime credit markets: that they are simultaneously instruments of financial inclusion and instances of exploitative, even predatory, lending. Such also is the logic of microfinance, for it allows the poor access to credit but on terms that are significantly different from those enjoyed by "prime" consumers—be they the high interest rates of Comparatamos or the intimate discipline enacted by the Grameen Bank. In other words, the subprime marks the limits of the democratization of capital.

The designation of microfinance as subprime lending is not unusual. Yunus himself refers to microfinance as "sub sub sub subprime" (Parker 2008). But accompanying such designations is a narrative that seeks to draw a sharp distinction between microfinance and other forms of subprime lending. The interlocutors and brokers of microfinance, from CGAP to Yunus, insist that microfinance embodies a new moral paradigm in the economy of finance, what may be designated as "responsible finance" or "ethical capitalism." Thus, at a recent conference in Tunisia, president of PlanetFinance, Jacques Attali, not only argued that microfinance could "seriously help cushion the impact of the global financial crisis on Africa," but also that it "could be a solution to the financial crisis given that it is based on ethics which is lacking in traditional finance cycles" (AFDB 2009). CGAP (2008c) insists that microfinance "operates very differently from US subprime markets": "The microfinance sector has also developed innovative risk-management techniques, prided itself on knowing customers, been scrupulous about ensuring repayment ability, and kept an eagle eye on delinquency." Not surprisingly, CGAP has been strongly advocating the adoption of its Code of Ethics, a new version of the Washington consensus on poverty. In Yunus's framework, such themes of transparency and discipline are repackaged as "trust." Once vilified by the *Wall Street Journal*, Yunus is now being celebrated by it as the "subprime lender" (Parker 2008). The reporter marvels at how microfinance has restored trust, and thus the original meaning of the term, credit, which derives from the Latin, *credere*, or "to believe." Yunus agrees, contrasting such trust-driven transactions with a credit system "entirely based on distrust." Indeed it seems that microfinance is remaking the forms of trust that are needed to facilitate the circulation of money through global networks (Gilbert 2005).

This resilience of microfinance, attributed to its unique ethics, raises the question: has microfinance unlocked the mystery of subprime capital? Above all, can it set the right price for risk? In a *New York Times* editorial, columnist Thomas Friedman (2009) boldly argued that the "capitalist engine doesn't need to be discarded; it needs some fixes." His is an attempt to come to terms with the brave new world of finance capital. Friedman thus laments a world of "just financial products" and calls for "more engineering of goods." But above all, he notes, this is a system that has been "mispricing risk," thus producing "toxic assets" and "destructive creation." Microfinance as poverty capital promises to set the right price for risk and to thus open up a new frontier of financial markets, those that are both pro-poor and profitable.

If poverty capital is to dominate the new millennium, then the material and discursive technologies detailed and analyzed throughout this book will soon become prominent. Financial institutions will make knowable subprime subjects who have hitherto remained at the margins of capital accumulation, such as the extreme poor. This will be a dataspace of heat maps and global rankings where risk can be tracked and rated. But such circuits of truth will require more than data. They will also require new stories to be told. One such story is the "parable of the cobbler and laid-off financier" told by Kate McKee (2009) on the CGAP blogs. In an interesting reversal, the Wall Street financier is presented as having wealth but lacking discipline. Without a job but with a "fat bonus check," he squanders time and money at the "Carnival in Rio" and "snorkeling in the Philippines." By contrast, the cobbler is busy serving a growing market, as consumers seek to repair worn-out shoes rather than purchasing new ones. Once asked to remake itself in the image of Wall Street, the microfinance sector is now asked to recognize that its clients are the cobblers. "It's a good time to be a cobbler again." This statement, made in the corridors of power in Washington DC, marks the consolidation, rather than end, of the Washington consensus on poverty. For it is in such a statement that "neoliberal populism" is most fully evident, as a celebration of both free-market ideologies and the people's economy. The cobbler's economic vulnerability is now recast as opportunity.

The making of poverty capital will also involve the remaking of geographies. Today microfinance conferences are titled "dollars without borders." Through microfinance a new global order of development is being envisioned, one where places that fail can be fixed. If once, as described by LiPuma and Lee (2004), the Arab world was portrayed as a periphery, lacking the "talent for cooperation" and "aptitude" required for banking and finance, then today it is this "other" geography that is a new frontier of capital accumulation. Islamic microfinance is a global niche market; cities such as Dubai are sites of a frantic and fantastic urban development; and nation-states such as Kuwait control vast Sovereign Wealth Funds, state-owned investment funds that can buy up the Wall Street giants and much more. The remaking of peripheral geographies as frontiers also requires the making of truths—poverty truths. It is thus that a wave of securitizations—be they those of BRAC and ASA or those of the Grameen Foundation—capitalizes on the truth of the Bangladesh model. After all, this model promises high rates of financial and social returns on investment. This too is poverty capital.

Above all the production of poverty capital will require new practices and meanings of debt. In the Katrina moment that is the financial crisis, credit has become visible as debt. What was once lauded as the vast scope and reach of a liquid financial market is now seen as greedy recklessness. Will there be, as Canadian novelist Margaret Atwood (2008) in a rumination on debt asks, "payback"? Can the microfinance sector remake debt as *credere*, as systems of credit based on trust? Or will it be an industry of "microsharks," a predatory subprime market? Rejecting Yunus's notion of "credit as a human right," a manager of a microfinance fund thus declared: "Can we please remember that credit means you owe something and you can get overly indebted?" (Bruck 2006).

Anthropologist Janet Roitman (2005: 73) asks a profound question: "How is it that some forms of wealth are socially sanctioned in spite of their origins in debt relations whereas others are denounced quite flatly as debt, being portrayed as a negative economic indicator, a disruption in the order of production and exchange?" In an age of poverty capital, it is microfinance that will have to renew

220

what Roitman calls the "productivity of debt." If in previous moments of crisis, microfinance was a social remedy for the harsh strictures of neoliberal adjustment, then today microfinance is an asset class, a circuit of accumulation, speculation, and profit. It is poverty capital.

Each genre of capital has its own truths. The truths are trades in promises, promises that are more often betrayed and fulfilled. In the case of production capital, the animating truth is the idea of Fordism, a system of wage-earning work that not only efficiently produces commodities but also ensures that those who produce can consume, with dignity. In the case of development capital, the animating truth is the teleology of modernization, the march up the ladder of development, through well-charted stages of economic growth. In the case of finance capital, the animating truth is the promise of an ownership society, one where risk is constantly transformed, through speculation, into prosperity. In the case of poverty capital, the animating truth is the democratization of capital, of the bottom billion gaining access to the instruments of capitalism and for this in turn to be the basis for a new generation of global capital. This is the subprime frontier of the new millennium.

But like other types of capital, poverty capital too is messy. Its generation of global capital is fragile, dependent on what the interlocutors of millennial development term the ability "to monetize the promise of a poor woman who had never touched a coin" in places "where one cannot drink the water." This, as I have shown, requires considerable and constant work. Poverty capital's truth-making enterprise is also fraught with contradiction. The animating truth of bottom-billion finance exists uneasily alongside other poverty truths, such as those concerned with social protection or development infrastructure or the tortoise-pace temporality of weekly savings. Like Kandinsky's compositions, poverty capital is made up of centralities as well as multiplicities.

I am concerned enough about the power and hegemony of poverty capital to have undertaken this research and written this book. But I am also convinced enough about the fractures and crises of poverty capital—its political possibilities, its double agents, the ideas that are weapons—to have found such an undertaking worthwhile. This is not the story of counter-geographies of resistance or native rebellions from "below." Instead it is the story of a "folding together," of complicities that are also subversions, of dissent in the creases and folds of the composition that is poverty capital.

NOTE

1   Alex Counts, president of the Grameen Foundation, 2006 Microcredit Summit, Halifax, Canada.

References

Abed, F. and Matin, I. (2007) "Beyond lending: how microfinance creates new forms of capital to fight poverty," *Innovations*, Winter and Spring, 3–17.

Abu-Lughod, L. (2009) "Dialects of women's empowerment: the international circuitry of the Arab Human Development Report 2005," *International Journal of Middle East Studies*, 41, 61–62.

AFDB (2009) "French economist underscores role of micro-finance in efforts at reducing poverty." Online. Available HTTP: http://www.afdb.org/en/news-events/article/french-economist-underscores-role-of-micro-finance-in-efforts-at-reducing-poverty-4446/ (accessed April 15, 2009).

Ahmed, M. (2002) *Key to Achieving Sustainability: Simple and Standard Microfinance Services of ASA*, Dhaka, Bangladesh: ASA.

Albright, M.K. and Doerr, J. (2004) "Micro-credit brings macro-benefits," *San Francisco Chronicle*, May 27. Online. Available HTTP: http://www.sfgate.com/cgi-bin/article.cgi?file=/chronicle/archive/2004/05/27/EDG7J6ROMA1.DTL (accessed July 14, 2004).

Alexander, P. (2007) "The big business of small loans." Online. Available HTTP: www.emergingmarkets.org (accessed November 20, 2007).

Ali, T. (2008) "Afghanistan: mirage of the good war," *New Left Review*, 50, 5–22.

Alterman, J. (2006) "The wrong way to sway Egypt," *Washington Post*, June 13. Online. Available HTTP: http://www.washingtonpost.com/wp-dyn/content/article/2006/06/12/AR2006061201286.html (accessed March 18, 2008).

AME Info (2008) "Islamic solidarity fund for development to support vocational education and microfinance." Online. Available HTTP: http://www.ameinfo.com/149911.html (accessed October 29, 2008).

Appadurai, A. (2001) "Deep democracy: urban governmentality and the horizon of politics," *Environment and Urbanization*, 13 (2), 23–44.

Armstrong, D. (2008) "Is bigger better?," *Forbes*, June 2. Online. Available: HTTP http://www.forbes.com/forbes/2008/0602/066.html (accessed June 15, 2008).

ASA (2001) *ASA Manual*, Dhaka, Bangladesh: ASA.

Atia, M. (2008) "Building a house in heaven: Islamic charity in neoliberal Egypt," unpublished dissertation, University of Washington, Seattle.

Atwood, M. (2008) *Payback: Debt and the Shadow Side of Wealth*, Toronto: House of Anansi Press.

AVID Consulting Corporation (2004) Final Report of Mid-term Evaluation of USAID/Egypt Small and Emerging Business Program, prepared for USAID. Online. Available HTTP: http://www.banyanglobal.com/pdf/micro_2004.12.15_usaid.pdf (accessed January 7, 2005).

Ayittey, G. (2004) *Africa Unchained: The Blueprint for Africa's Future*, New York: Palgrave Macmillan.

Ayres, R. (1983) *Banking on the Poor: The World Bank and World Poverty*, Cambridge, MA: MIT Press for the Overseas Development Council.

Badr El-Din, N. (2006) *The SFD's Microfinance Sector*, Cairo, Egypt: The Social Fund for Development, Government of Egypt.

Bajaj, V. and Leland, J. (2009) "Modifying mortgages can be a tricky business," *New York Times*, February 19. Online. Available HTTP: http://www.nytimes.com/2009/02/19/us/19loans.html?_r=1&fta=y (accessed February 19, 2009).

Barry, A. (2004) "Ethical capitalism," in W. Larner and W. Walters (eds) *Global Governmentality: Governing International Spaces*, New York: Routledge, 195–211.

Bayat, A. (2002) "Activism and social development in the Middle East," *International Journal of Middle East Studies*, 34 (1), 1–28.

Bayat, A. (2007) "Radical religion and the habitus of the dispossessed: does Islamic militancy have an urban ecology?," *International Journal of Urban and Regional Research,* 31 (3), 579–590.

Beblawi, H (1990) "The rentier state in the Arab world," in G. Luciani (ed.) *The Arab State*, Berkeley: University of California Press, 85–98.

Bello, W. (2006) "Microcredit, macro issues," *The Nation*, October 14. Online. Available HTTP: http://www.thenation.com/doc/20061030/bello (accessed February 10, 2007).

Bello, W. (2007) "Globalization in retreat: capitalist overstretch, civil society and the crisis of the globalist project," *Berkeley Journal of Sociology*, 51, 209–220.

Benetton (2008) "MFI started by Youssou N'Dour featured in Benetton's latest global communication campaign," February 13. Online. Available HTTP: http://www.benetton.com/africaworks-press/en/press_information/1_1.html (accessed January 20, 2009).

Bergeron, S. (2003a) "Challenging the World Bank's narrative of inclusion," in A. Kumar (ed.) *World Bank Literature*, Minneapolis: University of Minnesota Press, 157–171.

Bergeron, S. (2003b) "The post-Washington consensus and economic representations of women in development at the World Bank," *International Feminist Journal of Politics*, 5 (3), 397–419.

Bhide, A. and Shramm, C. (2007) "Phelps's prize," *Wall Street Journal*, January 29. Online. Available HTTP: http://online.wsj.com/article/SB117003072952090648.html (accessed February 18, 2007).

Blease, G. (2008) "Savings and souls," *The Economist*, September 4. Online. Available HTTP: http://www.economist.com/displaystory.cfm?story_id=12052687 (accessed November 11, 2008).

Bono (2007) "Guest editor's letter: message 2U," *Vanity Fair*, July. Online. Available HTTP: http://www.vanityfair.com/magazine/2007/07/bono200707 (accessed August 10, 2007).

Bono (2009) "It's 2009. Do you know where your soul is?," *New York Times*, April 19. Online. Available HTTP: http://www.nytimes.com/2009/04/19/opinion/19bono.html?_r=1 (accessed April 19, 2009).

Bornstein, D. (1996) *The Price of a Dream: The Story of the Grameen Bank and the Idea that is Helping the Poor Change their Lives*, New York: Simon & Schuster.

Boston Globe (2002) "Microprogress," March 18.

Bourdieu, P. (1985) "The social space and the genesis of groups," *Theory and Society*, 14 (6), 723–744.

Bourdieu. P. (2005) *The Social Structures of the Economy*, trans. C. Turner, Malden, MA: Polity Press.

Brandsma, J. and Burjrjee, D. (2004) *Microfinance in the Arab States: Building Inclusive Financial Sectors*, New York: UNCDF.

Bruck, C. (2006) "Millions for millions," *The New Yorker*, October 30. Online. Available HTTP: http://www.newyorker.com/archive/2006/10/30/061030fa_fact1 (accessed December 1, 2006).

Burgis, T. (2008) "Microfinance commercialisation warning," *Financial Times*, July 29. Online. Available HTTP: http://www.themix.org/press-clippings/2009/03/20/financial-times-microfinance-commercialisation-warning (accessed October 22, 2008).

Burns, J. and Thomas Jr, L. (2009) "Anglo-American capitalism on trial," *New York Times*, March 29. Online. Available HTTP: http://www.nytimes.com/2009/03/29/weekinreview/29burns.html (accessed March 29, 2009).

Bush, G.W. (2002) "State of the Union address." Online. Available HTTP: http://www.washingtonpost.com/wp-srv/onpolitics/transcripts/sou012902.htm (accessed September 5, 2008).

Business Week (2007) "Yunus blasts Compartamos," December 13. Online. Available HTTP: http://www.businessweek.com/magazine/content/07_52/b4064045920958.htm (accessed January 10, 2008).

Business Wire (2008) "Microfinance institution ASA International secures largest equity capital commitment ever to microfinance." Online. Available HTTP: http://www.pr-inside.com/microfinance-institution-asa-international-secures-r434429.htm (accessed February 1, 2009).

Buvinic, M. (1997) "Women in poverty: a new global underclass," *Foreign Policy*, 108, 38–52.

Bystrom, H. (2008) "The microfinance collateralized debt obligation: a modern Robin Hood?," *World Development*, 36 (11), 2109–2126.

Capital Plus (2004) *The Challenge of Development in Development Finance Institutions*, Chicago: Publication of the Development, Finance Forum.

Carapico, S. (2000) "NGOs, INGOs, GO-NGOs and DO-NGOs: making sense of non-governmental organizations," *Middle East Report*, 214. Online. Available HTTP: http://www.merip.org/mer/mer214/214_carapico.html (accessed March 11, 2008).

Carter, G. (2007) "Editor's letter: Annie get your passport," *Vanity Fair*, July. Online. Available HTTP: http://www.vanityfair.com/magazine/2007/07/graydon200707 (accessed August 10, 2007).

Caulfield, C. (1996) *Masters of Illusion: The World Bank and the Poverty of Nations*, New York: Henry Holt.

CGAP (2003) *Annual Report,* Washington DC: CGAP, The World Bank.

CGAP (2004a) *Key Principles of Microfinance,* Washington DC: CGAP, The World Bank.

CGAP (2004b) *Foreign Investment in Microfinance: Debt and Equity from Quasi-Commercial Investors?,* Focus Note 25, Washington DC: CGAP, The World Bank.

CGAP (2007) "Savings for poor people: good for clients, good for business." Online. Available HTTP: http://www.cgap.org/p/site/c/template.rc/1.26.2209/ (accessed September 12, 2008).

CGAP (2008a) *Islamic Microfinance: An Emerging Market Niche,* Washington DC: CGAP, The World Bank.

CGAP (2008b) *Foreign Capital Investment in Microfinance: Balancing Social and Financial Returns,* Focus Note 44, Washington DC: CGAP, The World Bank.

CGAP (2008c) "The global financial crisis: what does it mean for microfinance?," December 15. Online. Available HTTP: http://www.cgap.org/p/site/c/template.rc/1.26.4511/ (accessed February 26, 2009).

CGAP (2008d) "Building a microfinance industry from scratch," May 31. Online. Available HTTP: http://www2.cgap.org/p/site/c/template.rc/1.26.2213/ (accessed June 21, 2008).

Chamberlin, W. (2003) "USAID testimony before the senate foreign relations committee," March 26. Online. Available HTTP: http://www.globalsecurity.org/military/library/congress/2003_hr/cham0515.htm (accessed June 28, 2004).

Chambers, R. (1983) *Rural Development: Putting the Last First,* Hoboken, NJ: Wiley.

Chant, S. (2006) "Re-thinking the 'feminization of poverty' in relation to aggregate gender indices," *Journal of Human Development,* 7 (2), 201–220.

Chant, S. (2008) "The 'feminisation of poverty' and the 'feminisation' of anti-poverty programmes: room for revision?," *Journal of Development Studies,* 44 (2), 165–197.

Chant, S. and Brickell, K. (2010) "'The unbearable heaviness of being': reflections on female altruism in Cambodia, Philippines, the Gambia and Costa Rica," *Progress in Development Studies,* 10, 2, forthcoming.

Chazan, D. (2009) "Microcredit loans used to buy food," *Financial Times,* June 4. Online. Available HTTP: http://www.microfinancegateway.org/p/site/m/template.rc/1.1.2302/ (accessed July 1, 2009).

Chen, M. (1983) *A Quiet Revolution: Women in Transition in Rural Bangladesh,* Rochester, VT: Schenkman Books.

Chronic Poverty Research Centre (2008) *The Chronic Poverty Report 2008–09: Escaping Poverty Traps,* Manchester: Brooks World Poverty Institute, University of Manchester.

Chu, M. (2005) "Microfinance: the next ten years," in A. Pakpahan, E.M. Lokollo, and K. Wijaya (eds) *Microbanking: Creating Opportunities for the Poor Through Innovation,* Jakarta: Bank Rakyat Indonesia, 110–115.

Chu, M. (2007) "Profit and poverty: why it matters," *Forbes.com,* December 20. Online. Available HTTP: http://www.forbes.com/2007/12/20/michael-chu-microfinance-biz-cz_mc_1220chu.html (accessed December 2, 2009).

Clinton, W. (2006) "Speech: remarks at Guildhall on globalization, London." Online. Available HTTP: http://www.clintonfoundation.org/032806-sp-cf-gn-gl-gbr-sp-remarks-at-guildhall-on-globalization.htm (accessed February 10, 2007).

Coleman, T. (2008) "A new vision for bottom billion microfinance." Online. Available HTTP: http://www.microlinks.org/ev.php?ID=27639_201&ID2=DO_DISCUSSIONPOST_LIST (accessed May 20, 2009).

Collier, P. (2007) *The Bottom Billion: Why the Poorest Countries are Failing and What Can Be Done About It*, New York: Oxford University Press.

Comaroff, J. and Comaroff, J. (2000) "Millennial capitalism: first thoughts on a second coming," *Public Culture*, 12 (2), 291–343.

Cornia, G. and Reddy, S. (2001) *The Impact of Adjustment-related Social Funds on Income Distribution and Poverty*, Discussion Paper 2001/1. New York: United Nations University/World Institute for Development Economics Research (WIDER).

Counts, A. (2004) "Scarce use of public funds should facilitate greater depth of outreach," unpublished letter to the *New York Times*. Online. Available HTTP: http://www.micro financegateway.org/p/site/m/template.rc/1.26.9075/ (accessed September 1, 2004).

Covington, R. (2009) "Bangladesh's audacity of hope," *Aramco World*. Online. Available HTTP: http://www.saudiaramcoworld.com/issue/200903/bangladesh.s.audacity.of.hope.htm (accessed June 10, 2009).

CSRwire (2006) "Grameen–Jameel initiative engineers $2.5 million investment to boost microfinance in Egypt," September 26. Online. Available HTTP: http://www.csrwire.com/ press/press_release/20265-Grameen-Jameel-Initiative-Engineers-2-5-Million-Investment-to-Boost-Microfinance-in-Egypt (accessed February 22, 2008).

Dailey, J. (2005) "Data standards for connecting to commercial sources of capital," *Journal of Microfinance*, 7 (2), 33–45.

Daily Star (2007a) "Leading economist criticizes Yunus's microcredit policy," February 22. Online. Available HTTP: http://www.thedailystar.net/ (accessed December 1, 2007).

Daily Star (2007b) "Bangladesh academics ask Yunus to clarify position before joining politics," February 25. Online. Available HTTP: http://www.thedailystar.net/ (accessed December 1, 2007).

Danaher, K. (1995) *Fifty Years is Enough: The Case Against the World Bank and the International Monetary Fund*, Cambridge, MA: South End Press.

Das, M. (2008) *Whispers to Voices: Gender and Social Transformation in Bangladesh*, Washington DC: The World Bank.

Dash, E. and Creswell, J. (2008) "Citigroup pays for a rush to risk," *New York Times*, November 23. Online. Available HTTP: http://www.nytimes.com/2008/11/23/business/world business/23iht-23citi.18059343.html?_r=1 (accessed November 23, 2008).

Dash, E. and Story, L. (2009) "Citi Rescue may not be its last," *New York Times*, February 28. Online. Available HTTP: http://www.nytimes.com/2009/02/28/business/28citi.html (accessed February 28, 2009).

Deeb, L. (2006) *An Enchanted Modern: Gender and Public Piety in Shi'i Lebanon*, Princeton: Princeton University Press.

De Janvry, A. and Sadoulet, E. (2004) "Conditional cash transfer programs: are they really magic bullets?," *ARE Update*, 7 (6), 9–11. Online. Available HTTP: http://www.agecon. ucdavis.edu/extension/update/articles/v7n6_3.pdf (accessed December 2, 2008).

Denoux, G. (2005) "Promoting democracy and governance in the Arab world: strategic choices for donors," in S. Ben-Nafissa et al. (eds) *NGOs and Governance in an Arab World*, Cairo: American University of Cairo Press, 69–100.

Derrida, J. (1994) *Specters of Marx: The State of the Debt, the Work of Mourning, and the New International*, New York: Routledge.

De Soto, H. (2002) *The Mystery of Capital: Why Capitalism Triumphs in the West and Fails Everywhere Else*, New York: Basic Books.

Development Finance Forum (2004) *Capital Plus: The Challenge of Development in Development Finance Institutions*, Chicago: Shorebank Corporation.

Diacon, D. (1988) *World Habitat Awards*, Coalville, Leicestershire: Building and Social Housing Foundation.

Dowla, A. and Barua, D. (2006) *The Poor Always Pay Back: The Grameen II Story*, Bloomfield, CT: Kumarian Press.

Dugger, C. (2004) "Debate stirs over tiny loans for world's poorest," *New York Times*, April 29. Online. Available HTTP: http://www.nytimes.com/2004/04/29/world/debate-stirs-over-tiny-loans-for-world-s-poorest.html (accessed April 29, 2004).

Dugger, C. (2006) "Peace prize to pioneer of loans for those too poor to borrow," *New York Times*, October 14. Online. Available HTTP: http://www.nytimes.com/2006/10/14/world/asia/14nobel.html?scp=1&sq=peace%20prize%20borrowers&st=cse (accessed October 14, 2006).

Dunford, C. (1998) "Microfinance: a means to what end?," *NEXUS, SEEP*, Summer.

Dunford, C. (2004) "US legislation tests limits of helping the very poor to take advantage of microcredit services," unpublished letter to the *New York Times*. Online. Available HTTP: http://www.microfinancegateway.org/p/site/m/template.rc/1.26.9075/ (accessed September 1, 2004).

Easterly, W. (2006) *The White Man's Burden: Why the West's Efforts to Aid the Rest Have Done So Much Ill and So Little Good*, New York: Penguin Press.

The Economist (2009) "Banking on the fund," April 8. Online. Available HTTP: http://www.economist.com/opinion/displaystory.cfm?story_id=13446763&fsrc=rss (accessed June 11, 2009).

Elyachar, J. (2002) "Empowerment money: the World Bank, non-governmental organizations, and the value of culture in Egypt," *Public Culture* 14 (3), 493–513.

Elyachar, J. (2005) *Markets of Dispossession: NGOs, Economic Life, and the State in Cairo*, Durham, NC: Duke University Press.

Elyachar, J. (2006) "Best practices: research, finance, and NGOs in Cairo," *American Ethnologist*, 33 (3), 413–426.

EQI/NCBA (2005) *Technical Assistance for the Small and Emerging Business Project in Egypt, 2001–2005*, Cairo: EQI.

Falk Moore, S. (2001) "The international production of authoritative knowledge: the case of drought-stricken West Africa," *Ethnography* 2 (2), 161–189.

Fawaz, M. (2000) "Agency and ideology in the service provision of Islamic organizations in the southern suburb of Beirut," paper presented at the "NGOs and Governance in Arab Countries" UNESCO conference.

Ferguson, J. (2006) *Global Shadows: Africa in the Neoliberal World Order*, Durham, NC: Duke University Press.

Ferguson, N. (2002) *Empire: The Rise and Demise of the British World Order and the Lessons for Global Power*, London: Allen Lane.

Ferguson, N. (2008) *The Ascent of Money: A Financial History of the World*, New York: Penguin Press.

Ferguson, N. (2009) "Preface," in D. Moyo *Dead Aid: How Aid is Not Working and How There is a Better Way for Africa*, New York: Penguin Press, xiii–xvii.

Fernando, J.L. (2006) "Microcredit and empowerment of women: blurring the boundary between development and capitalism," in J.L. Fernando (ed.) *Microfinance: Perils and Prospects*, New York: Routledge, 1–42.

Fernando, N. and Meyer, R. (2002) "ASA: the Ford Motor model of microfinance," *Finance for the Poor*, Manila: Asian Development Bank.

Fikkert, B. (2003) *Christian Microfinance: Which Way Now?* Working Paper #205. Lookout Mountain, GA: Chalmers Center for Economic Development, Covenant College.

Fine, B. (2000) *Social Capital Versus Social Theory: Political Economy and Social Science at the Turn of the Millennium*, New York: Routledge.

Fine, B. (2001) "Neither the Washington nor the post-Washington consensus: an introduction," in B. Fine, C. Lapavitsas, and J. Pincus (eds) *Development Policy in the Twenty-first Century: Beyond the Post-Washington Consensus*, New York: Routledge, 1–27.

Finnemore, M. (1997) "Redefining development at the World Bank," in F. Cooper and R. Packard (eds) *International Development and the Social Sciences: Essays on the History and Politics of Knowledge*, Berkeley: University of California Press, 203–227.

Fischer, S. (2003) "Wall Street meets microfinance," WWB/FWA Lenore Albom Lecture Series, November 3. Online. Available HTTP: http://www.petersoninstitute.org/fischer/pdf/fischer110303.pdf (accessed October 10, 2004).

Fisher, M. and Downey, G. (2006) "The anthropology of capital and the frontiers of ethnography," in M. Fisher and G. Downey (eds) *Frontiers of Capitalism: Ethnographic Reflections on the New Economy*, Durham, NC: Duke University Press, 1–29.

Forster, S., Maurer, K., and Mithika, M. (2007) "CGAP phase III midterm evaluation (July 2003–June 2006)." Online. Available HTTP: http://www.cgap.org/ (accessed January 11, 2008).

Fouad, N., Refat, N., and Murcos, S. (2005) "From inertia to movement: a study of the conflict over the NGO law in Egypt," in S. Ben-Nafissa et al. (eds) *NGOs and Governance in the Arab World*, Cairo: American University of Cairo Press, 101–122.

Foucault, M. (1969; 1982 edition) *The Archaeology of Knowledge and the Discourse on Language*, New York: Pantheon.

Foucault, M. (1966; 1994 edition) *The Order of Things: An Archaeology of the Human Sciences*, New York: Vintage.

Frank, C. (2008) "Stemming the tide of mission drift: microfinance transformations and the double bottom line," *Women's World Banking*, April 17. Online. Available HTTP: http://www.swwb.org/stemming-the-tide-of-mission-drift (accessed July 15, 2008).

Friedman, T. (2002) "Globalization, alive and well," *New York Times*, September 22. Online. Available HTTP: http://www.nytimes.com/2002/09/22/opinion/globalization-alive-and-well.html (accessed September 22, 2002).

Friedman, T. (2009) "The price is not right," *New York Times*, April 1. Online. Available HTTP: http://www.nytimes.com/2009/04/01/opinion/01friedman.html (accessed April 1, 2009).

Fuglesang, A. and Chandler, D. (1988) *Participation as Process: What We Can Learn From the Grameen Bank*, Bangladesh, Dhaka: Pearl Printing.

Fukuyama, F. (1989) "The end of history?," *The National Interest*, 16, 3–18.

Fukuyama, F. (1992) *The End of History and the Last Man*, New York: Avon Books.

Gates, B. (2008) "How to fix capitalism," *Time*, July 31, 23–29.

Gereffi, G. and Korzeniewicz, M. (eds) (1993) *Commodity Chains and Global Capitalism*, Westport, CT: Greenwood Press.

Gilbert, E. (2005) "Common cents: situating money in time and space," *Economy and Society*, 34 (3), 356–387.

Goetz, A. (2001) *Women Development Workers: Implementing Rural Credit Programmes in Bangladesh*, Thousand Oaks, CA: Sage Publications.

Goetz, A.M. and Sengupta, R. (1996) "Who takes the credit? Gender, power, and control over loan use in rural credit programs in Bangladesh," *World Development*, 24 (1), 45–63.

Goldman, M. (2005) *Imperial Nature: The World Bank and Struggles for Social Justice in an Age of Globalization*, New Haven, CT: Yale University Press.

Gore, C. (2000) "The rise and fall of the Washington consensus as a paradigm for developing countries," *World Development*, 28 (5), 789–804.

Government of Bangladesh (2005) *Unlocking the Potential: National Strategy for Accelerated Poverty Reduction*, Dhaka, Bangladesh: General Economics Division, Planning Commission.

Government of Egypt (2005) *National Strategy for Microfinance in Egypt: A Sector Development Approach*, Cairo, Egypt: Social Fund for Development.

Gowan, P. (2009) "Crisis in the heartland: consequences of the new Wall Street system," *New Left Review*, 55, 5–29.

Grameen Foundation (2007a) "Grameen–Jameel Initiative secures $2.7 million for FONDEP," January 2. Online. Available HTTP: http://www.syminvest.com/market/news/micro finance/grameerijameel-initiative-secure-27-million-for-fondep/2007/1/2/242 (accessed May 11, 2008).

Grameen Foundation (2007b) "Grameen Foundation appoints Diane M. Smith to head Capital Markets Group," January 29. Online. Available HTTP: http://www.grameenfoundation. org/resource_center/newsroom/news_releases/~story=203 (accessed May 11, 2008).

Grameen Foundation (2009) "GF announces new social investing guidelines for microfinance," February 23. Online. Available HTTP: http://www.grameenfoundation.org/ resource_center/newsroom/news_releases/~story=372 (accessed April 2, 2009).

Grameen Trust (2003) *Notes from Grameen Dialogues*, Dhaka, Bangladesh: Grameen Bank.

Halawi, D. (2009) "Microfinance remains 'resilient' to global market trends," *Daily Star*, May 13. Online. Available HTTP: http://www.dailystar.com.lb/article.asp?edition_id=1& categ_id=3&article_id=101892 (accessed May 20, 2009).

Halder, S. and Mosley, P. (2002) *Working with the Ultra Poor: Learning from BRAC's Experiences*, RED BRAC Economic Studies, XVII, Dhaka, Bangladesh: BRAC.

Hamzeh, A. (2004) *In the Path of Hizbullah*, Syracuse: Syracuse University Press.

Haque, M.S. (2002) "The changing balance of power between the government and NGOs in Bangladesh," *International Political Science Review*, 23 (4), 411–435.

Harb, M. (2001) "Post-war Beirut: resources, negotiations, and contestations in the Elyssar project," in S. Shami (ed.) *Capital Cities: Ethnographies of Urban Governance in the Middle East*, University of Toronto: Centre for Urban and Community Studies, 111–134.

Harb, M. and Leenders, R. (2005) "Know thy enemy: Hizbullah, 'terrorism' and the politics of perception," *Third World Quarterly*, 26 (1), 173–195.

Harford, T. (2008) "The battle for the soul of microfinance," *Financial Times*, December 6. Online. Available HTTP: http://www.microcapital.org/microcapital-excerpt-the-battle-for-the-soul-of-microfinance-by-financial-times-senior-columnist-tim-harford/ (accessed December 10, 2008).

Harik, J. (1994) *The Public and Social Services of the Lebanese Militias*, Oxford: Centre for Lebanese Studies.

Harik, J.P. (1996) "Between Islam and the system: sources and implications of popular support for Lebanon's Hezbollah," *Journal of Conflict Resolution*, 40 (1), 40–67.

Harriss, J. (2001) *Depoliticizing Development: The World Bank and Social Capital*, London: Anthem Press.

Harvey, D. (2005) *A Brief History of Neoliberalism*, New York: Oxford University Press.

Harvey, D. (2009) "Why the US stimulus package is bound to fail," *Socialist Project*, E-Bulletin 184, Online. Available HTTP: http://davidharvey.org/2009/02/why-the-us-stimulus-package-is-bound-to-fail/ (accessed May 20, 2009).

Hashemi, S. (2001) *Linking Microfinance and Safety Net Programs to Include the Poorest: The Case of IGVGD in Bangladesh*, CGAP Focus Note 21, Washington DC: CGAP, The World Bank.

Hashemi, S. (2006) "What will the Nobel Prize mean for microfinance: an interview," October 16. Online. Available HTTP: http://web.worldbank.org/WBSITE/EXTERNAL/COUNTRIES/SOUTHASIAEXT/0,,contentMDK:21091923~pagePK:146736~piPK:14683 0~theSitePK:223547,00.html (accessed December 20, 2006).

Hashemi, S. (2007) *Beyond Good Intentions: Measuring the Social Performance of Microfinance Institutions*, CGAP Focus Note 41, Washington DC: CGAP, The World Bank.

Hashemi, S. and Rosenberg, R. (2006) *Graduating the Poorest into Microfinance: Linking Safety Nets and Financial Services*, CGAP Focus Note 32, Washington DC: CGAP, The World Bank.

Hashemi, S., Schuler, S.R., and Riley, A.P. (1996) "Rural credit programs and women's employment in Bangladesh," *World Development*, 24 (4), 635–653.

Hasso, F. (2009) "Empowering governmentalities rather than women: the Arab Human Development Report 2005 and Western development logics," *International Journal of Middle East Studies*, 41, 63–82.

Helms, B. (2006) *Access for All: Building Inclusive Financial Systems*, Washington DC: CGAP, The World Bank.

Higgins, A. (2006) "Branded terrorist by U.S., Israel, a microcredit czar keeps lending," *The Wall Street Journal*, December 29.

Hochberg, F. (2002) "Practical Help for Afghans," *New York Times*, January 5. Online. Available HTTP: http://www.nytimes.com/2002/01/05/opinion/practical-help-for-afghans.html (accessed June 19, 2008).

Hossain, N. and Matin, I. (2004) *Engaging Elite Support for the Poorest? BRAC's Experience with the Ultra Poor Programme*, CFPR-TUP Working Paper Series, 3, Dhaka, Bangladesh: BRAC.

Houston Chronicle (2002) "Microcredit: a way to fight poverty, terrorism in small bites," March 18.

Hulme, D. and Moore, K. (2006) "Why has microfinance been a policy success? Bangladesh and beyond," GPRG-WPS-041. Online. Available HTTP: http://www.gprg.org/pubs/workingpapers/pdfs/gprg-wps-041.pdf (accessed January 28, 2009).

Hulme, D. and Mosley, P. (1996) *Finance Against Poverty: Effective Institutions for Lending to Small Farmers and Microenterprises in Developing Countries*, London: Routledge.

Husseini, R. (1997) "Promoting women entrepreneurs in Lebanon: the experience of UNIFEM," *Gender and Development*, 5 (1), 49–53.

Ignatius, D. (2005) "Long road to the promised land," *Washington Post*, June 15. Online. Available HTTP: http://www.washingtonpost.com/wp-dyn/content/article/2005/06/14/AR2005061401343_pf.html (accessed June 19, 2008).

ING (2008) "A billion to gain? A study on global financial institutions and microfinance." Online. Available HTTP: http://www.ingmicrofinanciering.nl/uploads/ul_A%20Billion%20to%20Gain%20-Next%20Phase,%20March%202008%20Adobe%207.pdf (accessed March 1, 2009).

Ismail, S. (2006) *Political Life in Cairo's New Quarters: Encountering the Everyday State*, Minneapolis: University of Minnesota Press.

Jackson, C. (1996) "Rescuing gender from the poverty trap," *World Development*, 24 (3), 489–504.

Jacquand, M. (2005) "Measuring social performance: the wrong priority," *Microfinance Matters*, August. Online. Available HTTP: http://www.uncdf.org/english/microfinance/pubs/newsletter/pages/2005_08/news_measuring.php (accessed January 30, 2009).

Jad, I. (2009) "Comments from an author: engaging the Arab Human Development Report 2005 on Women," *International Journal of Middle East Studies*, 41, 61–62.

Jansen, A. (2002) "Preface," in D. Drake and E. Rhyne (eds) *The Commercialization of Microfinance: Balancing Business and Development*, Bloomfield, CT: Kumarian Press, vii–viii.

Kabeer, N. (2000) "Conflicts over credit: re-evaluating the empowerment potential of loans to women in rural Bangladesh," *World Development*, 29 (1), 63–84.

Kabeer, N. (2003) "Assessing the wider social impacts of microfinance services," *IDS Bulletin*, 34 (4), 106–114.

Kabeer, N. (2005) Gender Equality and Human Development: The Instrumental Rationale. United Nations Human Development Report Office Occasional Paper. Online. Available HTTP: http://hdr.undp.org/en/reports/global/hdr2005/papers/HDR2005_Kabeer_Naila_31.pdf (accessed April 20, 2009).

Kabeer, N. and Matin, I. (2005) *The Wider Social Impacts of BRAC's Group Based Lending in Rural Bangladesh: Group Dynamics and Participation in Public Life*, BRAC Research Monograph Series 25, Dhaka, Bangladesh: BRAC.

Kapur, D. (2002) "The changing anatomy of governance of the World Bank," in J. Pincus and J. Winters (eds) *Reinventing the World Bank*, Ithaca, NY: Cornell University Press, 54–75.

Kelly, R. (2006) "Bush administration defends US military aid to Egypt," *World Socialist Website*. Online. Available HTTP: http://www.wsws.org/articles/2006/may2006/egyp-m22.shtml (accessed April 7, 2008).

Khalili, L. (2007) "Standing with my brother: Hizbollah, Palestinians and the limit of power," *Comparative Studies in Society and History*, 49, 276–303.

Khandker, S. (1998) *Fighting Poverty with Microcredit: Experience in Bangladesh*, New York: Oxford University Press.

Khandker, S. (2003) *Micro-finance and Poverty: Evidence using Panel Data from Bangladesh*, Policy Research Working Paper 2945. Washington DC: World Bank.

Khandker, S. (2005) "Microfinance and poverty: evidence using panel data from Bangladesh," *The World Bank Economic Review*, 19 (2), 263–286.

Khechen, M. (2007) "Beyond the spectacle: Al-Saha Village, Beirut," *Traditional Dwellings and Settlements Review*, XIX (1), 7–21.

Kiviat, B. (2008) "Microfinance: women being cheated?," *Time*, April 17. Online. Available HTTP: http://www.time.com/time/world/article/0,8599,1731718,00.html (accessed March 30, 2009).

Klein, N. (2001) "A fete for the end of the end of history," *The Nation*, March 19. Online. Available HTTP: http://www.thenation.com/doc/20010319/klein (accessed April 10, 2009).

Klein, N. (2007) *The Shock Doctrine: The Rise of Disaster Capitalism*, New York: Penguin Books.

Knudsen, A. (2005) "Islamism in the diaspora: Palestinian refugees in Lebanon," *Journal of Refugee Studies*, 18 (2), 216–234.

Knudsen, A. (2007) *The Law, The Loss, and the Lives of Palestinian Refugees in Lebanon*, CMI Working Paper 1. Online. Available HTTP: http://www.cmi.no/publications/file/?2607=the-law-the-loss-and-the-lives-of-palestinian (accessed December 3, 2008).

Kraske, J. et al. (1996) *Bankers with a Mission: The Presidents of the World Bank, 1946–91*, New York: Oxford University Press (published for the World Bank).

Krugman, P. (2009) "America the tarnished," *New York Times*, March 30. Online. Available HTTP: http://www.nytimes.com/2009/03/30/opinion/30krugman.html?_r=1&adxnnl=1&adxnnlx=1246309244-xjApIMsjK/4HYsnbEc3EZQ (accessed March 30, 2009).

Lane, E. (1860; 2005 edition) *Manners and Customs of the Modern Egyptians*, New York: Cosimo Books.

Latifee, H.I. (2004) *Grameen Trust Experience, 1991–2003*, Dhaka, Bangladesh: Grameen Bank.

Levinson, C. (2004) "$50 billion later, taking stock of US aid to Egypt," *Christian Science Monitor*. Online. Available HTTP: http://www.csmonitor.com/2004/0412/p07s01-wome.html (accessed July 17, 2008).

LiPuma, E. and Lee, B. (2004) *Financial Derivatives and the Globalization of Risk*, Durham, NC: Duke University Press.

Littlefield, E. (2006) "The future of microfinance—and the World Bank's role in it," November 19. Online. Available HTTP: http://www.microfinancegateway.org/p/site/m/template.rc/1.26.9106/ (accessed December 15, 2006).

Littlefield, E. (2007) "The changing face of microfinance funding," *Forbes.com*, December 20. Online. Available HTTP: http://www.forbes.com/2007/12/20/elizabeth-littlefield-microfinance-biz-cz_el_1220littlefield.html (accessed December 28, 2007).

Littlefield, E. and Rosenberg, R. (2004) "Microfinance and the poor: breaking down the walls between microfinance and formal finance," *Finance and Development*, 41 (2), 38–40.

Lovell, C. (1992) *Breaking the Cycle of Poverty: The BRAC Strategy*, West Hartford, CT: Kumarian Press.

Luciani, G. (ed.) (1990) *The Arab State*, Berkeley: University of California Press.

McKee, K. (2009). "The parable of the cobbler and the laid-off financier," *CGAP Microfinance Blog*, March 2. Online. Available HTTP: http://microfinance.cgap.org/2009/03/02/the-parable-of-the-cobbler-and-the-laid-off-financier/ (accessed April 8, 2009).

Mahajan, S. (2007) *Bangladesh: Strategy for Sustained Growth*, Washington DC: World Bank.

Mahbub, A. et al. (2001) *Changes in Women's Status at the Village Level: The Contribution of BRAC Development Programme*, RED BRAC Social Studies, XXVII, Dhaka, Bangladesh: BRAC.

Mahmood, S. (2005) *The Politics of Piety: The Islamic Revival and the Feminist Subject*, Princeton: Princeton University Press.

Mahmud, S. (2004) "Microcredit and women's empowerment in Bangladesh," in S. Ahmed and M.A. Hakim (eds) *Attacking Poverty with Microcredit*, Dhaka, Bangladesh: Dhaka University Press, 153–188.

Malkin, E. (2008) "Microfinance's success sets off a debate in Mexico," *New York Times*, April 5. Online. Available HTTP: http://www.nytimes.com/2008/04/05/business/worldbusiness/05micro.html (accessed April 5, 2008).

Mallaby, S. (2004) *The World's Banker: A Story of Failed States, Financial Crises, and the Wealth and Poverty of Nations*, New York: The Penguin Press.

Marcos, Subcomandante (2000) "Do not forget ideas are also weapons," *Le Monde Diplomatique*. Online. Available HTTP: http://mondediplo.com/2000/10/13marcos (accessed August 8, 2005).

Margolis, M. (2007) "Lining up the loan angels," *Newsweek International*, April 9. Online. Available HTTP: http://www.newsweek.com/id/35845 (accessed April 15, 2007).

Martin, R. (2002) *The Financialization of Daily Life*, Philadelphia: Temple University Press.

Masterson, K. (2009) "Tufts learns how far a big gift can go," *Chronicle of Higher Education*, March 13. Online. Available HTTP: http://chronicle.com/free/v55/i27/27a00102.htm (accessed March 20, 2009).

Matin, I. (1997) "The renegotiation of joint liability: notes from Madhupur," in G. Wood and I. Sharif (eds) *Who Needs Credit?: Poverty and Finance in Bangladesh*, London: Zed Books, 262–270.

Matin, I. (2004) *Delivering Inclusive Microfinance with a Poverty Focus: Experiences of BRAC*, BRAC Research Reports. Online. Available HTTP: http://www.bracresearch.org/reports_details.php?scat=23&tid=32&v= (accessed September 22, 2008).

Matin, I. and Begum, S.A. (2002) *Asset-ing the Extreme Poor: Experiences and Lessons from BRAC Project*, RED BRAC Economic Studies, XVIII, Dhaka, Bangladesh: BRAC.

Matin, I., Hulme, D., and Rutherford, S. (2002) "Finance for the poor: from microcredit to microfinancial services," *Journal of International Development*, 14 (2), 273–294.

Maurer, B. (2005) *Mutual Life, Limited: Islamic Banking, Alternative Currencies, Lateral Reason*, Princeton: Princeton University Press.

Maurer, B. (2006) "The anthropology of money," *Annual Review of Anthropology*, 35, 15–36.

Maurer, B. (2008) "Re-socialising finance? Or dressing it in mufti? Calculating alternatives for Cultural Economies," *Journal of Cultural Economy*, 1 (1), 65–78.

Microcapital (2008) "Pioneers in Microfinance: Shafiqual Haque Choudhury," June 25. Online. Available HTTP: http://www.microcapital.org/pioneers-in-microfinance-shafiqual-haque-choudhury-founder-and-president-of-asa-of-bangladesh/ (accessed February 11, 2009).

Microfinance Gateway (2008) "Microfinance multiplied: an interview with Fazle Abed." Online. Available HTTP: http://www.microfinancegateway.org/p/site/m/template.rc/1.26.9120/ (accessed August 16, 2008).

Mill, J.S. (1859; 1982 edition) *On Liberty*, New York: Penguin Books.

Miller-Adams, M. (1999) *The World Bank: New Agendas in a Changing World*, London: Routledge.

Milobsky, D. and Galambos, L. (1995) "The McNamara Bank and its legacy 1968-1987," *Business and Economic History*, 24 (2), 167-195.

Mitchell, T. (1988) *Colonising Egypt*, Cambridge: Cambridge University Press.

Mitchell, T. (2002) *Rule of Experts: Egypt, Techno-politics, Modernity*, Berkeley: University of California Press.

Mitchell, T. (2006) *Rule of Experts: Egypt, Techno-politics, Modernity*, Berkeley: University of California Press.

MIX (2003) *Benchmarking Arab Microfinance 2003*. Online. Available HTTP: http://www.themix.org/publications/2003-arab-microfinance-analysis-and-benchmarking-report-arabic (accessed May 2, 2004).

MIX (2008) *Benchmarking Arab Microfinance 2006*. Online. Available HTTP: http://www.themix.org/sites/default/files/Arab%20Benchmarking%20Report%202006.pdf (accessed January 15, 2009).

Mjøs, O.D. (2006) "Presentation speech: Nobel Peace Prize award ceremony." Online. Available HTTP: http://nobelprize.org/nobel_prizes/peace/laureates/2006/presentation-speech.html (accessed January 7, 2007).

Mohanty, C.T. (1991) "Under western eyes: feminist scholarship and colonial discourses," in C.T. Mohanty et al. (eds) *Third World Women and the Politics of Feminism*, Bloomington: Indiana University Press, 51-80.

Molyneux, M. (2006) "Mothers at the service of the new poverty agenda: Progresa/Oportunidades, Mexico's conditional transfer programme," *Social Policy and Administration*, 40 (4), 425-449.

Morduch, J. (1998) *Does Microfinance Really Help the Poor? New Evidence from Flagship Programs in Bangladesh*, Research Program in Development Studies Working Papers 198. Princeton: Princeton University Press.

Morduch, J. (1999a) "The microfinance promise," *Journal of Economic Literature*, XXXVII: 1569-1614.

Morduch, J. (1999b) "The role of subsidies in microfinance: evidence from the Grameen Bank," *Journal of Development Economics*, 60 (1), 229-248.

Moyo, D. (2009) *Dead Aid: How Aid is not Working and How There is a Better Way for Africa*, New York: Penguin Press.

Munk, N. (2007) "Jeffrey Sachs's $200 billion dream," *Vanity Fair*, July. Online. Available HTTP: http://www.vanityfair.com/politics/features/2007/07/sachs200707 (accessed August 10, 2007).

Naipaul, V.S. (1961; 2001 edition) *A House for Mr. Biswas*, New York: Vintage Books.

Narayan, D. and Ebbe, K. (1997) *Design of Social Funds: Participation, Demand Orientation, and Local Organizational Capacity*, Washington DC: The World Bank.

Narayan, D. and Petesch, P. (2002) *Voices of the Poor: From Many Lands*, Washington DC: The World Bank.

Narayan, D. and Pritchett, L. (1997) *Cents and Sociability*, World Bank Policy Research Working Paper No. 1796. Washington DC: The World Bank.

New York Times (1997) "Micro-loans for the very poor," February 16.

New York Times (2001) "Liberating the women of Afghanistan," November 24.

New York Times (2003) "Banking for the world's poor," November 19.

New York Times (2004) "Microcredit's limits," May 5.

Norton, A. (1999) *Hizballah of Lebanon: Extremist Ideals vs. Mundane Politics*, New York: Council on Foreign Relations.

Otero, M. (2008) "Microfinance at the crossroads," *Forbes.com*. Online. Available HTTP: http://www.forbes.com/2008/05/19/micro-finance-accion-oped-cx_mot_0519accion.html (accessed February 1, 2009).

Paglen, T. and Thompson, A.C. (2006) *Torture Taxi: On the Trail of the CIA's Rendition Flights*, Brooklyn, NY: Melville House.

Pal, A. (2006) "Microsharks," *The Economist*, August 16. Online. Available HTTP: http://www.economist.com/businessfinance/displayStory.cfm?story_id=7803631 (accessed November 23, 2006).

Parker, E. (2008) "Subprime lender," *Wall Street Journal*, March 1. Online. Available HTTP: http://online.wsj.com/article/SB120432950873204335.html (accessed March 1, 2008).

Pearl, D. and Phillips, M. (2001) "Grameen Bank, which pioneered loans for the poor, has hit a repayment snag," *Wall Street Journal*, November 27. Online. Available HTTP: http://online.wsj.com/public/resources/documents/pearl112701.htm (accessed June 23, 2004).

Peet, R. (2003) *The Unholy Trinity: The World Bank, IMF, and WTO*, London: Zed Books.

Pender, J. (2001) "From 'structural adjustment' to 'comprehensive development framework': conditionality transformed?," *Third World Quarterly*, 22 (3), 397–411.

Peteet, J. (1996) "From refugees to minority: Palestinians in post-war Lebanon," *Middle East Report*, 200, 27–30.

Phillips, K. (2008a) *Bad Money: Reckless Finance, Failed Politics, and the Global Crisis of American Capitalism*, New York: Viking Press.

Phillips, K. (2008b) "Why Wall Street socialism will fail," *Huffington Post*, April 18. Online. Available HTTP: http://www.huffingtonpost.com/kevin-phillips/why-wall-street-socialism_b_96772.html (accessed October 7, 2008).

Pieterse, J.N. (2001) *Development Theory: Deconstructions/Reconstructions*, Thousand Oaks, CA: Sage Publications.

Pincus, J. and Winters, J. (eds) (2002) "Reinventing the World Bank," in *Reinventing the World Bank*, Ithaca, NY: Cornell University Press, 1–25.

Pitt, M. and Khandker, S. (1998) "The impact of group-based credit programs on poor households in Bangladesh: does the gender of participants matter?," *Journal of Political Economy*, 106 (5), 958–996.

Polanyi, K. (1944; 2001 edition) *The Great Transformation: The Political and Economic Origins of Our Time*, Boston: Beacon Press.

Portes, A. and Landolt, P. (2000) "Social capital: promise and pitfalls of its role in development," *Journal of Latin American Studies*, 32, 529–547.

Prahalad, C.K. (2004) *The Fortune at the Bottom of the Pyramid: Eradicating Poverty through Profits*, Cambridge, MA: Wharton School Publishing.

PR Newswire (2008) "S&P announces program to develop global ratings framework for microfinance institutions," February 6. Online. Available HTTP: http://www.prnewswire.com/cgi-bin/stories.pl?ACCT=109&STORY=/www/story/02-06-2008/0004750914& EDATE= (accessed August 22, 2008).

Putnam, R. (2000) *Bowling Alone: The Collapse and Revival of American Community*, New York: Simon & Schuster.

Rahman, A. (1999) "Micro-credit initiatives for equitable and sustainable development: who pays?," *World Development*, 27 (1), 67–82.

Rankin, K. (2001) "Governing development: neoliberalism, microcredit, and rational economic woman," *Economy and Society*, 30 (1), 18–37.

Rankin, K. (2002) "Social capital, microfinance, and the politics of development," *Feminist Economics*, 8 (1), 1–24.

Rankin, K. (2008) "Manufacturing rural finance in Asia: institutional assemblages, market societies, entrepreneurial subjects," *Geoforum* 39, 1965–1977.

Rawe, J. (2003) "Why micro matters: Wall Street is figuring out how to profitably package tiny loans to Third World entrepreneur," *Time*, November 24. Online. Available HTTP: http://www.time.com/time/magazine/article/0,9171,1006292,00.html (accessed December 22, 2003).

Ray, R. and Qayum, S. (2009) *Cultures of Servitude: Modernity, Domesticity, and Class in India*, Palo Alto, CA: Stanford University Press.

Reich, R. (2008a) "A modest proposal for ending socialized capitalism." Online. Available HTTP: http://robertreich.blogspot.com/2008/07/modest-proposal-for-ending-socialized.html (accessed February 9, 2009).

Reich, R. (2008b) "Why Wall Street is melting down, and what to do about it." Online. Available HTTP: http://robertreich.blogspot.com/2008/09/why-wall-street-is-melting-down-and.html (accessed October 1, 2008).

Reille, X. and Glisovic-Mezieres, J. (2009) *Microfinance Funds Continue to Grow Despite the Crisis*, CGAP brief, April, Washington DC: CGAP, The World Bank. Online. Available HTTP: http://www.cgap.org/p/site/c/template.rc/1.9.34437/ (accessed May 23, 2009).

Reinke, J. (1998) "Does solidarity pay? The case of the Small Enterprise Foundation, South Africa," *Development and Change*, 29, 553–576.

Results (2008) "Kenyan crisis shouldn't hide importance of ladders out of poverty, not just safety nets." Online. Available HTTP: http://www.results.org/website/download.asp?id= 3193 (accessed April 24, 2009).

Reuters (2009) "TIAA-CREF makes $40 million investment in developing world markets microfinance equity fund." Online. Available HTTP: http://www.reuters.com/article/pressRelease/idUS176313+24-Feb-2009+BW20090224 (accessed June 1, 2009).

Rhyne, E. (2001) *Mainstreaming Microfinance: How Lending to the Poor Began, Grew, and Came of Age in Bolivia*, Bloomfield, CT: Kumarian Press.

Rich, B. (2002) "The World Bank under James Wolfensohn," in J. Pincus and J. Winters (eds) *Reinventing the World Bank*, Ithaca, NY: Cornell University Press, 26–53.

Rich, F. (2009) "Has a 'Katrina Moment' Arrived?," *New York Times*, February 22. Online. Available HTTP: http://www.nytimes.com/2009/03/22/opinion/22rich.html?_r=1 (accessed February 22, 2009).

Robinson, M. (2001) *The Microfinance Revolution: Sustainable Finance for the Poor*, Washington DC: The World Bank and the Open Society Institute.

Rogaly, B. (1996) "Micro-finance evangelism, 'destitute women', and the hard selling of a new anti-poverty formula," *Development in Practice*, 6 (2), 100–112.

Roitman, J. (2005) *Fiscal Disobedience: An Anthropology of Economic Regulation in Central Africa*, Princeton: Princeton University Press.

Rosenberg, R. (2006) *Aid Effectiveness in Microfinance: Evaluating Microcredit Projects of the World Bank and UNDP*, CGAP Focus Note 35, Washington DC: CGAP, The World Bank.

Rosenberg, R. (2007) *CGAP Reflections on the Compartamos Initial Public Offering: A Case Study on Microfinance Interest Rates and Profits*, CGAP Focus Note 42, Washington DC: CGAP, The World Bank.

Roy, Ananya (2009) "Civic governmentality: the politics of inclusion in Beirut and Mumbai," *Antipode*, 41(1), 159–179.

Roy, Arundhati (2003) "The day of the jackals: on war and occupation," *Counterpunch*, June 2. Online. Available HTTP: http://www.counterpunch.org/roy06022003.html (accessed December 3, 2003).

Rutherford, S. (1995) *ASA: The Biography of an NGO*, Dhaka, Bangladesh: ASA.

Rutherford, S. et al. (2004) "Grameen II: a 'grounded VIEW' of how Grameen's new initiative is progressing in the villages," Microsave. Online. Available HTTP: http://www.safesave.org/GRAMEEN%2011%20Status%20report%20Final%2019%20Apr%202004.pdf (accessed November 11, 2006).

Saad-Ghorayeb, A. (2002) *Hizbullah: Politics and Religion*, London: Pluto Press.

Sachs, J. (2002) "Weapons of mass salvation," *The Economist*, October 24. Online. Available HTTP: http://www.unmillenniumproject.org/documents/Economist_oct24_2002.pdf (accessed January 18, 2003).

Sachs, J. (2005) *The End of Poverty: Economic Possibilities for Our Time*, New York: Penguin Press.

Sachs, S. (2000) "Helping hand of Hezbollah emerges in South Lebanon," *New York Times*, May 30.

Said, E. (1979) *Orientalism*, New York: Vintage Books.

Saliba, R. (2000) "Emerging trends in urbanism: the Beirut post-war experience. A presentation at the Diwan al-Mimar," Center for the Study of the Built Environment, Jordan. Online. Available HTTP: http://www.csbe.org/Saliba-Diwan/essay1.htm (accessed May 17, 2006).

Sassen, S. (2002) "Governance hotspots," in C. Calhoun et al. (eds) *Understanding September 11*, New York: W.W. Norton & Company, 106–120.

Sawalha, A. (2001) "Post-war Beirut: place attachment and interest groups in Ayn Al-Mreisi," in S. Shami (ed.) *Capital Cities: Ethnographies of Urban Governance in the Middle East*, University of Toronto: Centre for Urban and Community Studies, 89–110.

Scully N.D. (2001) "Women see gaps, can't give Bank credit for new loan program," *Bank Check Quarterly*. Online. Available HTTP: http://www.igc.org/dgap/women.html (accessed March 10, 2004).

Scully, N.D. (n.d.) "Microcredit no panacea for poor women." Online. Available HTTP: http://www.gdrc.org/icm/wind/micro.html (accessed May 1, 2009).

Seattle Times (1997) "Not-so-petty cash," April 9.

Sevcik, K. (2003) "What liberation?," *Mother Jones*, July/August. Online. Available HTTP: http://www.motherjones.com/politics/2003/07/what-liberation (accessed July 15, 2008).

Shahe, E., Morshed, M., Mahbub, A.K.M., and Stiglitz, J. (2007) "Microfinance and missing markets," *Social Science Research Network*, March. Online. Available HTTP: http://papers.ssrn.com/sol3/papers.cfm?abstract_id=1001309 (accessed May 11, 2008).

Shakya, Y. and Rankin, K. (2008) "The politics of subversion in development practice: an exploration of microfinance in Nepal and Vietnam," *Journal of Development Studies*, 44 (8), 1214–1235.

Shiva, V. (1998) "Biodevastation," *Synthesis/Regeneration*, 17, Fall. Online. Available HTTP: http://www.greens.org/s-r/17/17-15.html (accessed December 2, 2004).

Silva, S. (2002) "Quantum leap: microcredit boosted by technology," *Microenterprise Americas*, 33–35. Online. Available: http://www.iadb.org/sds/mic/micamericas/eng/2/p32-35.pdf (accessed June 11, 2004).

Singer, P. (2009) "America's shame: when are we going to do something about global poverty?," *The Chronicle Review*, March 13: B6–B10.

Smillie, I. (2009) *Freedom from Want: The Remarkable Success Story of BRAC, the Global Grassroots Organization That's Winning the Fight Against Poverty*, Sterling, VA: Kumarian Press.

Smith, A. (1776; 1991 edition) *The Wealth of Nations*, London: Prometheus Books.

Smith, A. (1759; 2000 edition) *The Theory of Moral Sentiments*, London: Prometheus Books.

Smith, N. (2004) *The Endgame of Globalization*, New York: Routledge.

Smith, P. and Thurman, E. (2007) *A Billion Bootstraps: Microcredit, Barefoot Banking, and the Business Solution for Ending Poverty*, New York: McGraw Hill.

Solomon, D. (2009) "The anti-Bono," *New York Times*, February 22. Online. Available HTTP: http://www.nytimes.com/2009/02/22/magazine/22wwln-q4-t.html (accessed February 22, 2009).

Soros, G. (2008) *The New Paradigm for Financial Markets: The Credit Crisis of 2008 and What It Means*, New York: PublicAffairs.

Sparke, M. (2007) "Everywhere but always somewhere: critical geographies of the Global South," *The Global South*, 1 (1), 117–126.

Spivak, G.C. (1994) "Responsibility," *boundary 2*, 21 (3), 55–57.

Spivak, G.C. (1999) *A Critique of Postcolonial Reason: Toward a History of the Vanishing Present*, Cambridge, MA: Harvard University Press.

Standing, G. (2000) "Brave new words? A critique of Stiglitz's World Bank rethink," *Development and Change*, 31, 737–763.

Stiglitz, J. (1998) "More instruments and broader goals: moving toward the post-Washington consensus," WIDER Annual Lecture, Helsinki, Finland. Online. Available HTTP: http://www.globalpolicy.org/component/content/article/209/43245.html (accessed August 8, 2005).

Stiglitz, J. (1999) "The World Bank at the millennium," *The Economic Journal*, 109 (459), 577–597.

Stiglitz, J. (2000a) "What I learned at the world economic crisis," *The New Republic*, April 17. Online. Available HTTP: http://www2.gsb.columbia.edu/faculty/jstiglitz/download/opeds/What_I_Learned_at_the_World_Economic_Crisis.htm (accessed August 8, 2005).

Stiglitz, J. (2000b) "Formal and informal institutions," in P. Dasgupta and I. Serageldin (eds) *Social Capital*, Thousand Oaks, CA: Sage Publications, 59–70.

Stiglitz, J. (2001) "Information and the change in the paradigm in economics," *Nobel Prize Lecture*, December 8. Online. Available HTTP: http://nobelprize.org/nobel_prizes/economics/laureates/2001/stiglitz-lecture.pdf (accessed September 1, 2005).

Stiglitz, J. (2002) *Globalization and Its Discontents*. New York: Norton.

Stiglitz, J. (2008) "Is there a post-Washington consensus consensus?," in N. Serra and J. Stiglitz (eds) *The Washington Consensus Reconsidered: Towards a New Global Governance*, New York: Oxford University Press, 41–56.

Stolberg, S.G. (2009) "Critique of housing plan draws quick White House offensive," *New York Times*, February 20. Online. Available HTTP: http://www.nytimes.com/2009/02/21/us/politics/21obama.html (accessed February 20, 2009).

Stolz, A.C. (2008) "Norway launches USD117Mln microcredit fund," *Reuters*, June 2. Online. Available HTTP: http://www.microfinancegateway.org/p/site/m/template.rc/1.26.7663/ (accessed September 27, 2008).

Suleiman, J. (1997) "Palestinians in Lebanon and the role of non-governmental organisations," *Journal of Refugee Studies*, 10: 397–410.

Suleiman, J. (1999) "The current political, organizational, and security situation in the Palestinian refugee camps of Lebanon," *Journal of Palestine Studies*, 29 (1), 6680.

Surowiecki, J. (2008) "What microloans miss," *The New Yorker*, March 17. Online. Available HTTP: http://www.newyorker.com/talk/financial/2008/03/17/080317ta_talk_surowiecki (accessed March 20, 2008).

Swibel, M. (2007) "Forbes analyzes microfinance investment, releases first-ever list of top 50 MFIs," *Forbes*, December 20. Online. Available HTTP: http://www.forbes.com/2007/12/20/top-philanthropy-microfinance-biz-cz_1220land.html (accessed February 16, 2009).

Tavernise, S. (2006) "Charity wins deep loyalty for Hezbollah," *New York Times*, August 6. Online. Available HTTP: http://www.nytimes.com/2006/08/06/world/middleeast/06tyre.html?_r=1 (accessed August 6, 2006).

Tendler, J. (2000) "Why are social funds so popular?," in S.J. Evenett, W. Wu, and S. Yusuf (eds) *Local Dynamics in an Era of Globalization: 21st Century Catalysts for Development*, New York: Oxford University Press (published for the World Bank), 114–129.

Tendler, J. and Serrano, R. (1999) *The Rise of Social Funds: What Are They a Model Of?* DURP/MIT mimeo, MIT/UNDP Decentralization Project.

Thomson, A. (2009) "Microfinancing still resilient in Mexico," *Financial Times*, February 26. Online. Available HTTP: http://www.ft.com/cms/s/0/37addbce-0270-11de-b58b-000077b07658.html (accessed March 15, 2009).

Thys, D. (2004) "Legislation promotes life-enhancing investments in the bankable poor," unpublished letter to the *New York Times*. Online. Available HTTP: http://www.microfinancegateway.org/p/site/m/template.rc/1.26.9075/ (accessed September 1, 2004).

Tierney, J. (2006) "Shopping for a Nobel," *New York Times*, October 17. Online. Available HTTP: http://select.nytimes.com/2006/10/17/opinion/17tierney.html (accessed October 17, 2006).

Tsing, A. (2004) *Friction: An Ethnography of Global Connection*, Princeton: Princeton University Press.

Tulchin, D. (2003) *Microfinance's Double Bottom Line: Measuring Social Return for the Microfinance Industry*, Seattle, WA: Social Enterprise Associates.

UNDP (2003a) *Human Development Report: Millennium Development Goals: A Compact Among Nations to End Human Poverty*, New York: Oxford University Press.

UNDP (2003b) *Subjective Poverty and Social Capital: Towards a Comprehensive Strategy to Reduce Poverty*, Cairo, Egypt: UNDP.

UNDP (2005) *Human Development Report: International Cooperation at a Crossroads: Aid, Trade, and Security in an Unequal World*, New York: UNDP.

UNDP (2007) *Human Development Report. Fighting Climate Change: Human Solidarity in a Divided World*, New York: UNDP.

UNESCO (2009) "Global crisis hits the most vulnerable," March 3. Online. Available HTTP: http://portal.unesco.org/en/ev.php-URL_ID=44687&URL_DO=DO_TOPIC&URL_SECTION=201.html (accessed March 15, 2009).

UNIFEM (2008) *Who Answers to Women? Gender and Accountability*, New York: United Nations Development Fund for Women.

UNRWA (2003) "12 years of Credit to Microenterprise." Online. Available HTTP: http://www.un.org/unrwa/publications/pdf/mmp_ar2003.pdf (accessed June 1, 2006).

USAID (2002) "Lebanon revisited: a transition strategy, 2003–2005." Online. Available HTTP: http://www.usaid.gov/lb/documents/lebanon_strategy.doc (accessed May 7, 2004).

Vivian, J. (1995) "How safe are 'social safety nets'? Adjustment and social sector restructuring in development countries," in J. Vivian (ed.) *Adjustment and Social Sector Restructuring*, London: Frank Cass (for the United Nations Research Institute for Social Development), 1–25.

Wade, R. (2001) "Showdown at the World Bank," *New Left Review*, 7, 124–137.

Wallis, W. (2009) "Lunch with the Financial Times: Dambisa Moyo," *Financial Times*, January 30. Online. Available HTTP: http://www.ft.com/cms/s/2/4121b1fa-ee5a-11dd-b791-0000779fd2ac.html (accessed April 11, 2009).

Waly, G. (2005) "Building a national strategy for microfinance in Egypt: international year of microcredit inspires collaborative process." Online. Available HTTP: http://www.uncdf.org/english/microfinance/pubs/newsletter/pages/2005_07/year_update.php (accessed December 20, 2005).

Watkins, K. and Montjourides, P. (2009) "The Millennium Development Goals—bankable pledge or sub-prime asset?," presentation to the UNESCO Future Forum, March 2. Online. Available HTTP: http://portal.unesco.org/en/ev.php-URL_ID=44385&URL_DO=DO_PRINTPAGE&URL_SECTION=201.html (accessed June 1, 2009).

Weber, H. (2002) "The Imposition of a global development architecture: the example of microcredit," *Review of International Studies*, 28 (3), 537–555.

Weber, H. (2006) "The global political economy of microfinance and poverty reduction: locating local 'livelihoods' in political analysis," in J.L. Fernando (ed.) *Microfinance: Perils and Prospects*, New York: Routledge, 43–63.

White, S.C. (1999) "NGOs, civil society, and the state in Bangladesh: the politics of representing the poor," *Development and Change*, 30, 307–326.

Williamson, J. (1990) "What Washington means by policy reform," in J. Williamson (ed.) *Latin American Adjustment: How Much Has Happened?*, Washington, DC: Institute for International Economics, 5–20.

Williamson, J. (2000) "What should the World Bank think about the Washington Consensus?," *World Bank Research Observer*, 15 (2), 251–264.

Williamson, J. (2004) "A short history of the Washington consensus," paper presented at a conference from the Washington Consensus towards a new Global Governance, Barcelona. Online. Available HTTP: http://www.iie.com/publications/papers/williamson0904-2.pdf (accessed September 27, 2008).

Wolfensohn, J. (2000) "How the World Bank is attacking poverty through small enterprise development and microfinance," *Small Enterprise Development*, 11 (1), 5–7.

Wolfowitz, P. (2007) "Resignation statement." Online. Available HTTP: http://web.worldbank.org/WBSITE/EXTERNAL/NEWS/0,,contentMDK:21339650~pagePK:64257043~piPK:437376~theSitePK:4607,00.html (accessed May 30, 2007).

Woller, G., Dunford, C., and Woodworth, W. (1999) "Where to microfinance?," *International Journal of Economic Development*, 1 (1), 29–64.

Wood, G. and Sharif, I. (eds) (1997) *Who Needs Credit?: Poverty and Finance in Bangladesh*, London: Zed Books.

Woods, N. (2006) *The Globalizers: The IMF, the World Bank, and Their Borrowers*, Ithaca, NY: Cornell University Press.

Woolcock, M. (1998) "Social capital and economic development: toward a theoretical synthesis and policy framework," *Theory and Society*, 27, 151–208.

Woolcock, M. (1999) "Learning from failures in microfinance: what unsuccessful cases tell us about how group based programs work," *The American Journal of Economics and Sociology*, 58 (1), 17–42.

World Bank (2000) *Annual Report*, Washington DC: The World Bank.

World Bank (2006a) "Microfinance comes of age." Online. Available HTTP: http://web.worldbank.org/WBSITE/EXTERNAL/NEWS/0,,contentMDK:21153828~pagePK:64257043~piPK:437376~theSitePK:4607,00.html (accessed December 20, 2006).

World Bank (2006b) "The future of microfinance—and the World Bank's role in it." Online. Available HTTP: http://www.microfinancegateway.org/content/article/detail/36645 (accessed December 20, 2006).

World Bank (2009) "Crisis hitting poor hard in developing world," February 12. Online. Available HTTP: http://web.worldbank.org/WBSITE/EXTERNAL/NEWS/0,,contentMDK:22067892~pagePK:64257043~piPK:437376~theSitePK:4607,00.html (accessed March 3, 2009).

Worth, R. and Fattah, H. (2006) "Villagers cheer as Lebanese army marches into the south," *New York Times*, August 19.

Wyly, E. et al. (2008) "Subprime mortgage segmentation in the American urban system," *Tijdschrift voor Economische en Social Geografie*, 99 (1), 3–23.

Yom, S. (2008) "Washington's new arms bazaar," *Middle East Report*, 246. Online. Available HTTP: http://www.merip.org/mer/mer246/yom.html (accessed December 15, 2008).

Yunus, M. (2002a) *Grameen Bank II: Designed to Open New Possibilities*, Dhaka, Bangladesh: Grameen Bank.

Yunus, M. (2002b) "Grameen Bank, micro-credit, and the Wall Street Journal," *Grameen Bank Dialogue*, January newsletter of the Grameen Trust, Dhaka, Bangladesh.

Yunus, M. (1999; 2003 edition) *Banker to the Poor: Micro-Lending and the Battle Against World Poverty*, New York: Public Affairs.

Yunus, M. (2006a) "Nobel lecture," Oslo. Online. Available HTTP: http://nobelprize.org/nobel_prizes/peace/laureates/2006/yunus-lecture-en.html (accessed January 15, 2007).

Yunus, M. (2006b) *Ten Indicators to Assess Poverty Level*, Dhaka, Bangladesh: Grameen Bank.

Yunus, M. (2008) *A World Without Poverty: Social Business and the Future of Capitalism*, New York: Public Affairs.

Yunus, M. and Abed, F. (2004) "Poverty matters," unpublished letter to the *New York Times*. Online. Available HTTP: http://www.microfinancegateway.org/p/site/m/template.rc/1.26.9075/ (accessed September 1, 2004).

Zaatari, Z. (2006) "The culture of motherhood: an avenue for women's civil participation in southern Lebanon," *Journal of Middle East Women's Studies*, 2 (1), 33–64.

Zafar, A. (1988) *Subsistence Level Development Trap in an Empowerment Strategy: Is BRAC Coming Out of It?*, RED BRAC Economic Studies 10, Dhaka, Bangladesh: BRAC.

Zoellick, R. (2003) "America will not wait for the won't-do countries." Online. Available HTTP: http://montevideo.usembassy.gov/usaweb/paginas/41-00EN.shtml (accessed June 5, 2009).

Zoellick, R. (2009) "Time to herald the age of responsibility," *Financial Times*, January 25. Online. Available HTTP: http://web.worldbank.org/WBSITE/EXTERNAL/NEWS/0,,contentMDK:22045260~pagePK:64257043~piPK:437376~theSitePK:4607,00.html (accessed May 3, 2009).

Zohir, S. and Matin, I. (2002) *Wider Impacts of Microfinance Institutions: Towards Defining the Scope and Methodology*, RED BRAC Economic Studies, Vol. XVII, Dhaka, Bangladesh: BRAC.

Index